AMERICA'S

REBUILDING

By the Cuomo Commission on Competitiveness

LEWIS B. KADEN,
CHAIRMAN OF THE COMMISSION

AGENDA

ECONOMIC STRENGTH

Introduction by
MARIO M. CUOMO
GOVERNOR OF NEW YORK STATE

LEE SMITH, DIRECTOR OF THE
COMMISSION AND EDITOR OF THE REPORT

M.E. Sharpe   Armonk, New York   London, England

Available in the United Kingdom and Europe from M.E. Sharpe,
Publishers, 3 Henrietta Street, London WC2E 8LU.

Library of Congress Cataloging-in-Publication Data

America's agenda: rebuilding economic strength / by the Cuomo Commission
on Competitiveness ; introduction by Mario M. Cuomo; Lewis B. Kaden,
Chairman; Lee Smith, editor of the report.
p. cm.

Includes index.

ISBN 1–56324–086–6.—ISBN 1–56324–094–7 (pbk.)
1. United States—Economic conditions—1981- 2. United States—
Economic policy—1981- 3. United States—Foreign economic relations.
4. United States—Commercial policy. 5. Competition—United States.
I. Smith, Lee (Lee Orr) II. Cuomo Commission on Trade and
Competitiveness (N.Y.)
HC106.8.A454 1992
338.973—dc20
92–26858
CIP

Printed in the United States of America

The paper used in this publication meets the minimum requirements
of American National Standard for Information Sciences—
Permanence of Paper for Printed Library Materials, ANSI Z39.48–1984.

∞

MV 10 9 8 7 6 5 4 3 2 1

CONTENTS

Contents

Contents

LIST OF CHARTS

LISTS OF FIGURES AND TABLES

PREFACE

AMERICA'S AGENDA is a report of the Commission on Competitiveness appointed by New York Governor Mario M. Cuomo in 1987. The report begins by recognizing the obvious reality that the end of the Cold War and the emergence of a highly competitive global economy have produced a transformation of our economic, social, and political institutions. It notes that during this period of great change, the choices we make are exceedingly important, because they will determine the kind of nation we will be in the next century.

The report then attempts to help Americans make the right choices about the policies needed to rebuild our economic strength, provide widespread opportunity, and preserve our social cohesion. It offers both a broad understanding of our problems and comprehensive reforms. The Commission believes a piecemeal program will not suffice: our economic and social problems are intertwined; what we do internationally directly affects what we do domestically.

We have tried to make our report as useful as possible to policymakers and the public by offering an agenda of specific recommendations. We have also attempted to avoid the vague generalities so often produced by study groups representing diverse constituencies.

The report expresses the views of the commissioners and contains their recommendations to Governor Cuomo. Not every commissioner agrees with every word, phrase, idea, or recommendation. Separate statements by individual commissioners are included as an appendix.

MEMBERS OF THE COMMISSION:

Owen Bieber
President
United Automobile Workers
    of America (UAW)

Donald P. Brennan
Managing Director
Morgan Stanley & Co.

Edward J. Cleary
President
New York State AFL-CIO

William C. Ferguson
Chairman and CEO
NYNEX Corporation

Jeffrey E. Garten
Managing Director
The Blackstone Group

Hernand V. Gonzalez, Jr.
National Ethnic Marketing
    Manager
Pepsi-Cola Company

David D. Hale
Senior Vice President and
    Chief Economist
Kemper Financial Services,
    Inc.

Brad Johnson
Director
New York State Office of
    Federal Affairs

Lewis B. Kaden
Partner
Davis Polk & Wardwell
Chair, International Policy
    Task Force

Eugene J. Keilin
Senior Partner
Keilin and Bloom

Mitchell E. Kertzman
Chairman and CEO
Powersoft Corporation
Chair, Industrial Competi-
    tiveness Task Force

Lawrence R. Klein
Benjamin Franklin Professor
    of Economics (Emeritus)
Wharton School, University
    of Pennsylvania

Perla M. Kuhn
Senior Partner
Kuhn and Muller, Esqs.

Karin Lissakers
Director of Business and
    Banking Studies
Columbia University
Chair, Latin America Task
    Force

Gerald W. McEntee
President
American Federation of
    State, County, and Mu-
    nicipal Employees
    (AFSCME)

Ira M. Millstein
Senior Partner
Weil, Gotshal & Manges

Ramon H. Orange
President and Chairman
Ebonex Inc.

Addison Barry Rand
Executive Vice President
Xerox Corporation

Felix G. Rohatyn
Senior Partner
Lazard Frères & Company
Chair, Investment Task Force

Robert E. Rubin
Senior Partner and Co-Chair
Goldman, Sachs & Company
Chair, Poverty and Labor
    Markets Task Force

Stephen C. Schlesinger
Director of International
    Organizations
New York State Department
    of Economic Development

Jack Sheinkman
President
Amalgamated Clothing and
    Textile Workers Union
    (ACTWU)

Lee Smith
Executive Director
Governor's Commission on
    Competitiveness

John J. Sweeney
President
Service Employees Interna-
    tional Union (SEIU)
Chair, Healthcare Task Force

Vincent Tese
Director of Economic
    Development
State of New York

Laura D'Andrea Tyson
Professor of Economics and
    Business Administration
University of California,
    Berkeley
Research Director, BRIE

Lynn R. Williams
President
United Steelworkers of
    America (USWA)

Andrew J. Zambelli
Secretary to the Governor
New York State

To develop these recommendations, the Commission organized itself into individual task forces to explore specific issues. Each task force was chaired by a commissioner and drew upon members of the Commission, outside experts, and representatives of constituencies. From the task forces' efforts we drew the substance of the chapters on investment, competitiveness, urban poverty, healthcare, international strategy, and Latin America.

The report addresses many—although not all—of the major issues facing America. For example, we do not have a chapter on the relationship between the environment and economic growth, while we recognize that addressing this is one of the most important challenges of our time. We also know that the nation's economic security requires a sensible long-term energy policy, and we urge policymakers not to ignore energy matters. We leave detailed study of these important subjects to other individuals and groups.

Although the Commission benefited from the efforts of all its members and outside experts, it was especially helped by the chairs of the individual task forces: Investment—Felix Rohatyn; Competitiveness—Mitchell Kertzman; Urban Poverty—Robert Rubin; Healthcare—John Sweeney; International Strategy—Lewis Kaden; and Latin America—Karin Lissakers.

The Commission expresses its appreciation to Governor Cuomo for forming the Commission in 1987, encouraging us to publish our first report, *The Cuomo Commission Report: A New American Formula for a Strong Economy*, and then giving us the opportunity to broaden the Commission's mandate to produce this additional report. Governor Cuomo asked the commissioners for their best ideas. Throughout the process he has remained keenly interested and supportive of our independence.

The commission also wishes to express its gratitude to Lee Smith. As was the case in our first report, he pulled the project together, articulated common themes, and mediated different views. I speak for each commissioner in expressing our admiration for his insight and our respect for his deep concern for policies that promote a better future for our families and our country.

Lewis B. Kaden
Chairman of the Commission
New York City
July 1992

ACKNOWLEDGMENTS

FOUR years ago we melded the diverse views of the members of the Cuomo Commission on Trade and Competitiveness into a well regarded book, *The Cuomo Commission Report: A New American Formula for a Strong Economy*. It described the new domestic and international policies the country needed to restore the competitiveness of its production system. Much of the analysis of the first book remains valid, and we have drawn upon that report when drafting this one.

Preparing this new report was a challenge in several respects. Competitiveness was no longer the nation's major problem so the Commission had to address a broader array of concerns. In addition to the economic problems of slow growth and low investment, we had to address critical social problems such as poverty and the need for a better system of healthcare. The end of the Cold War required us to think about a new foreign policy appropriate for a world where economic security was now at least as important, if not more so, than military security.

It took the efforts of a talented and hardworking group of individuals to meet these new challenges. Particular mention is due to the assistant director of the Commission, Martin Kohli, who made a large contribution to all aspects of the Commission's work. John Berry and Suzy Im provided valuable assistance throughout the Commission's life. Jeff Levin, Mel Friedman, Mark Levitan, Tammy Mitchell, Loretta Mock, and Didi Charney provided editorial support. Gerri Goeller was very helpful in the production of the book, as were Phil White and Sophia Hernandez. In addition, Tim Wendt and Sarah Bernstein also contributed to the Commission's work.

The staff was immeasurably aided in its work by the commissioners who chaired the individual task forces. Lewis Kaden and Bob Rubin were particularly helpful and supportive of the Commission's work, as were Mitchell Kertzman, Karin Lissakers, Felix Rohatyn, and John Sweeney. Also providing input and encouragement were commissioners Jack Sheinkman, Laura D'Andrea Tyson, Jeff Garten, and Steve Schlesinger. Larry Klein generously made his macroeconomic model available to us. Ron Blackwell, Rob McGarrah, Gerry Shea, and Gene Gibson provided important assistance, as did our advisers David Aaron, Sherle Schwenninger, David Hamburg, Tony Jackson, Craig Fields, Jerry Levinson, Lorraine Klerman, and Walter Maher. The Commission is grateful to the McArthur Foundation for its support of our work on Latin America. The Commission also benefited from the support and advice of Vincent Tese, Alan Sullivan, and Harold Holzer.

Finally, I particularly want to thank our editor at M.E. Sharpe, Richard Bartel, for his interest and support of this project.

Lee Smith
Director of the Commission
Editor of the Report
New York City
July 1992

INTRODUCTION

Setting a New Course

by Mario M. Cuomo
Governor of New York

Losing Confidence in the Future

THE American faith in a better, brighter future for our children and our children's children is being tested. Not since the Great Depression have so many Americans questioned whether the next generation would earn at least the comfort, security, and dignity of the one before it. This quintessential American faith has sustained us and helped us define ourselves as a nation. If that vision of America is lost, we will lose the nation as we have known it.

This need not happen: we *can* change course.

Currently, real average hourly wages are at their lowest level in almost 30 years. While the wealthiest 1 percent of all Americans nearly doubled their incomes during the 1980s, 70 percent of Americans saw their real incomes decline. Important benefits, such as health insurance, are less available, making it more difficult for American breadwinners to support their families.

Much of this painful decline could have been avoided. Washington's flawed economic policies of the last decade have squandered our national assets. The nation has failed to invest adequately in its children. It has also failed to sustain and improve the public infrastructure: roads, bridges, and schools. Altogether this imprudence has eroded our global competitiveness, just as the competition is growing more challenging.

Ironically, as the European Community unites, becoming stronger, the United States is fragmenting its strength, becoming weaker. For the past 12 years, under a policy called the New Federalism, the national government has withdrawn investments for education, job training, and housing, and has shifted more of that burden to state and local governments. This new burden, together with the revenue-shrinking recession and problems such as AIDS, crack, and homelessness, have driven state and local governments into a primitive struggle for fiscal survival, forcing them to slash spending, raise taxes, and pick the pockets of neighboring states for scraps of job-producing business.

The national government has, in effect, pitted states against one another in a "state-eat-state" combat that is wounding many of them. Instead of consolidating our strengths, we are moving back toward the failed wisdom of the Articles of Confederation, which we replaced more than 200 years ago with our Constitution and its unique form of intelligent federalism.

As a result, America has fallen from its position as the world's largest creditor to the ignominious status of the world's largest debtor. Today we send billions of dollars to Germany, Japan, and other nations to buy from them goods that we used to make and sell to them. Then we borrow back the dollars, paying billions more in interest, decreasing our ability to invest, and perpetuating the debilitating cycle.

Now more and more Americans see clearly that the short-sightedness of the 1980s has wounded the heart and the soul of our economy. It is time to make a new beginning.

An Agenda for Fundamental Change

In 1987 I called together a group of experts from business, labor, government, and academia and asked them to serve on the Commission on Competitiveness. I asked the group to provide recommendations on what we in New York and the nation could do to overcome our economic problems. Their first report, published in 1988, focused on the enormous trade deficit and debunked what was then the conventional wisdom—that the trade deficit was simply the result of the high dollar and the federal budget deficit. The Commission argued that changes in our fiscal and monetary policy were necessary but not sufficient. It showed that a nation's competitiveness also depends on microeconomic factors, such as the ability of individual firms and industries to innovate and produce high-quality goods. Every industry has unique strengths and unique problems that macroeconomic policies cannot address. Taking a back-to-basics approach, the report demonstrated that new relationships in the workplace, such as employee participation, were essential ingredients in the formula to increase productivity so as to meet new global competition.

The commissioners were confident that America's growing interdependence with the world economy would not lead to a decline in our standard of living, if we could rebuild our competitiveness and reform the global economic system to promote worldwide growth. The report also emphasized the importance of exports and the need for economic growth in our traditional markets, such as Latin America. Written with commendable clarity and common sense, the first report was, in the opinion of many experts, a high point in the debate about competitiveness.

Today many of the first report's insights and arguments are widely accepted. America's economic policies, however, have not yet changed, and our economy has continued to perform poorly.

In an effort to advance our new thinking about economic policies and move more swiftly toward implementation, in 1990 I reconvened the Commission. I asked the group to re-examine the nation's economic condition in light of the new challenges and opportunities presented by the end of the Cold War. I called on the Commission members to offer positive policy proposals and to identify practical measures that might be carried out at both the state and national levels . . . right now!

Once again they have done an excellent job. The Commission's latest report offers its readers a thorough analysis of our problems and a bold and workable set of solutions, not all of which I subscribe to *in his verbis*, but all of which are worthy of consideration.

America is entering a new era in its history. Cold War policies are obsolete. The primary challenge now, as the Commission rightly emphasizes, is rebuilding our economic strength—the ability of each of us to earn a rising standard of living by producing goods and services that meet the test of international markets.

The success of tomorrow's economy will rest, in large measure, on the ability of workers, managers, and public officials to fashion cooperative and participatory relationships. For too long government has limited its economic policy to incentives, offering them mostly to companies and investors. No more. The past decade has taught us that incentives are not enough. Washington cut taxes so that the wealthy had incentives to save, cut welfare so that the poor had incentives to work, and cut regulations so that industry had incentives to produce. Never in recent history has federal economic policy been so oriented toward incentives. And seldom have policies had such meager results in terms of growth and opportunity.

The United States needs new national economic policies that go beyond simply freeing up capital in the hands of the wealthy. Capital is, of course, essential, and we must provide incentives for its creation. But America needs a more comprehensive approach that integrates all the elements vital to generating long-term prosperity: infrastructure, technology, energy, free and fair trade policies, and, most important, labor—educated, skilled, motivated human beings—people who will create the nation's wealth in the 21st century.

Government can encourage economic growth by investing in all these elements, without dangerously swelling the federal deficit over the long term.

We need an approach that fosters a balance between co-operation and competition. We need long-term, cooperative relationships between labor and management, between companies and their suppliers, between business and government. Only by tapping the knowledge and the commitment of all participants in the production process can we produce the top-quality goods that will afford Americans a high standard of living. Increasing participation—a democratic ideal—makes good economic sense.

In Chapter 1 the report gets right to the point. There is no mystery about the nation's basic problem: neither the private sector nor the public sector has been making the investments America needs. Government has neglected investment in children, in education, and in the infrastructures of the next century. Business has pursued short-term speculation rather than long-run productive investment.

For over a year we in New York have been calling for policies to promote investment-led growth. I wholeheartedly support the Commission's recommendations for increasing investment. A net investment tax credit will spur private investment. The proposal to inject capital into the banks will make it easier for banks to lend to credit-starved small- and medium-size businesses. An ambitious public investment agenda will reverse the neglect of our infrastructure and make industry more productive. As the Commission points out, public investment can support and spur private investment. By rebuilding our transportation and communications systems, by fostering an educated and motivated workforce, government can create an environment in which business *wants* to invest. It is clear to me that the 1990s must be a decade of rebuilding—and this means committing much of the peace dividend to promoting public and private investments.

I also agree that we need a new approach to international strategies. The next president should create what we are naming the Economic Security Council to give higher priority to our national and international economic interests. Just as our domestic policies must focus on increasing investment to spur growth, so must our international policies. By encouraging the World Bank and the International Monetary Fund to support needed investments overseas, the United States can stimulate growth in our export markets. The business and political leaders of the world must continue to come together, not out of a compassionate impulse by the haves to share with the have-nots—that is an elegant but unreliable impulse—but because they understand that individual nations will eventually find greater power in the strength of a whole world.

By providing an accurate diagnosis and offering thoughtful recommendations toward rebuilding a strong economy, the Commission has, in my judgment, met its mandate. And it has done more. It has also shown us how intertwined economic and social problems have become. The distinction between economic policy and social policy is becoming less and less useful. Economic deprivation in Latin America has contributed to the increased availability of drugs in North America. The absence of a comprehensive system for providing quality healthcare to all Americans, including mothers and small children, is resulting in escalating costs that are passed back and forth between the private and the public sectors. The alienation of the inner-city poor is imposing costs on society as a whole, in lost productivity and in additional welfare and criminal justice expenses. So the Commission's recommendations on how to relieve inner-city poverty are especially welcome. The recent tragedy in Los Angeles has prompted many Americans to look again at and to listen more closely to the misery in the nation's urban areas.

Policy debates about the inner-city poor too often fall into blame games: either we blame society for not providing inner-city residents with jobs, quality education, and medical care, or we blame the inner-city poor themselves for dependency on welfare, dropping out of school, and having children while they themselves are still children. Fixing blame is not the most effective way to change things. What will help us change are programs that can give the poor the hope of success—a strategy that begins with prenatal care, continues with preschool and other programs, and ends with measures to promote more jobs in our cities, such as New York's "Decade of the Child."

As I have noted, I do not agree with every one of the Commission's ideas and recommendations. I would prefer more specificity about how to deal with the deficit, and the Commission's treatment of international economic policy could also have contained more concrete proposals on how to help the struggling nations of Eastern Europe. For example, federal assistance to U.S. firms exporting critical goods, such as pollution-abatement equipment, to this region would yield benefits both to Americans and to Eastern Europeans.

In a few policy areas I think that the Commission has not gone far enough. For instance, I believe it has not paid sufficient attention to energy and to the environment. The nation needs to develop an energy plan such as the one we have in New York, a plan that is pro-growth as well as pro-environment.

On the whole, however, the Commission has given us an extremely useful strategy with many excellent recommendations. It is comprehensive and fair, and I am confident this report will be as well received as was the Commission's previous effort.

If Americans are looking for new ideas, they will find them here. If Americans want change, and I know they do, here is a program. As a nation, we would be well served by its adoption. But to do that will require something even more difficult to achieve than formulating a strategy—forging a national consensus behind it, then mustering the political will and leadership to carry it out.

The Need for Leadership

This election year is the moment to debate such a plan—and to envision a future in which we solve our problems, while maintaining our traditions of inclusion, fairness, and participation.

To the dismay of most Americans, our political process still makes it difficult for policymakers to deal with substantive issues. Too often our elected leaders present us with a politics of denial and evasion: *denial* of the nation's problems in order to make easier the *evasion* of the remedies needed to cure the problems.

In 1988 we were treated to the unworthy spectacle of a presidential campaign about diversions—the Pledge of Allegiance, Boston Harbor, and Willie Horton. The partisan impulse behind such politics remains with us today. Much of the current political rhetoric deploys divisiveness to avoid the real issues: it argues that we can solve our problems by getting tough on the poor and on immigrants. Some have cynically suggested that welfare is a significant part of the nation's economic problem, even though federal aid to families with dependent children constitutes only 1 percent of our budgetary load.

In 1992 Americans can expect to hear more about "family values," which are often left undefined. No one denies the importance of stable, intact families, and these are difficult times for raising a family and keeping it together. Part of the problem is economic. To support children, adults need jobs—and not jobs that pay the minimum wage and fail to offer medical benefits. The diminishing portion of jobs that pay decent wages has undercut the ability of Americans to provide for their families. And Washington's reluctance to support day care programs and its opposition to parental leave policies have imposed further strains on the nation's families.

Children need more than material sustenance. They also need moral examples—examples of adults who can and do put the good of the family and community above their own individual desires. Children and young adults look not only to their parents for such examples but also to our public leaders—especially in our nation's capital. Here again Washington's performance over the last 12 years has been dismal. The involvement of Washington insiders in frauds at the savings and loans, with defense contractors, and at federal agencies sends the message that enriching oneself while abusing a public trust is perfectly normal. These are the kind of values that are hurting American families.

We need to construct a new American economy based on

the principle of inclusion, not exclusion. We must promote a progressive free enterprise economy with policies that empower all Americans—not just those at the top—to participate and prosper, to be both workers and shareholders in America's future.

In its past, at moments of critical juncture, America has been among the more fortunate of nations. In those moments it has been blessed with leaders who understood historic necessity and opportunity, and acted with courage to lead in ways that united Americans.

Abraham Lincoln refused to accept the breakup of the Union and guided the country through the agonizing Civil War. He also helped the United States make the transformation from agrarian capitalism to industrial capitalism through federal education, housing, and trade policies.

Franklin Delano Roosevelt, before successfully leading the nation in war, confronted and overcame a domestic economic and social crisis, thus laying the groundwork for decades of growth and prosperity.

Harry S. Truman, thrust abruptly into the presidency at Roosevelt's death, quickly grasped the profound threat that the Soviet Union posed, reorganized our government to meet that challenge, and in the process opened up a whole new world to returning soldiers.

These were leaders who did not shrink from the responsibilities of leadership, leaders that did not blame the past for their own failures. Nor did they hide in platitudes from the storm of crisis. No. They had instead the boldness to be honest about hard realities, to acknowledge them, and then to do what needed to be done.

This again is a time for such leaders, men and women who do not fear the truth. But such leaders can only arise if the American people shoulder their responsibility to themselves and to their children and insist that those who lead us offer more than hollow rhetoric.

I have faith in the greatness of this nation because I have faith in the strength of our people. We can change our course.

But that will require resurrecting and reasserting the basic values and strengths that made us strong in the first place: the intelligence to think and to plan; the eagerness to work, to save, and to invest; and the willingness to bite our lips and make the sacrifices our families need now. I believe we can find the will and the wallet to regain our economic strength, restore our sense of national purpose, and preserve the American dream for future generations.

PART I

America in Transition

CHAPTER 1

The Need for a New Course

A Nation Adrift

Two notable eras in American history have simultaneously come to an end. One is the era of the Cold War, brought to a close by the stunning dissolution of the Soviet Union. Paralleling the Cold War was another era—marked by the success of America's remarkable 20th-century economic system, a system that made us the world's economic giant. The end of these eras begins the transition to the next stage in our history.

Americans are worried about what kind of society will emerge from this period of change. Our economic strength has been weakened by mistakes and omissions made in the public and private sectors. The nation's international policies seem increasingly irrelevant to our real concerns. We sense that the Cold War's end is an opportunity—for now the nation can address its long neglected domestic problems. We know that our economy must be redirected toward the challenges of the future. We are fearful that we will not seize the moment.

The modest economic recovery apparently under way will have little effect on our long-term problems. In many respects our economy is stagnant. Wages and salaries are in depression. Instead of investing the funds needed to maintain our infrastructure and invigorate the private sector, the nation has had to spend its money covering the enormous debts—public and private—accumulated in the 1980s. Huge federal budget deficits now discourage the governmental initiatives that could help America regain its vitality.

Our economic problems exacerbate our social problems. Lack of growth means falling tax revenues, which in turn force local and state budget cutbacks of services and aid to education. The healthcare system is failing: costs are out of control, access restricted, and quality uneven. Entrenched poverty is making American cities less livable for millions, while imposing enormous costs on society as a whole.

Instead of enjoying the fruits of the Cold War's end, we are losing ground in a competitive world market, where strength is measured economically, not militarily. We lack an effective international strategy to advance our economic interests and help solve pressing global economic, environmental, and social problems.

In this climate of anxiety, intolerance by some Americans grows, threatening our traditions of compassion, fairness, and willingness to compromise, just at the moment when these virtues are needed more than ever. Without compassion and a shared sense of fairness, cooperation will vanish and society will be divided into the haves and the have-nots.

Most Americans recognize that we all rise fastest when we rise together. Growth and equity should coincide. Pervasive poverty saps the nation's prosperity.

If America is to retain its goal of opportunity for all, its traditions of pluralism, and its capacity for compassion, we must rebuild our economic strength. We can restore our economy. But not by palliatives. To remedy deeply rooted economic and social problems will require a fundamental shift in the nation's priorities—and across-the-board reform of our policies and institutions. Only in this way can the nation progress.

America confronts a choice. We can accept our slow, gradual decline as an economic power—or we can hasten the evolution of a stronger America. But to start society moving forward again, we must do the hard work of reinvigorating our major social and economic institutions. Because our present problems are complex and interconnected, small, incremental reforms will not work. A decade of comprehensive reforms will be needed to renew the promise of America.

This conclusion—that only fundamental economic and social change can restore our nation—was not arrived at quickly by the Commission. Our members, drawn from all walks of life—business, labor, government, finance, and academia—have studied America's problems for over five years. Established in early 1987 by Governor Mario M. Cuomo of New York, the Commission issued its first report in 1988. In it we found that the United States had not adjusted to the competitive demands of the global economy. That report articulated four principles—still relevant today—of a new economic strategy. First, national security is now as much a matter of economic strength as it is of military strength. Second, competitiveness is the primary determinant of our ability to maintain our standard of living and our traditions of opportunity and inclusion. Third, economic strength is determined by the health of our economic and social institutions as well as by proper macroeconomic policies. Lastly, positive, active government is necessary to make the economy more competitive and to insure our national and personal security.

In 1988 we predicted that if the nation failed to heed these four principles and did not become more competitive, in the 1990s we would experience slower economic growth and a declining standard of living. Painfully, much of that prophecy is coming true even faster than we predicted.

In the face of growing social problems and the dramatic global change resulting from the end of the Cold War, Governor Cuomo expanded the Commission's mandate. He asked the Commission for advice and recommendations on how New York and the nation could address the challenges of the post–Cold War era. In response the Commission focused on six critical issues: public and private investment, industrial competitiveness, urban poverty, healthcare, international strategies, and our relationship with Latin America.

The Commission established task forces for each of these

topics. Each task force was composed of Commission members and outside experts. Through meetings and correspondence over the following year and a half, the task forces formulated a series of policy recommendations that form the basis of this report.

We offer this report as a contribution to the process of national self-examination already under way. We are hopeful that a consensus for economic renewal will emerge. In our report we propose practical ways to reform our major policies and institutions. We recognize that the federal budget deficit is a serious problem, but reject the notion that it rules out a comprehensive economic and social program. Likewise, we challenge the belief that government lacks the ability to implement a national economic strategy.

History teaches that nations decline if they do not adjust to their changed circumstances. We are convinced that if this generation of leaders does not take action, the next one may not be able to. We are equally sure the American people want change. Distressed by the condition of their nation, they are demanding that their leaders address the central economic and social issues. They will support new policies if they are convinced those policies will restore America's ability to compete in the global economy and ameliorate our pressing social and economic problems at home.

Ten Signs of the Nation's Distress

To carry out effective, fundamental reform first requires a full appreciation of the problems we face. The Commission identified ten signs of the nation's distress:

1. *Insufficient Public and Private Investment: The Third Deficit*
Most people have heard about the dangers of the federal budget and trade deficits. Equally important is the third deficit—the shortfall between badly needed public and private investment and our actual expenditures.

To invest means spending money on the assets, either publicly or privately owned, that will be used to produce or maintain wealth. The public sector invests in highways, bridges, water systems, pollution control, airports, schools, training, and research and development (R&D). In the United States public investment has fallen during the last ten years. After averaging 2.8 percent of gross national product (GNP) from 1976 to 1981, public investment dropped to 2.2 percent in 1982 and fell to 1.9 percent in 1990, the lowest level on record.[1]

World-class companies succeed by tapping the abilities and knowledge of educated and skilled workers. Yet federal investments in training and education declined steadily over the past decade. By 1996 training outlays are projected to reach their lowest level in over 30 years.[2] The United States ranks 14th out of 16 industrialized nations in expenditures for grades kindergarten through 12.[3]

Throughout the 1980s our industrial rivals consistently devoted larger portions of their national product to public investment. Japan's public investments amounted to 5.7 percent of its gross domestic product (GDP), while France, Germany, and Italy spent between 2.0 and 4.8 percent.[4] (See Chart 1.1.) Not surprisingly, all of them experienced higher rates of growth of output and productivity than did the United States.

Today France is investing in an advanced, high-speed rail system. Great Britain and France are sharing the costs of building the ambitious Channel tunnel and the next generation of supersonic aircraft. Germany is investing tens of billions of deutschemarks in new facilities and infrastructure. By 1994 Japan, Germany, and France are all expected to have fully operational advanced telecommunications networks that can carry voice and data information concurrently. Because the rate of American telecommunications investment dropped an average of 8 percent a year in the 1980s, such systems are expected to be less than half complete in the United States by 1994.[5]

To maintain our ability to produce wealth requires a strong

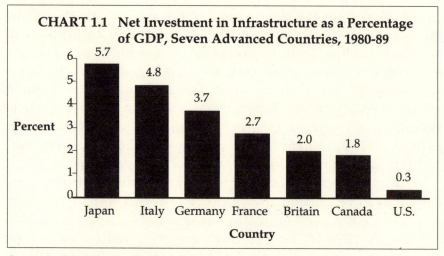

CHART 1.1 Net Investment in Infrastructure as a Percentage of GDP, Seven Advanced Countries, 1980-89

Sources: Organization for Economic Cooperation and Development and the Bank for International Settlements
Note: The latest year available is 1989.

investment in the most advanced technologies and the newest capital equipment. High rates of private capital investment can boost the productivity of workers, making possible higher wages.

Unfortunately, our record in private investment is no better than in public investment. In the 1980s, as Chart 1.2 illustrates, net domestic private investment, as a percentage of GNP, was only about three-fourths as large as it had been during the three preceding decades.[6] In 1989, for the first time since World War II, the United States ceded its lead in total capital investments to Japan, a country whose economy is half the size of ours.[7] Of the world's leading industrial nations, the United States ranked last over the past three years in terms of the share of income it devoted to new investment.[8]

2. Loss of Manufacturing and Technological Leadership and Lagging Productivity
Many American companies are rebuilding their competitiveness. Yet many others continue to struggle. As a recent report observed, the nation's "consumer electronics and factory

automation industries have been practically eliminated by foreign competition; the U.S. share of the world machine tool market has slipped from about 50 percent to 10 percent. . . . Even such American success stories as chemicals, computers and aerospace have foreign competitors close on their heels."[9] Although the U.S. position in the semiconductor industry is improving, its current share of the world market remains markedly lower than in 1970.[10] Some U.S. companies still undervalue quality; others lag behind in the race to master techniques for continuously improving quality.

We must also do better in developing the critical technologies for competitiveness during the decade ahead. In materials and associated processing technologies, we remain competitive, except for the important area of electronics applications. In many engineering and production technologies, we are lagging; in electronic components, we are losing badly.[11]

To create and apply new technical knowledge, we must invest more in research and development. The U.S. government currently spends $70 billion annually on R&D, but much of it is for military purposes.[12] As a result the United States trails its

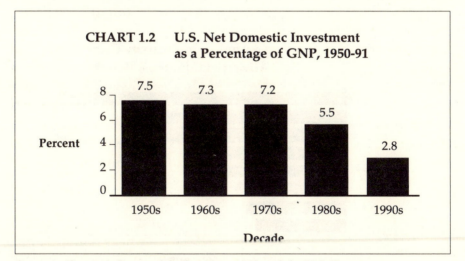

CHART 1.2   U.S. Net Domestic Investment as a Percentage of GNP, 1950-91

Percent

8 — 7.5 (1950s)
7.3 (1960s)
7.2 (1970s)
5.5 (1980s)
2.8 (1990s)

Decade

Sources: *Economic Report of the President*, 1992 and the U.S. Department of Commerce, *Survey of Current Business*
Note: *The 1990s includes 1990 and 1991.*

major competitors in civilian R&D investment. In 1978 public and private expenditures for nondefense research and development as a share of GNP were: Japan, 2.0 percent; Germany, 2.1 percent; and the United States, 1.6 percent. By 1989 the gap had widened: Japan, 3.0 percent; Germany, 2.8 percent; and the United States, 1.9 percent.[13]

Along with low investment, our tenuous hold on global technological leadership is one reason for the nation's lagging productivity. Between 1950 and 1973, labor productivity, measured as output per hour, grew at an average annual rate of 2.3 percent, a rate sufficient to double per-capita real incomes every 28 years. But from 1973 to 1979, productivity growth slowed to an average rate of 1 percent per year, a rate at which it will take 70 years to double per-capita income.[14] In the 1980s manufacturing productivity improved, yet service sector productivity barely grew at all. Overall productivity actually dropped in 1989 and 1990. Over the 1979-90 period, the United States ranked last among advanced industrialized nations in productivity growth, as Chart 1.3 shows.[15] As a

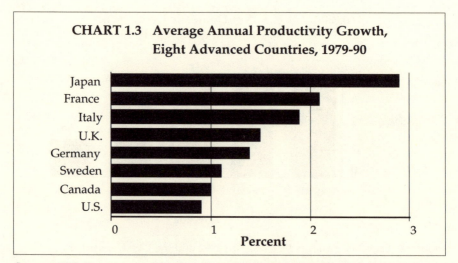

CHART 1.3 Average Annual Productivity Growth, Eight Advanced Countries, 1979-90

Source: U.S. Department of Labor, Bureau of Labor Statistics

consequence of slow productivity growth and the weak dollar, the United States now ranks behind all but one other advanced country in the value of output per employee. (See Chart 1.4.)

Productivity, understood as value added per worker, is a fundamental determinant of national income. Steady increases in productivity over long periods of time make a decisive difference in a country's wealth and well-being.

3. *A Persistent Trade Deficit*

For most of its history, the United States has exported more goods than it imported. But in the 1970s the nation began importing more than it exported—and we have ever since.

Because of American industry's declining competitiveness and our openness to the global economy, the economic demand spurred by federal budget deficits in the early 1980s precipitated a huge inflow of imports. At the same time our exports increased much more slowly. The trade deficit jumped from $38 billion in 1982 to $170 billion in 1987, before easing downward to $74 billion in 1991.[16]

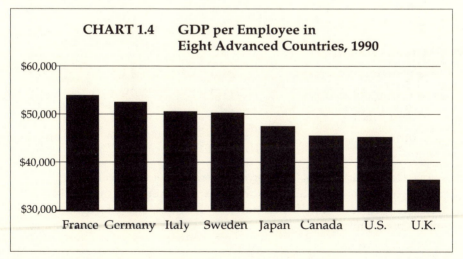

CHART 1.4   GDP per Employee in Eight Advanced Countries, 1990

Source: U.S. Department of Labor, Bureau of Labor Statistics

11

In 1991, despite the growth in exports and a fall in demand for imports caused by the recession, we still had a substantial trade deficit. The single largest bilateral trade deficit, $44 billion, remained the one with Japan. This deficit and that with China widened between 1990 and 1991, as Table 1.1 shows, while our trade deficits with most other countries contracted. We also have persistent deficits with oil exporters, the Asian newly industrializing countries (Hong Kong, Singapore, South Korea, and Taiwan), and with advanced, high-wage countries such as Canada, Germany, and Italy.

TABLE 1.1 Merchandise Trade Balance, by Region, 1990 and 1991
(in billions of dollars)

Region	1990	1991	Change
Advanced countries	−45.1	−33.1	12.0
Canada	−9.5	−8.0	1.5
France	0.6	2.1	1.5
Germany	−9.7	−5.3	4.4
Italy	−4.8	−3.2	1.6
Japan	−41.7	−44.1	−2.4
United Kingdom	3.0	3.2	0.2
Oil–exporting countries	−24.6	−14.8	9.8
Developing countries	−41.0	−29.8	11.2
Asian NICs	−20.6	−14.8	5.8
China	−10.4	−12.7	−2.3

Source: U.S. Department of Commerce, Bureau of Economic Analysis
Note: Advanced countries include countries other than the six listed; the Asian Newly Industrializing Countries (NICs) are Hong Kong, Singapore, South Korea, and Taiwan.

4. *A Nation in Hock*

The total federal debt soared to $3,599 billion in 1991, up from $909 billion in 1980.[17] In 1991 we paid close to $200 billion annually—15 cents of every dollar the federal government collects—in interest payments on the federal debt.[18] (See Chart 1.5.) The national debt is not something we owe only to ourselves: foreigners hold over $300 billion in federal debt.[19] Interest payments on the debt to foreigners more than tripled from $12.6 billion in 1980 and are expected to reach $39.8 billion in 1992.[20]

In 1992 the federal deficit is expected to climb higher still— rising to $352 billion, from $269 billion in 1991.[21] (See Chart 1.6.) At the present rate, more than $1 trillion of additional federal debt will accumulate in the next three years. Federal borrowing on this scale puts upward pressure on long-term interest rates, making private investments in new plant, equipment, and R&D more costly.

The private sector is also burdened by debt. Corporate debt increased from $829 million in 1980 to $2.2 trillion in 1991.[22] Net

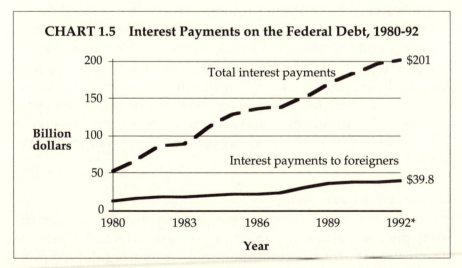

CHART 1.5   Interest Payments on the Federal Debt, 1980-92

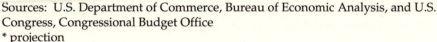

Sources: U.S. Department of Commerce, Bureau of Economic Analysis, and U.S. Congress, Congressional Budget Office
* projection

13

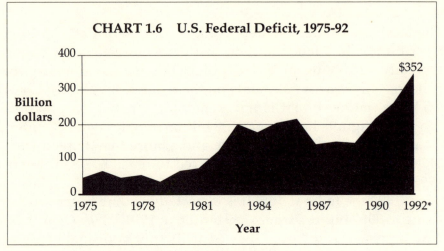

CHART 1.6   U.S. Federal Deficit, 1975-92

Source: *Economic Report of the President,* 1992
* projected by the U.S. Congress, Congressional Budget Office

interest payments consumed 19 percent of corporate earnings in 1977; by 1991 these payments had risen to 41.7 percent.[23] (See Chart 1.7.) As a result, companies have fewer resources for investments.

Consumers have debt problems, too. The sum of home mortgages and outstanding consumer debt rose from $1.4 trillion at the end of 1980 to almost $4.0 trillion by the end of 1991.[24] This average annual increase of 10 percent was much higher than the average annual growth in aftertax income. As Chart 1.8 shows, in 1991 total consumer debt was equal to nearly 94 percent of disposable personal income, compared to 71 percent in the early 1980s and a previous peak of 75 percent in the late 1970s.[25]

5. *A Weak Financial Sector*
A healthy financial sector—savings and loans, banks, securities firms, and insurance companies—is essential to the process of investment. Yet the combination of recent regulatory policies and difficult economic conditions has seriously weakened this critical sector. Financial deregulation in the 1980s allowed

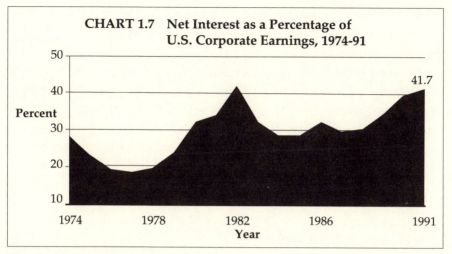

CHART 1.7 Net Interest as a Percentage of U.S. Corporate Earnings, 1974-91

Source: *Economic Report of the President*, 1992

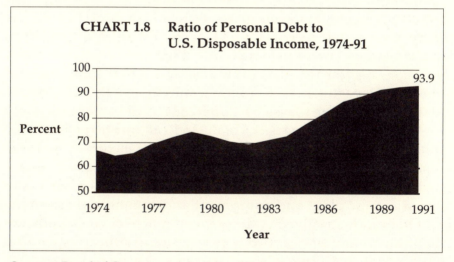

CHART 1.8 Ratio of Personal Debt to U.S. Disposable Income, 1974-91

Sources: Board of Governors of the Federal Reserve System and the
U.S. Department of Commerce, Bureau of Economic Analysis
Note: The 1991 estimate is based on data through the third quarter.

the savings and loan industry to put large sums of federally insured deposits into real estate loans, junk bonds, and many other speculative investments. The estimated cost of the savings and loans cleanup now tops $500 billion—a staggering sum that could easily finance massive investments in highways, bridges, high-speed rail, schools, training, research, and the environmental infrastructure.

In the 1990s many commercial banks and insurance companies are in precarious positions. Also hurt by the collapse of real estate prices and by bad loans to Latin America, the commercial banks are now forced to increase their capital bases to meet international capital adequacy requirements. Last year 124 banks holding $64 billion in assets folded.[26] (See Chart 1.9.) The federal government expects a similar number of bank failures in 1992.

6. *A Flawed Healthcare System*

America is less and less able to afford its healthcare system. We spent more than $800 billion on healthcare in 1991—approximately 12.3 percent of our gross national product. In 1992 the share is expected to climb to 14 percent.[27] During the 1980s, while average family income barely kept pace with the rate of inflation, healthcare costs grew one and a half times faster.[28] The U.S. Department of Commerce anticipates that healthcare costs will continue to rise by 12 percent to 15 percent annually over the next five years.[29] Total medical care expenses now consume 19 percent of the average family's income.[30] As these costs rise, American families have less to spend on other needs—such as housing and education—and corporations have less to invest in new plant and equipment and commercial research.

Other industrialized nations spend much less on healthcare than the United States. If our per-capita healthcare spending were equal to Germany's and Japan's, we would save $300 billion per year.[31] Internationally, American firms are at a competitive disadvantage against foreign firms that enjoy the benefits of full government financing of healthcare for their employees.

The rising healthcare bill for business, which now amounts to 25 percent of corporate profits, is forcing some employers to drop medical benefits.[32] Consequently, employer-provided insurance covers a smaller portion of the work force than it did

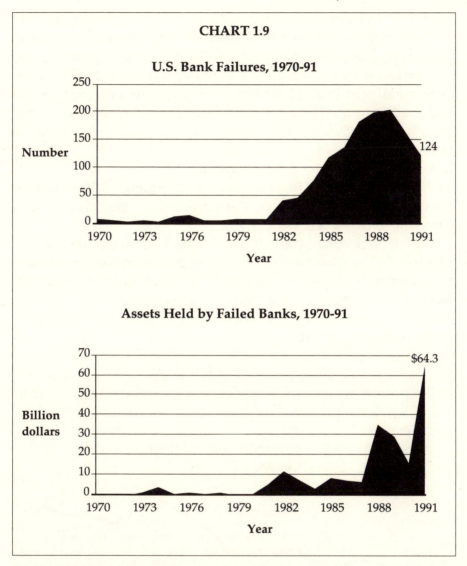

CHART 1.9

U.S. Bank Failures, 1970-91

Number

124

Year

Assets Held by Failed Banks, 1970-91

Billion
dollars

$64.3

Year

Source: The Federal Deposit Insurance Corporation

in the past. Because of the escalating costs to families and corporations alike, some 35 million Americans today lack health insurance.[33] The majority of these people live in families where at least one member works full-time. Holding a full-time job no longer necessarily provides the rewards and the security that it used to.

Many of those without coverage are our most vulnerable

citizens. One-quarter of the uninsured are children, and an additional one-quarter are women of childbearing age.[34] Approximately 26 percent of all women between the ages of 15 and 44 currently lack insurance for maternity care. In addition, nearly half a million pregnant women are uninsured, increasing the likelihood that they will give birth to unhealthy babies.[35]

7. *Entrenched Poverty: A Less Inclusive Society*

In 1990 the official U.S. poverty count stood at 33.6 million Americans—13.5 percent of the population—the highest rate since the 1981-82 recession.[36]

Almost one out of four children under the age of six lives in poverty.[37] (See Chart 1.10.) The number of families on welfare increased more between 1990 and 1991 than it did in the previous 16 years.[38] Welfare and food stamp enrollments have shot up. A record 25 million Americans—almost one in ten—now depend on the federal food stamp program to put groceries on the table.[39]

The poor are more likely to be homeless, to be out of work, to die prematurely from sickness, to be victims of crime, or to

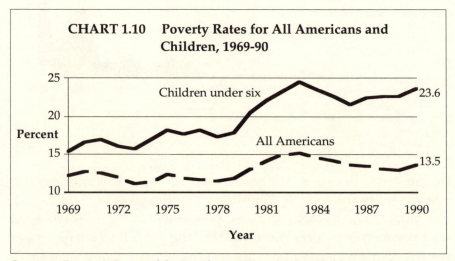

CHART 1.10   Poverty Rates for All Americans and Children, 1969-90

Sources: *Economic Report of the President*, 1987 and 1992, Children's Defense Fund, *The State of America's Children 1991*, and the U.S. Bureau of the Census

commit crimes. Chronic poverty is a terrible waste of human resources—a drag on the nation's economy in terms of lost productivity, higher social service costs, and impaired competitiveness.

8. *Slow Growth*
The growth of the national economy in the 1980s, stimulated by immense federal budget deficits, began grinding to a halt in 1989. After adjusting for inflation, the U.S. economy in 1991 was no larger than it was in 1989, arguably the worst three-year economic performance in the postwar era.[40] (See Chart 1.11.)

Most experts predict only a sluggish recovery in 1992—one unlikely to achieve better than 3 percent annual growth. If this proves true, it would be one of the weakest U.S. rebounds in recent memory. In eight of the last ten recoveries, for example, first-year GNP growth averaged a healthy 6.7 percent.[41]

9. *High Unemployment*
With slow growth, unemployment has risen. Few families have remained untouched by the current slump. Nearly 9 million Americans—7.1 percent of the labor force—were unemployed

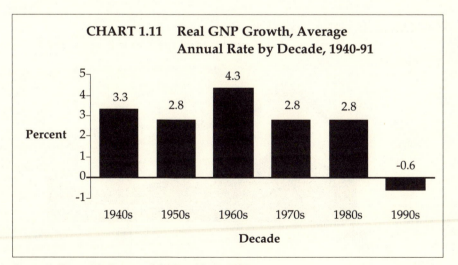

CHART 1.11   Real GNP Growth, Average Annual Rate by Decade, 1940-91

Source: *Economic Report of the President, 1992*

at the end of 1991, a five-and-a-half-year high.[42] According to some estimates, one out of five people in the work force has experienced unemployment in 1991.[43] When the jobless eventually secured new jobs, there was an even chance that the new jobs paid less than the old ones. In addition, more than 6 million part-time workers could not find full-time work, and 1 million others were so discouraged that they no longer looked for jobs. All told, 16 million Americans—12.4 percent of the labor force—lacked full-time employment in 1991.[44] (See Chart 1.12.)

In countless communities across the country, poverty and homelessness are on the rise. Among those hardest hit are minorities and the young. According to recent reports, for example, widespread government layoffs have had a disproportionate effect on minority groups because those groups have historically found more job opportunities in the public sector than in private industry.[45] The nationwide loss of manufacturing jobs has also adversely affected the newest and youngest members of the labor force. Many of the jobs lost were in urban areas. Virtually all of the estimated 1 million jobs lost

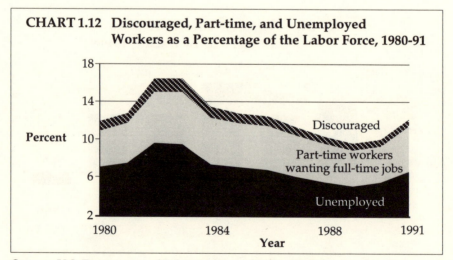

CHART 1.12   Discouraged, Part-time, and Unemployed
Workers as a Percentage of the Labor Force, 1980-91

Source: U.S. Department of Labor, Bureau of Labor Statistics

since the recession began in July 1990 were held by workers 16 to 24 years old.[46]

10. *Declining Middle-Class Incomes and Growing Inequality*
Slow growth has taken its toll on the average person's standard of living. Wage and salary levels for a majority of American families have declined steadily. In 1991, for example, the average worker was receiving pay 4 percent smaller, in inflation-adjusted terms, than in 1980.[47] (See Chart 1.13.) According to the U.S. Census Bureau, in 1990 median family income, which reflects changes in the number of workers as well as in their wages, was $36,915, only about $1,400 more than in 1973.[48] All of the increase was due to expanded participation in the labor market. Between 1980 and 1989 working America's average fringe benefits fell by 14 percent while its taxes rose.[49]

As average incomes stagnated or declined, inequality increased—a trend that was exacerbated by changes in federal taxes. Between 1980 and 1985, the average of the richest 1 percent of families benefited from $37,880 in tax cuts while the

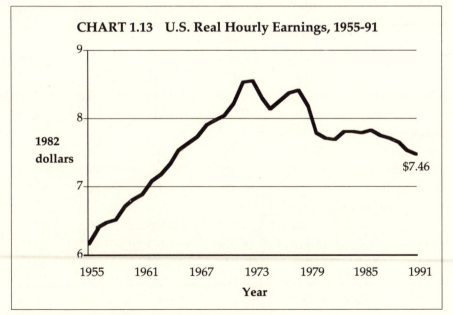

CHART 1.13   U.S. Real Hourly Earnings, 1955-91

Source: *Economic Report of the President*, 1992

21

typical middle-class family received only a $250 tax cut.[50] The increase in the Social Security tax then erased these small gains for the middle class.

The distribution of wealth also became more concentrated. In 1983 the top 1 percent of households held 31 percent of all assets. By 1989 this had risen to 37 percent, more than the bottom 90 percent of all households.[51]

Income growth has been stymied by the shift of jobs from high-paying to low-paying industries, caused by the competitive difficulties of our goods-producing industries and by the slow productivity growth of many service industries. As Table 1.2 shows, 88 percent of the new jobs created in the 1980s were in retail trade and services, two industries of the service-producing sector that pay below-average wages. High-wage

TABLE 1.2 The Shift of Employment from High-Wage to Low-Wage Industries

Industry	Employment (in thousands) 1979	1991	Change	Share of job growth	1991 average weekly earnings
Mining	958	697	−261	−1.6	$631
Construction	4,463	4,696	233	1.4	534
Manufacturing	21,040	18,426	−2,614	−15.7	455
Durable goods	12,730	10,556	−2,174	−13.0	483
Nondurable	8,310	7,870	−440	−2.6	420
Transportation and public utilities	5,136	5,824	688	4.1	512
Wholesale trade	5,221	6,072	851	5.1	425
Retail trade	14,972	19,346	4,374	26.3	200
Finance, insurance, and real estate	4,975	6,708	1,733	10.4	373
Services	17,112	28,779	11,667	70.0	333
Total private	73,876	90,548	16,672	100.0	$355

Source: U.S. Bureau of Labor Statistics

industries in the services sector (transportation, public utilities, and wholesale trade) grew little during the 1980s. Most serious for the American living standard, 2.6 million high-paying manufacturing jobs disappeared during the decade.

Some families have managed to keep their heads above water by working longer hours or taking second jobs; others, by relying on the second income of a spouse or by sending their teenage children to work. Still, the bills for food, shelter, medical care, child care, and college tuition keep rising. Millions of Americans are now wondering if their redoubled efforts will be enough to carry them through the uncertainties of the 1990s.

Needed: Fundamental Reform

The ten signs of the nation's distress persuasively indicate that the present deficiencies in our economic system are not small and isolated, but deep and systemic. The present system is no longer working. To make America work again, we must reform our major economic and social policies and institutions.

Many Americans are worried not only by the breakdown of the existing economic and social system but also because the strategies thus far offered by Washington are in no way commensurate with the problem. Instead of contemplating fundamental reforms, Washington proposes small changes or no change at all.

The discontent with the status quo has led to a number of proposals that are partial reforms, albeit reforms that often contain important elements of a comprehensive agenda. But by themselves they cannot begin to remedy the present system's inadequacies.

Washington has proposed tax cuts to encourage consumer spending since such spending makes up two-thirds of the gross national product. Unfortunately, consumers are in no mood or position to spend the nation to a strong recovery. According to numerous opinion polls, Americans harbor deep economic anxieties. Consumers are less confident today than in 1982, the depth of the last recession, even though unemployment and inflation are lower now than they were ten years ago. And while the *willingness* of consumers to spend is important, so is their *ability* to spend. As we have seen, consumers have less spending ability because their incomes are stagnant or falling. Worries about job security and large increases in consumer debt and interest payments have further sapped consumer confidence.

Some people hope that the recent growth of exports will provide enough stimulation, so that eventually we can grow out of our problems. But the United States cannot expect much help from the global economy. While U.S. exports, especially in high value-added sectors, have been an important source of growth over the past several years, they are not likely to increase in the coming year because demand from many important foreign economies is slowing. The rise in Germany's interest rates has slowed Europe's growth, dampening demand for U.S. goods. Japan's economy seems headed for recession; the United Kingdom is already in one. The major nations are pursuing independent, not coordinated, economic policies. The outlook for global economic growth is not favorable.

What about new incentives for private investment as a way to spur growth? Some have proposed a combination of capital gains tax cuts and new business incentives to stem the long-term decline in private investment. But without other measures to promote growth, there is little hope for reversing the sharp drop in business-sector confidence. When office buildings are half empty and factories are not operating at high levels of capacity, companies will not invest—no matter how favorable the tax climate. As long as Washington lacks a strategy for rebuilding economic strength, private-sector investment will likely remain subdued.

The traditional economic remedies cannot succeed in restoring our economy's strength for one basic reason: the economic problems we confront are structural, not cyclical. We need fundamental changes to reinvigorate our economic system.

Viewed from a historical perspective, America's economic

system has entered a historic period of transformation, similar to other eras of transition in our history. In the 19th century we moved from agrarian to industrial capitalism as the rapid expansion of industrial manufacturing centered in the North propelled the American economy into a new century and a new position of prominence in the world of nations. In the 20th century a new form of capitalism emerged in America—a manager-dominated capitalism built on the new production systems that evolved in the 1910s and 1920s, shaped by the economic and social reforms of the New Deal, and solidified into a powerful national system by the Cold War. The distinctive feature of the new system was the prominence of large, diversified companies run not by owners but by powerful corporate managers, using hierarchical lines of authority. It was this economic system—which we have called New Deal capitalism—that not only made us the world's preeminent economic power but, more importantly, provided our nation with the growing prosperity required to sustain increasing opportunity, education, and fairness.

Today that system is proving unequal to the task of securing our present and future prosperity. We find ourselves in competition with other countries—in particular, Germany and Japan—that have developed different national systems of capitalism directed more than ours toward global markets.[52] We must evolve a system, predicated on the end of the Cold War, that is capable of meeting the demands of the global economy. As we will see in Chapter 2, a major lesson we can take from the experience of other nations is that comprehensive strategies, supported by a consensus between the private and public sectors, are more likely to succeed at rebuilding economic strength than are a series of patchwork reforms.

We need a strategy that tackles our immediate and long-term problems at the same time—a program that not only spurs a strong recovery from the recession but also helps rebuild national economic strength. The program must restore America's ability to sustain strong growth. Strong growth, 3 to

4 percent a year, expands markets, increases sales, and raises rates of factory utilization—thereby boosting profits, investment, and the rate of technological change. When an economy grows rapidly, living standards rise, new doors of opportunity are opened, and social justice is more easily attained.

To shape and implement a comprehensive strategy, government must reassert its traditional leadership role. No one sector—business, labor, finance, scientific—speaks for all of society and has the duty to advance the common good. Only government can do this. Only government can bring together the diverse elements of American life, not by dictating an agenda but by encouraging a consensus for renewing our country from the ground up.

A comprehensive strategy would increase public and private investment. We need strong business investment in the most advanced technologies and capital equipment, as well as investment in the skills of workers. Private investment must be matched by public investment in physical infrastructure and greatly expanded investments in human capital. The focus of public funding for technology research should shift dramatically from military to commercial purposes.

A comprehensive strategy would support and encourage American firms to produce high-quality, high-value goods through the implementation of high-performance forms of work organization—systems that allow for greater teamwork, employee participation, more flexible work rules, and more decentralized decision making. We need compensation schemes that align the risks and rewards for managers, owners, and workers. The best of our corporations cultivate cooperative, long-term relationships with their suppliers, employees, and customers. They make investments for the future, not only in plant and equipment but also in the relationships necessary to produce quality products. They have compensation systems that reward performance of *all* employees, not just the performance of chief executive officers. Government policies should nurture these positive approaches.

A comprehensive strategy would revitalize our primary

and secondary educational systems—especially in the inner cities—so that children who could make a contribution to society do not wind up being burdens on society. It would also reform our healthcare system, so that quality treatment is both available and affordable to all. These are not only desirable economic goals. They also fulfill America's promise of realizing individual human potential as a means of advancing the common good.

A comprehensive strategy would include effective international policies. We presently lack clear policies that advance our economic interests and foster a cooperative, stable, and high-growth world economy.

We must also meet the challenge of the newly emerging regional trading blocs. As Japan builds up its Eastern Asian markets and Germany rebuilds Eastern Europe and anchors the new European Community, the United States should implement a comprehensive new policy toward its closest regional partner—Latin America. We need policies with objectives beyond liberalizing trade and investment, policies linked to the mutual concerns of North and South Americans—immigration, environmental degradation, drug trafficking, and economic growth. In short, we need a new hemispheric strategy.

Finally, we need to change the priorities of our international endeavors. With the collapse of the Soviet Union, the United States should significantly reduce its security commitments and bring military spending in line with the new global realities. It is our *economic* security that now requires attention.

New Guiding Principles

A comprehensive strategy for rebuilding America's economic strength is possible only if it is founded upon a new national consensus for reform. That the American people are ready, indeed eager for change, is increasingly apparent.

Change will come one way or another. Confronted by discontented voters, governments will have to act. What we need is a plan for effective action—a strategy that incorporates an understanding of our historical situation and is designed to take advantage of the prevailing economic and social trends.

Though it is difficult to describe in detail the next stage in our economic system's evolution, we have identified some of its key operating principles. Heeding them will help America succeed in the new global economy. In our view U.S. policies must be shaped by these operating principles if the nation is to achieve security and prosperity.

1. *Creating and sustaining economic strength requires long-run strategies.* America's time horizons are too short. Too often our markets and managers focus on the next quarter—not the next four years. The federal budget process enervates long-term public investment efforts. The education and training system underinvests in people, and our labor relations policies do not foster long-term loyalty. The policies of most pension funds, the largest sources of investment, do not incorporate active ownership strategies to maximize the long-term potential of the companies whose shares they own. These undermine the average person's willingness to seek mutual gain and share risks and rewards. Instead, people think they have to "get it while they can." Since these attitudes and institutions, geared toward short-term profit, are tied to one another, reform must proceed on all fronts.

The direction of reform is clear. American industry, to achieve excellence in production, needs to foster long-term relationships with its shareholding owners, suppliers, customers, and employees. The private sector must plan for the future—and government must create a business climate that rewards long-term strategies.

2. *To maintain and increase our standard of living, we need to develop more participatory economic institutions.* The way for American capitalism to succeed is through encouraging more participation at all levels.

We do not have the cultural cohesion of the Japanese or the strong links between government, business, finance, and labor that characterize Germany. Their styles of capitalism work for them. They would likely not work for us. We need instead a system that draws from our entrepreneurial spirit, diversity, and democratic ethos.

Within corporations, horizontal, not just vertical, linkages that strengthen participation should be encouraged. For example, by creating more ties between the research scientist, the engineer, and the process of production, we can speed up the processes of technological innovation and quality improvement. At the same time, corporations should build new links to their network of suppliers to help improve their performance.

Partnerships between business and labor and, in some cases, government can be formed based on an enlightened awareness of shared interests and the understanding that increased participation can bring with it the rewards of increased quality and productivity. These partnerships may take a number of forms, such as employee ownership and participation plans, government-supported research consortiums that include universities and corporations, and employment training panels governed jointly by business, labor, and government.

3. *Rebuilding our economic strength will require a more active role for government and a new balance between markets and government.* One of the enduring features of the American system is government's role as guardian of the public welfare, which has been broadly defined as building a prosperous society. Throughout U.S. history, the federal government has served as a catalyst for economic development and social renewal.

Activist governments are as old as the Republic itself. Both George Washington and Alexander Hamilton called for public investments to stimulate domestic industries. In the early 19th century, the federal government promoted economic development through "national improvements"—roads, bridges, and canals. Later in the century, Abraham Lincoln established a national banking system, provided joint public-private funding for transcontinental railroads, and founded our system of public land-grant colleges.

Twentieth-century presidents—Wilson, Roosevelt, Truman, Eisenhower, Kennedy, Johnson, Nixon, Ford, and Carter—all used their power to insure that government met its economic responsibilities. Even Herbert Hoover believed that government had a significant role to play; although his interventions proved too little and too late to ward off the Great Depression, his Reconstruction Finance Corporation broke new ground in government's participation in the economy.

The philosophy of recent U.S. leadership has departed from the traditional American belief that government can play a positive economic role, holding instead that government action is by definition negative, and that market forces are always better. As the last few years have confirmed, blind allegiance to the ideal of the market is naive. Market forces do not operate in a vacuum—they are either influenced by, or are nothing more than, the economic strategies of our competitors and their governments. For the last 12 years, American industry and workers have faced aggressive international competition from nations whose governments set national economic objectives and encourage business to meet those objectives. Our failure to emulate this approach places us at a disadvantage.

An activist federal government does not mean unwieldy regulations, government-run industries, or bloated and unresponsive social welfare bureaucracies. It does mean carefully targeted government actions that advance national economic interests. It means responsible regulation of the financial system. It means making needed investments in education, infrastructure, and children—even as government itself becomes more responsive to users of its services.

It also means encouraging a new mix of competition and cooperation. The federal government must create incentives to encourage greater collaboration and cooperation domestically in order to increase American industry's ability to compete internationally.

4. *Macroeconomic balance is necessary but not sufficient for economic strength: we also need structural, that is, microeconomic*

policies. A much smaller deficit and a much higher national savings rate are important long-term objectives. But deficit reduction is not sensible in the midst of a recession or at the beginning of a recovery—and fiscal imbalance is only a small part of what ails America. The way to solve these immediate problems is to confront our fundamental problems.

Besides striking the right macroeconomic balance, macroeconomic policy must be coordinated with structural policies, which aim at specific sectors or institutions—such as reforming inner-city schools. Structural measures to reduce poverty will not work if macroeconomic policy is restricting growth. And macroeconomic policies to promote growth will not succeed unless structural policies improve the competitiveness of industry.

5. *Economic and social policy must be considered together.* Traditionally, the federal government has made economic policy without much coordination with social policy. Given the magnitude and pervasiveness of our present social problems and their connection to our economic problems, to continue this separation in policy development would be foolish.

Our studies of urban poverty, healthcare, and of Latin America have convinced us of the value of a developmental perspective. This approach looks at the stages in the process of human development and considers how failure at one stage in the life of an individual undermines future development and how, left unaddressed, that failure will eventually lead to higher social costs and loss of economic opportunity for that individual. The costs of stunted human lives are enormous—costs in lost productivity, welfare, social services, police, and prisons. A diminished quality of life is perhaps the most important cost.

6. *Increasing opportunities for individuals and increasing their responsibilities should be linked.* The task force on industrial competitiveness found that new forms of work organization that require workers to take more responsibility for the quality

31

of their products work best when linked to compensation policies that reward workers for improvements. The task force on urban poverty, while calling for measures to help inner-city residents develop into productive citizens, also believes that inner-city residents must take greater responsibility for their own lives.

   7. *In an interdependent global economy, the United States needs global growth to sustain its domestic growth.* Our efforts at domestic rebuilding will require that our trading partners also grow. We need healthy export markets to restore balance between imports and exports. Furthermore, our international strategies must insure that global credit conditions facilitate the high rates of investment needed in the United States and elsewhere.

   In the new global economy policymakers can no longer focus exclusively on national economies. The U.S. economy is open to, and interdependent with, the global economy, and policymakers must take this new condition into account if their policy prescriptions are to succeed.

Toward the Next American System

With the end of the Cold War and the loss of our undisputed industrial preeminence, the global economy is entering a new era. The distinctive feature of this new era will be the intensifying economic competition between Europe, Japan, and the United States. For America to succeed, it must move beyond the New Deal capitalism of the last 50 years and hasten the development of a new and more participatory economic system.

   We are confident that America will rise to the challenge, for our country still possesses valuable assets. No other nation matches our natural resources: temperate climate, fertile soil, mineral wealth, and abundant waterways and harbors.

   Despite setbacks, a number of U.S. manufacturing industries retain significant shares of world markets. In machinery, transportation equipment, and chemicals, the U.S. portion of world exports is 16 percent or more.[53]

The size of the American market is another strength. It is our "home field advantage." In this era of rapidly changing markets, the ability to respond quickly is increased by access and proximity—and no one has better access and proximity to America than Americans do. By taking full advantage of our position through flexible, market-responsive production, we can do much to restore our competitiveness. At the same time, we can use access to our markets as leverage for trade negotiations.

We can build on the strength of our open, democratic society. A nation that thrives on exchange and communication, that has always encouraged exploration and rewarded innovation, can do well in the global marketplace because it is open to change and new ideas. The large number of American scientific breakthroughs and Nobel Prize winners testifies to this spirit. Our extensive system of public universities remains a tremendous resource, providing many Americans with the chance to participate in society.

Finally, there is our most important source of strength—our vast, hardworking people. America's greatest asset is its work force. That means blue-collar and white-collar workers, industrial and service workers, entrepreneurs and employees, professionals and bricklayers and farmers—everyone who needs to work for a living. This group, over 110 million strong, forms much of America's middle class. It makes up the bulk of American consumers and producers. If it falters, the nation falters.

Most of the changes America must make are already known. We can take heart from the fact that with most problems, proven remedies exist. American companies, unions, foundations, state and local governments, the federal government in decades past, and, in some instances, foreign governments have developed effective programs we can use or adapt. The challenge now is to build on our existing strengths and on what works.

Change will not be easy. But for Americans that should not be an insurmountable obstacle. Our country was founded on the principles of hard work, democratic participation, and expanding opportunity. The American legacy of rising living standards was, after all, not foreordained—it was earned. It depended on our nation's ability to produce and spread wealth equitably throughout society, creating millions of individual stakeholders in the success of the American experiment. To generate wealth the country relied on political strategies and institutions that promoted competition and cooperation: competition to insure continued excellence in production and cooperation to insure that everyone received a fair chance to excel.

The Commission believes we can make a better nation for all Americans if we work together and defer the pursuit of short-term goals for far better long-term rewards. This is a choice Americans have willingly made when faced with adversity.

The following chapter retraces our economic path over the past four decades. By understanding how the American system developed and functioned and how the economic and social systems of our competitors worked, we can better hasten the evolution of a successful system for the century to come.

CHAPTER 2

The American System, 1945-90

Setting Priorities

THE United States and other advanced nations spent the years between 1945 and 1950 building and reforming their institutions. At home we put the finishing touches on a system of capitalism—we have chosen to call it New Deal capitalism— that had been evolving since the 1920s. Abroad, we helped Japan and Germany begin the rebuilding of their societies and the evolution of their distinctive market economies. During this half-decade, governments around the world set the priorities that governed their policies throughout the postwar period.

THE HOME FRONT: NEW INSTITUTIONS AND STRATEGIES
At the end of World War II, the economic strength of the United States, the only major industrial power to survive the war with its economy intact, was unquestioned. Many American firms dominated international markets. Our productivity was the highest of any nation. Modern factories, often built to supply the war effort, were retooled to serve large domestic and international markets. Foreign competition was almost nonexistent. The Defense Department was continuing its generous support for innovation in new industries—aerospace, electronics, and others—thus providing them with a competitive advantage. The primary challenges for the United States were to shift from military to civilian production, to avoid another depression, and to secure international stability.

The Great Depression and World War II led the public to

accept active government intervention in the economy. Between 1939 and 1944, military expenditures increased the federal budget deficit from $2.2 billion to $54.5 billion. During those years, real gross national product grew by an astounding average annual rate of 18.5 percent. Unemployment plummeted from 17.2 percent to 1.2 percent of the civilian labor force.[1] At the same time, the government was able to keep inflation under control and interest rates low, so that servicing the growing government debt remained manageable.

Unresolved, however, were the other roles that the federal government might play in the economy. President Truman and many of his advisers wanted to complete the unfinished agenda of the New Deal, with an "Economic Bill of Rights" that included the right to a job and to a minimum income. Senators Wagner of New York, Murray of Montana, and Thomas of Utah proposed the Full Employment Act of 1945, which called for a federal spending program sufficient to assure full employment. Because of congressional opposition, the bill was softened. The bill that actually passed, the Employment Act of 1946, created the president's Council of Economic Advisers, which advised the president on macroeconomic policy.

The economists who staffed the council believed that, with the proper macroeconomic policies, the government could counter downturns in the business cycle and help assure full employment. Since America's industries were the most advanced in the world, the council gave little attention to the issues of productivity and the development of new industries.

Policies to manage the business cycle complemented a national commitment, born in the Great Depression, to promote mass consumption. Managing the business cycle and promoting mass consumption were ideas that grew out of the work of British economist John Maynard Keynes.[2]

Keynes was able to explain why the market had not been able to generate a recovery from the depression, and he pointed to practical policy solutions. The depression illustrated his contention that the private sector might not by itself generate an adequate level of "effective demand"—demand backed up by consumer and business purchasing power. Government could spur demand by running a budget deficit.

The government could also support demand by encouraging a system of industrial relations that let workers increase their wages through collective bargaining. In the words of H. M. Robertson, general counsel to Brown and Williamson Tobacco:

> It became obvious to the management of our company that no mass production could long be carried on unless there was increased purchasing power by the great masses of people. To us this meant there must be increases in wages and shortening of hours. . . . The more difficult question was how this should be accomplished, and we arrived at the conclusion that collective bargaining by employer and employee . . . was the only means by which, under our system, any adjustment in the equitable distribution of income could be accomplished.[3]

The underlying premise of collective bargaining was that adequate levels of effective demand also required high wages. The nation accepted the principle, which we called the American formula, that its wealth depended on increasing the buying power of its citizens.[4] Production and consumption contribute to each other. Rising wages also stimulate technological progress and higher productivity by giving management an incentive to develop new technology. Labor, in turn, demands a share of the productivity gains, leading to a rising standard of living—and creating an incentive for a new round of productivity-enhancing technological progress.

Collective bargaining was so successful that policymakers used it to tackle social issues such as healthcare. During World War II, government controls of wages and prices encouraged unions and employers to devote more attention to bargaining over health insurance and other benefits. The expansion of hospital insurance helped both labor, which gained additional benefits for its members, and hospitals, which were paid more promptly. For business the costs were relatively small. In 1945 employers spent $21 per employee on health benefits, up from $7 per employee five years earlier. By the end of the war, health insurance coverage had tripled and was well on its way to becoming established in the unionized sectors of the economy.[5] In 1945 President Truman proposed a program for national health insurance, but Congress rejected it, preferring to rely instead on the system of employer-provided insurance.

The period between 1945 and 1950 thus saw the completion of New Deal capitalism. It relied on the high-productivity, mass production strategies that American industry had developed in the 1920s. It included the regulatory safeguards of the 1930s, macroeconomic policies to counter recessions, an industrial policy for militarily important industries, infrastructure investment, collective bargaining, and a social safety net. Companies were expected to innovate and share productivity gains with workers in the form of higher wages and improved benefits such as health insurance. It was a system that helped us achieve unprecedented domestic prosperity. It was complemented by international institutions that helped expand global trade and promote international peace.

ESTABLISHING INTERNATIONAL ORDER

In the years after World War II, we had two international problems—the possibility of Soviet expansion and the need to promote global growth. Even before Japan's surrender, the alliance between the United States and the Soviet Union was beginning to unravel. Despite agreements at Yalta, Stalin crushed democratic governments in Eastern Europe. At the Potsdam conference in 1945, Stalin resisted Roosevelt's proposals for cooperation between the great powers in the reconstruction of Germany. After the conference the temporary division of Germany hardened into a seemingly permanent partition.

Washington considered how to respond. In February 1946 George Kennan, a State Department official in Moscow, supplied the answer with his proposal on containment. Kennan detected in the Soviet leadership a reluctance to take risks. If, he argued, the United States amassed sufficient force and made clear its readiness to use force, America could contain the Soviet threat. Under the circumstances the United States would rarely need to employ force, he reasoned. He also emphasized the importance of offering a positive alternative to the Soviet model:

> Much depends on the health and vigor of our own society. World communism is like a malignant parasite which feeds only on diseased tissue. This is the point at which domestic and foreign policies meet. . . . We must formulate and put forward for other nations a much more positive and constructive picture of the world we would like to see than we have put forward in the past.[6]

Kennan's views gained widespread acceptance. Within a year Americans, who had been wary of entanglements with Europe, began to support the reconstruction of Europe as the centerpiece of the high politics of the Cold War.

President Truman recognized that our new foreign policy required the federal government to organize itself appropriately. A sweeping new national approach to America's global role was called for. He consequently proposed the National Security Act, which created the National Security Council (NSC) to advise the president on domestic, foreign, and military policies concerning national security.

The NSC, once authorized by Congress, strengthened the presidency in several ways. It allowed the president to take the initiative in making security policy, rather than wait for cabinet agencies to act. The staff of the NSC also helped the president to find out what the State Department and the Pentagon were doing and to follow up on the implementation of his policies. The NSC enhanced the president's abilities to anticipate problems, to see opportunities, to manage the national security bureaucracy, and to formulate and carry out both domestic and international policies.

Our efforts to organize ourselves for the Cold War were complemented by our international efforts to promote global prosperity. The American agenda included measures to rebuild a world economic system that had been ravaged by depression and war. The first task was to revive the devastated economies of Europe and Japan, but that was soon extended to establishing international institutions that would foster world trade.

In the short term, America's domestic needs and international goals neatly coincided. At home, demobilization and the conversion to civilian production were the immediate priorities. Manufacturers had to adjust to the loss of demand caused by the end of wartime spending. While the pent-up domestic desire for consumer goods could replace some of this demand, without export markets U.S. manufacturers would have to cut back on their production, possibly plunging the country into a recession.

But those markets could only be created with U.S. assistance to its war-weakened trading partners. Americans recognized that the postwar recovery depended on the ability of European countries to purchase capital goods from America. Since Europe lacked dollars or gold to buy the needed goods, the United States would have to supply the dollars, in the form of loans. The Marshall Plan for European recovery became a chief mechanism by which the United States provided the necessary capital.

The need for an enduring structure to foster international commerce and finance had become clear during the depression. In the 1930s virtually every nation had to confront both the collapse of domestic demand and rising unemployment. Many nations sought to increase employment and total output by running a trade surplus at the expense of the output and employment of other countries. Seeking to raise the price of their imports and cheapen their exports, countries cut themselves loose from the gold standard and devalued their currencies. In effect, such beggar-thy-neighbor strategies were designed to secure domestic prosperity by exporting unemployment. As other countries retaliated by devaluing their currencies or erecting barriers to trade, international trade began to dry up. One tactic used by the United States and other countries was to raise tariffs in an attempt to restrict imports. This led to further decline in world trade, which only served to make the depression more severe.

American policymakers were determined to create an institutional framework that could safeguard the world economy from repeating the history of the 1930s. Their aim was to find a middle ground between the overly rigid gold standard and the uncertainties of floating exchange rates.[7] During a week-long conference held in July 1944 at Bretton Woods, New Hampshire, the United States and its Allies agreed on the structure of a new international economic system. The system was composed of a set of institutions and agreements designed to sustain a growing and stable world economy.

At the center of the new financial order was the U.S. dollar. The participants at Bretton Woods agreed that the dollar would serve as the world's reserve currency—the currency that countries use to settle their international accounts. In the 19th century gold performed this function, as countries paid their international bills by redeeming foreign holdings of their currencies with gold. By the end of World War II, nearly every country, save the United States, was drained of its gold reserves. The United States agreed to step in and provide the world with a means of payment. In the new system every participant in world trade would accept dollars as payment for its exports, and America guaranteed that it would redeem dollars for gold at the fixed rate of $35 per ounce.

The liquidity needed for a dynamic, open system of world markets now depended on the power of the U.S. economy. By lending to our trading partners and by purchasing imports, the U.S. economy would supply the world economy with dollars. Only the United States had the productive capacity and the financial reserves for such a role.

The Bretton Woods system was also designed to end the practice of competitive devaluations. The solution was a return to fixed exchange rates. Member nations were obligated to buy or sell their currencies in the international money market in order to maintain their value. Countries in danger of exhausting their international reserves could apply to a new international institution, the International Monetary Fund (IMF) for loans. Countries with persistent foreign balance-of-payment problems would be allowed to devalue their currencies subject to the approval of the fund. The goal of the system was to discourage the earlier practice of solving economic problems by exporting unemployment.

On the commercial side the United States was determined to lower the barriers to international trade that had existed before World War II. Previously trade between the nations had taken place under bilateral agreements. Given the large number of nations involved and the huge number of products traded, this had gradually led to a chaotic and inefficient system. One of the proposals that emerged from the Bretton Woods conference was to establish an International Trade Organization (ITO), a supranational organization with jurisdiction over all global trade. Unfortunately the countries trying to negotiate the terms and design of the ITO had different visions of what the new trading order should look like. The United States wanted, for the most part, a global economy that would be open to U.S. exports and investments. Developing countries sought distinct privileges. The United Kingdom wanted special treatment for its relationship with its colonies. The proposal that resulted was a hodgepodge that Congress eventually rejected.[8]

Instead of the ITO, the leading nations of the world settled for the less ambitious General Agreement on Tariffs and Trade (GATT). Under GATT, nations extended to other countries the treatment afforded to "the most favored nation" in any bilateral agreement. The result was to substitute a multilateral and global network for bilateral agreements, so that world trade became simpler.

In subsequent years Bretton Woods would be modified. But the institutions it established—most notably the World Bank, the International Monetary Fund, and GATT—formed a system that made possible the great postwar expansion in Europe, America, and Japan.

Our Competitors Rebuild

While the United States was constructing its American system, Europe and Japan were also refashioning their institutions and reviving their economies. Japan and the nations of Western Europe confronted unusable harbors, ruined railroads, damaged roads and bombed-out factories. Banks and financial markets had been disrupted. The American dollar was the de facto hard currency, but only Americans had dollars. Because these countries were poor, they all recognized the need to sell to overseas markets—especially to the large and affluent U.S. market. The issue for them was how they could rebuild and regain their economic strength.

All of these countries were committed to private ownership and to reliance on the market. They used government to develop strategies, create and regulate institutions, and to forge consensus between labor and management. Thus, as a first step toward rebuilding, each country developed mechanisms for fostering cooperation among major economic constituencies—managers and owners of industrial enterprises, trade unions, banks, and the government. The French planning system, the advisory councils of Japan's Ministry of International Trade and Industry, and regular German roundtables all provided forums in which constituencies could debate their priorities and their ideas for improvement. In Germany and Japan these forums were facilitated by traditions of industrial management associations and strong trade unions; labor and management improved company training programs and instituted procedures for cooperating in production.[9] Inspired by American management experts such as W. Edwards Deming and J. M. Juran, Japanese companies established quality programs which shifted more of the responsibility for quality to workers on the shop floor.[10]

Steps were also taken to insure that government had the organizational abilities to effectively guide industrial development. In 1949 Japan created its Ministry of International Trade and Industry, which assumed much of the responsibility for rebuilding Japan's industrial base. In 1950 the Japan Export Bank was established to finance exports.[11] Throughout the postwar period, the Japanese agencies responsible for overseeing the economy recruited the best students from the elite universities to create a greatly respected civil service. A Japanese businessman, when asked why Japanese companies still follow the advice given by the Ministry of Industry and International Trade, replied, "Our government employs some of the best educated and intelligent people. Naturally we follow their advice."[12]

Development strategies of these nations relied upon increasing investment, especially in the infrastructure. In the public sector, the Marshall Plan and the World Bank played a key role in financing new highways and the reconstruction of ports and rail lines. The government also recognized the need for directing investment into such key industries as steel, coal, and cement, whose products were crucial inputs for other industries. Modernizing these strategic industries became a national priority. Policies that favored investment in new and efficient technologies resulted in handsome productivity gains—more than 5 percent per year in Germany through the 1950s, with similar gains elsewhere.[13]

Promoting cooperation, creating a competent government, and encouraging investment were critical to rebuilding the private sector. Equally important was the financial industry. The recovering nations reorganized their banking systems to place priority on industrial development. In some cases, public investment banks were created to finance basic industry and infrastructure. These included the Japan Development Bank, which made loans to designated industries to finance new plant and equipment. France had its Economic and Social Fund administered by the Ministry of Finance, and Germany created a fund to administer Marshall Plan dollars.[14] Here again Japan went furthest. In 1950 its Ministry of Finance pooled postal savings accounts, national pension funds, and various other accounts to create a so-called Fiscal Investment and Loan Program. By 1990 this fund amounted to $250 billion.[15]

Financing was directed by these governments according to long-term plans for rebuilding important industries and penetrating the lucrative American markets. The Volkswagen, the transistor radio, the Datsun, and a host of other products that appeared in the United States were among the fruits of these strategies. Although there were many difficulties and failures along the way, governments in Europe and Japan were very successful in orchestrating national recoveries through careful economic planning and public- and private-sector partnerships.

The years between the end of World War II and the middle of the 1960s saw the development of three versions of capitalism. The U.S. version—New Deal capitalism—was shaped by our unique dominance after World War II, by the Cold War, and by a belief in positive government. A clear division between public- and private-sector responsibilities ensured that government's role was not unlimited. The European social-democratic and the Japanese consensus-oriented versions of capitalism relied upon different political traditions. In both cases government played a major role, particularly in organizing reconstruction after the war. The economic priority was to build a strong production base able to export. These different types of capitalism were compatible and mutually reinforcing as long as the United States was strong enough both to shoulder the expense of the West's security and the smooth operation of the international economy.

The Golden Age of the 1950s and 1960s

The postwar arrangements worked well. The U.S. economy grew vigorously—a result of the competitive advantages of U.S. industries and of the generally skillful application of macroeconomic policies. During the 1950s the Eisenhower administration launched several initiatives that reshaped the economy and paved the way for a period of sustained economic growth at home. Citing the need to move armed forces and supplies quickly around the country, President Eisenhower proposed the creation of a continent-wide network of highways. The interstate highway system illustrated how programs launched for one purpose could have other, perhaps unintended, benefits. The new transportation networks allowed business to reach large markets more efficiently. More importantly, with new interstate highways to use, middle-class Americans bought automobiles. This benefited not only Detroit but the communities across America where factories made steel, glass, and rubber. Another stimulus came from the efforts of the Veterans Administration and the Federal Housing Authority to promote home ownership, which spurred the construction industry and its suppliers.

American business and labor were well positioned to profit from the expansion of demand. With many of Japan's and Europe's factories destroyed or damaged, American industry set the pace. A well-educated work force, modern factories, the world's best scientists and engineers, ample supplies of low-cost credit, and the world's largest domestic market gave American industry tremendous competitive advantages. In turn these competitive advantages meant that increases in domestic demand were largely met by increases in domestic production, not increased imports.

Few storm clouds darkened the economic horizon. After a boom in the early 1950s, in 1954 the economy slipped into a modest recession. The Eisenhower administration did not propose any jobs or public works programs to counter the recession. This administration was not committed, as the Roosevelt administration had been, to the Keynesian idea of using government spending to pull the economy out of downturns. On the other hand, it left in place the so-called automatic stabilizers, such as unemployment insurance, created by the New Deal. Nor did the Eisenhower administration interfere with the efforts of the Federal Reserve to combat the recession. During the 1954 recession, the Federal Reserve cut its discount rate, the rate at which it lends to member banks, and pumped money into the system. A similar pattern occurred in 1958, when the Federal Reserve and the automatic fiscal stabilizers helped pull the economy out of a somewhat sharper recession. Although growth resumed, the unemployment rate in the late 1950s hovered around 6 and 7 percent—much higher than the 2 to 3 percent of the early 1950s.[16]

With growing domestic markets, industry thrived. Labor

and management bargained over wages and benefits within the legal framework established in the 1930s. In 1954 the Internal Revenue Code confirmed that employer contributions to health benefit plans were deductible, thus providing further impetus for collective bargaining, which in turn led to greater provision of employment-based health insurance.[17]

When President Kennedy took office, the nation's industries were still preeminent at home and overseas. The banks and the financial markets helped industry finance new investments and enabled middle-class Americans to buy homes. Productivity and real wages were rising steadily. Yet millions of Americans did not share in this prosperity, as the new president and his advisers were keenly aware. Hundreds of thousands of families—black and white, urban and rural, in all regions of the country—were living without adequate food, shelter, and medical care in what Michael Harrington called "the other America."[18]

The new administration developed a number of proposals for bettering the lives of the most disadvantaged Americans. Secretary of Labor Arthur Goldberg proposed—in the "Full Employment Act of 1961"—to create a permanent public works program and to establish new job-training programs, especially in the new technologies. The new members of the Council of Economic Advisers, led by Walter Heller, took another approach. They were more concerned with achieving aggregate economic objectives—especially increasing the rate of economic growth. Heller and his colleagues favored tax cuts over spending programs.

The council's strategy of favoring tax cuts prevailed over the Labor Department's strategy of public employment. In 1961 the Kennedy administration liberalized the treatment of depreciation allowances. In 1963 Congress passed an investment tax credit and other tax cuts—but few spending increases, in part because Congress could not agree on how to allocate the money. The labor market programs that were agreed upon were aimed at the most disadvantaged, who lacked needed skills. Because these skills deficiencies were thought to be a temporary problem, no effort was made to link these training programs with more permanent labor market institutions such as the unemployment insurance system.

The tax cuts worked. Real, fixed nonresidential investment by the private sector, which had risen little between 1955 and 1959, surged from $165 billion in 1959 to $277 billion in 1966. Between 1962 and 1966 the economy grew by more than 5 percent a year.[19]

In 1964 Congress turned to one of the unfinished pieces of the New Deal: health insurance. Top officials at the Social Security Administration proposed legislation that would provide health insurance to the elderly who were already beneficiaries of the Old Age and Survivors' Insurance program. This strategy reinforced the tactic taken by the original Social Security Act, which directed social programs to the people who had "earned" their benefits through working rather than linking eligibility to citizenship. (Other countries followed a different approach, beginning their health insurance programs on a universal basis.) Intending to offer an alternative to the Social Security proposal, the American Medical Association proposed a bill that would provide health insurance for those too poor to afford private healthcare. Congress decided to do both, creating the Medicare program for the elderly, which would be administered by the Social Security Administration, and the Medicaid program for recipients of Aid to Families with Dependent Children, which would be administered by the states. Since neither the elderly nor poor women and children were commonly employed in the formal job market, these reforms complemented the existing system of employer-provided insurance.

By the mid-1960s President Johnson and his advisers confronted a set of problems that would set the stage for the troubled decade of the 1970s. First, there was a macroeconomic problem. With high rates of growth, the unemployment rate had fallen below 4 percent for the first time since the mid-1950s. The president was committed to more social spending and to greater involvement in the war in Vietnam. His advisers believed that the additional spending increases would place too much strain on an economy that was already producing as much as it could. America did not have idle factories and unemployed labor that could be put to use producing war materials and medical supplies. If we required such goods, then we needed to reduce the demand for other goods, so that people and resources could be shifted into the military and medical-care sectors. The president's advisers recommended tax increases as a way of reducing overall demand. Otherwise, demand that exceeded overall supply would generate inflation.

President Johnson realized that these tax increases would be resisted. Worried about his popularity, he decided, as would later presidents, that he wanted everything—large spending increases, robust economic growth and no new taxes. The economy did not oblige him. As the Treasury wrote larger and larger checks for Vietnam and the Great Society, it bought less and less. Prices edged upward. Inflation, which had been at 1 percent in the early 1960s, tripled to 3 percent in 1967 and then doubled to 6 percent by 1969.[20] In an effort to halt the inflationary spiral, the Federal Reserve raised interest rates. Economic growth slowed. When the Nixon administration took office it sought to balance the budget by cutting spending. The economy was pushed into a recession. The longest economic expansion of the postwar period had been ended by poor macroeconomic decisions and the unwillingness of the outgoing Johnson administration to recognize that the macroeconomy had its own logic.

A second problem was the changing relationship between wages and productivity growth. Throughout the postwar period, real wages and labor productivity grew at roughly the same rate. Between 1964 and 1968, for example, productivity grew at a 2.4 percent annual rate while wages advanced at a 2.5 percent pace. But between 1969 and 1973, productivity growth slowed to 1 percent a year while wage growth remained at 2 percent.[21] The productivity slowdown placed American firms in a difficult position. Either they had to raise their prices to cover their increased costs, or they had to accept lower profit margins.

American industry also faced new challenges overseas. The competitive preeminence of American industry—the other key factor in the strong growth of the Golden Age—was diminishing. The resurgence of the European and Japanese economies had been a source of American pride, since we helped bring it about. But their success changed the world's economic balance. As the 1960s progressed, the United States began to seem less like an economic superpower and more like the first among equals of several great industrial countries. In 1964 the United States produced 23 percent of the total exports of the advanced countries; by 1974 that percentage was down to 18 percent, and the percentage would continue to decline through the next two decades. (See Chart 2.1.) As U.S. industry lost market shares, the merchandise trade balance worsened.[22]

The U.S. military presence overseas also strained the international financial system. European countries gained dollars not only from the rapid growth of their exports to the United States and from private loans, but also from the huge expense

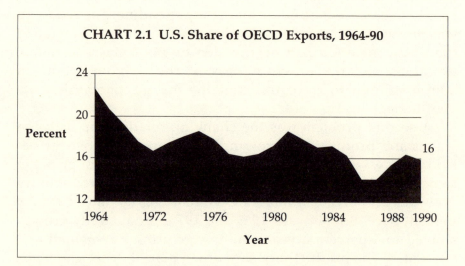

CHART 2.1 U.S. Share of OECD Exports, 1964-90

Source: Organization for Economic Cooperation and Development

incurred by American bases. Similarly, Japan benefited enormously from American spending on the Korean War.

In those days foreign holders of dollars could still demand
redemption of their paper currency in gold at $35 an ounce.
(Until the 1970s Americans were forbidden to own gold currency by a depression-era law.) In the first years after the war,
Europeans wanted America's products—its food and its capital
goods—more than they wanted its gold. But by the 1960s
European nations had accumulated more dollars than they
needed to buy the American goods. As their dollar surpluses
grew, many Europeans came to feel that the dollar was
overvalued. The French began presenting claims on the American Treasury for payment in gold. It was the beginning of the
end for the dollar as international reserve currency.

The postwar order, which seemed so permanent in the good
years of the 1950s and 1960s, could not go on forever. America's
economic dominance immediately following the war was recognized by our leaders as an unusual situation, and the postwar
plan for reconstruction and development was a deliberate effort to bring the world economy back into a stable balance. As
balance was gradually achieved, there was less and less need
for the United States to bear the full responsibility for keeping
the world economy growing. Unfortunately the same quality of
statesmanship that went into creating the postwar order was
not available for the task of replacing it with more equitable
arrangements.

"The characteristic danger of great nations is that they may
at last fail from not comprehending the great institutions which
they have created," Walter Bagehot warned his contemporaries
in 19th-century Britain.[23]   In the 1970s and 1980s America
suffered the consequences of failing to tailor its institutions to
the changes created by the institutions themselves.

A Decade of Discontent

On August 15, 1971, President Nixon ended the commitment of
the United States to redeem dollars for gold at $35 an ounce. In

the weeks that followed the world's bankers and finance officials attempted to set up a substitute system but could reach no
agreement. Floating exchange rates and the abandonment of
the gold standard, originally presented as a temporary measure, became permanent. Soon the dollar would be just another
commodity in the global marketplace.

The end of Bretton Woods and the subsequent devaluation
of the dollar opened a decade of discontent marked by two
upsurges in oil prices and a global slowdown in economic
growth. As Chart 2.2 shows, the rapid growth rates of Japan
and Germany fell by more than half—from an average annual
rate of 9.7 percent in Japan to 3.6 percent, and from 6.0 percent
in West Germany to 2.3 percent. In the United States the fall
was more modest, from a rate of 3.7 percent for 1950-73 to 2.5
percent during 1973-79.

There is no single, simple explanation for the growth slowdown. The oil price increases damaged the confidence of consumers and investors and triggered an upsurge in inflation,
which in turn prompted central banks in the advanced countries to tighten monetary policy.[24] With the collapse of the
Bretton Woods system, exchange rates fluctuated wildly,

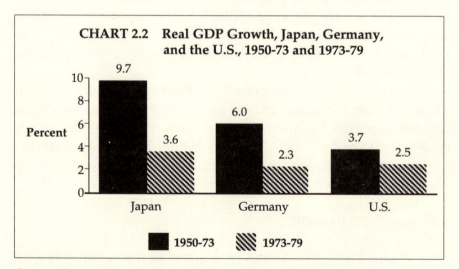

CHART 2.2   Real GDP Growth, Japan, Germany,
and the U.S., 1950-73 and 1973-79

Source: Organization for Economic Cooperation and Development

making international transactions riskier. Countries with competitiveness problems, such as the United Kingdom, found that slow growth was the only way they could avoid widening trade deficits and speculative attacks on their currencies. Just as important was a change in the priorities of policymakers. As the decade continued, policymakers attached greater weight to combating inflation and less to keeping the economy at full employment.[25]

STAGFLATION
Keynesian policies for the economy emphasized the importance of demand. When demand was too low, relative to supply, unemployment rose; when it was too high, inflation increased. Within this framework, it did not seem possible for high unemployment and high inflation to coexist. Yet during the 1970s the U.S. economy experienced this combination of simultaneous high inflation and high unemployment—stagflation.

The United States began the 1970s recovering from a recession that promised to relieve the inflationary pressures that had been building up since the late 1960s. The promise was not kept. Although civilian unemployment climbed to 5.9 percent in 1971, consumer prices still rose to unacceptable levels—until President Nixon imposed wage and price controls in the fall of 1971.

Nixon's controls seemed to work. Inflation soon declined to mid-1960s rates. But the controls only temporarily masked the pressures at work below. Then, as price controls were being phased out in 1973, the Organization of Petroleum Exporting Countries (OPEC) stunned the world economy with its fourfold increase in crude oil prices. By 1974 inflation was galloping along at a 12.3 percent annual pace, twice the rate that had caused so much concern in the late 1960s.

Another recession soon hit the economy, and the unemployment rate reached 8.3 percent in 1975, the highest it had been since 1941. The inflation rate did come down—but only to 4.9 percent, a pace that would have been unacceptable ten years earlier.[26]

This rather modest improvement was also short-lived. As the economy revived in the second half of the decade, growth remained sluggish. (See Chart 2.3). Unemployment declined to only 5.8 percent, a rate once considered recessionary.[27] Despite slow growth and high unemployment, inflation roared back, peaking at 13.3 percent in 1979.

PRODUCTIVITY GROWTH SLOWS

Nineteen seventy-three was the year that the real wages of blue-collar workers peaked. The high unemployment of the mid- and late-1970s was one factor that exerted downward pressure on wages. Another key factor was the slowdown in productivity growth. Without improvements in productivity, business was less able to pay for real wage increases. During the 1950s and 1960s output per hour of labor grew at an annual rate of 2.8 percent. After 1973 productivity growth crawled to a 1.0 percent annual rate, as Chart 2.4 shows.[28] (Germany and Japan also experienced large drops in productivity growth but their rates of growth remained higher than America's.)

One reason for the slowdown in productivity growth was the decline in economic growth. Output advanced by only 2.5

CHART 2.3   Inflation and Unemployment, 1950-73 and 1973-79

Source: *Economic Report of the President*, 1992

percent annually during the 1973-79 business cycle.[29] Without the pull of vigorous growth, which utilizes existing capacity, business has little incentive to modernize or expand its plant and equipment. In the 1970s investment in new plant and equipment declined. One important source of productivity growth—more modern factories and equipment—was now lagging.

Another cause for the productivity slowdown was the growing obsolescence of management's methods for organizing production. From the turn of the 20th century, Americans had been wedded to "scientific management," the idea that labor could be made more productive by the ever greater subdivision and simplification of production tasks. One aspect of this process was taking skills off the shop floor, so that management could have better control of the flow of production.[30] Another aspect was close supervision; supervisors and middle managers proliferated.

This strategy worked from the 1940s through the 1960s. But by the 1970s the mass production strategy began to reach its limits. American corporations increased the amount of supervision of shop-floor workers. In manufacturing, for example, the number of supervisors per 100 production workers rose

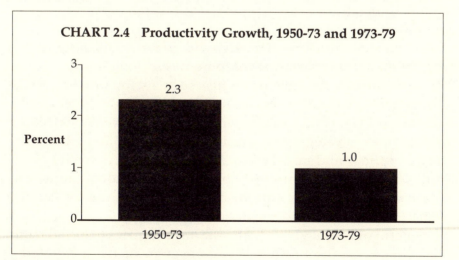

CHART 2.4 Productivity Growth, 1950-73 and 1973-79

Source: *Economic Report of the President*, 1992

from 4.8 in 1970 to 8.0 by 1979.[31] But this had little effect on output per hour and did not promote harmony in the workplace. The contentious strike at the General Motors assembly plant in Lordstown, Ohio, came to symbolize labor relations in the decade.

THE GLOBALIZATION OF PRODUCTION AND FINANCE

The 1970s saw startling changes in the global economic landscape. Breakthroughs in communications made it possible to link financial markets and institutions around the globe. Japanese life insurance companies and Saudi princes became major forces in the U.S. Treasury bond market. American interest rates became more sensitive to global developments.

At the same time large industrial corporations reorganized themselves to produce and sell around the globe. Even though U.S. companies had maintained overseas operations for years, their international operations expanded during the 1970s.

In Japan the 1970s saw the maturation of the export-led recovery strategy initiated in the darkest days of the 1940s. During the decades when Japan was exporting cheap plastic goods and textiles, the nation was also developing strong shipbuilding, steel, electronics, and automobile industries. From scratch, Japan built industries whose products were as good as any in the world—or better.

At the same time, the Third World experienced a decade of revolutionary industrial development. No longer were Third World countries thought to be just sources for raw materials like minerals and oil or agricultural commodities like rubber and cotton. Over time the newly industrializing countries (NICs) initiated new strategies for production. Just as Japan, between the early 1960s and mid-1970s, moved up the economic ladder from simple manufacturing to higher value-added goods, the new competitors were able to do the same in the 1970s and 1980s.

Several of the newly industrializing countries profited from the collapse of the Bretton Woods system of fixed exchange rates. When the dollar began to float in 1973, it fell against the currencies of our industrialized trading partners, making imports from those countries more expensive in the United States. Korea, Taiwan, and other NICs kept their currencies fixed against the dollar, so that exporters in these countries benefited from a more stable exchange-rate climate.

Easy access to foreign technology and capital, low wages, and a variety of tax, credit, regulatory, exchange rate, and import restrictions helped the NICs develop their industries. Often these countries were encouraged on the path of export-led growth by both the U.S. government and U.S.-based multinational corporations. "Export-processing zones" played an important role in this strategy. The local host government would designate a certain area as an export-processing zone and lay out the infrastructure (harbor access, ground and air transportation links, reliable power service, etc.) for an industrial district. Companies locating in these zones enjoyed special treatment under tax laws and were excused from certain labor-rights requirements, antipollution controls, and other regulations.

Not surprisingly export-processing zones boomed. The first one was established near Shannon Airport in Ireland in 1967; by the end of the 1970s there were more than 80 such zones in Third World countries.[32] In Mexico the border region along the United States became a giant export-processing zone with the support of the governments of both countries. In the United States, importers of garments, electronics, automobile parts, and other goods from this *maquiladora* zone pay U.S. tariffs only on the value added in Mexico, not on the full value of the imports. Since wages in Mexico are very low—as little as $4 or $5 a day— the tariff charges are minimal. The region continues to attract large investments from many U.S. companies that use *maquiladora* factories for the final assembly of goods.

When only a handful of countries pursued export-led growth, the side effects were limited, but as more and more countries jumped on the bandwagon, the limits of this approach became apparent. Countries following this model seemed to expect a free ride on the world economy, in that they depended on the willingness of others to absorb the increased output that comes with higher productivity and rising capacity. This is particularly true when they shelter their own markets from imports. In effect, this strategy assumes that other countries will take responsibility for growth in world demand. This was the role shouldered by the United States after World War II, but the United States no longer has the unlimited ability to absorb foreign goods.

By the start of the 1980s world trade with the United States was becoming unbalanced. Foreign nations were more dependent than ever before on America's demand and on America's willingness to accept lopsided commercial relationships. Europe, Japan, and the Third World all saw the U.S. market as their best hope for growth. Imports, which had less than 4 percent of the U.S. market in 1970, took more than 8 percent by 1979, as we see in Chart 2.5. Without America's commitment to be the "consumer of last resort," every country in the non-Communist world would have faced serious economic problems. Yet the United States was less and less capable of playing this role without suffering serious internal problems.

The globalization of production in the 1970s was made

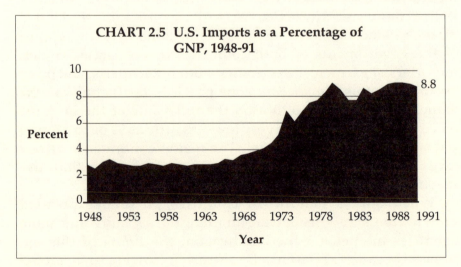

CHART 2.5 U.S. Imports as a Percentage of GNP, 1948-91

Source: U.S. Department of Commerce

possible by the globalization of finance. The emergence of global financial markets and the new mobility of capital dramatically altered the nature of the world economy. Capital flows began to dwarf trade flows. The financial markets became continuous, around-the-clock, worldwide exchanges.

OPEC's price increases forced the financial system to cope with huge new flows of dollars. The OPEC countries accumulated enormous hoards of surplus dollars; they wanted to invest these surpluses in safe, profitable, interest-bearing accounts. The international banks were the only agencies capable of handling investments on such a scale, and OPEC was only too happy to see them take the risks.

Providentially—or so it seemed to many at the time—the same increase in the price of oil that created these hoards of petrodollars also created a demand for huge loans. Developing countries needed to import fuel to run their industries; what was more natural than for these countries to borrow the surplus dollars of the exporters to finance their imports? The developing countries, even those with oil revenues, such as Mexico, also realized that they needed to accelerate their industrial development. To make these investments—including investments in oil exploration that might reduce their import bills—these countries turned to the banks.

Bank vaults were filled with petrodollars to lend; governments, including the American government, were concerned with the developing countries' limited access to capital. The result: massive loans to Third World countries, which amounted to over $1.1 trillion by the early 1980s.[33]

By 1980 the outline of the Third World debt crisis was beginning to emerge. Unlike the crisis of 1974, the Third World debt issue would have a long-term effect on the world's economy as well as on its banking system. Some of the largest banks in the world had made enormous loans to countries that could not meet their obligations on schedule. For the first time since World War II, the prospect of a global financial crisis became a real factor in the day-to-day thinking of bankers and regulators. Since production and finance were forging stronger links between nations, the United States was increasingly affected by international developments.

The world had traveled an immense distance since the early postwar period, and the institutions developed in that era looked increasingly inadequate in light of the vastly expanded scope of world finance.

THE TURN AWAY FROM KEYNESIAN MACROECONOMICS

Stagflation, the productivity slowdown, and increasing international competition made the 1970s a rough ride for most Americans. Policies that had seemed effective in the 1950s and 1960s were now regarded with skepticism. As many promises of the 1960s went unfulfilled, government was viewed less as a means by which citizens could act together to solve social problems and more as the *source* of many of those problems. Lyndon Johnson had promised the Great Society; many Americans felt they got high inflation and high unemployment instead.

In the United States and overseas, Keynesian economics, with its optimism about the ability of government policy to manage growth, was under fire. The internationalization of the economy meant that government stimulation of domestic demand was leaking out of the United States—drawing in a rising tide of imports. The inflation of the 1970s posed problems for the Keynesians. They had little to say about the underlying causes of inflation—namely, the rise in oil prices and the productivity slowdown. Their only solution was to cool the economy off by plunging it into recession. Eventually this would work, but it was often at a great cost—high unemployment—and the cure did not seem to be permanent. The drop in inflation after the 1973-75 recession proved to be temporary. By 1979 inflation was again in double digits—and accelerating. The recommended solution: higher interest rates to trigger another recession. The public, on the other hand, was demanding something new.

The Failed Restoration

In January 1981 President Reagan took office, vowing to restore economic growth and at the same time reassert U.S. military supremacy. The new administration sought to give Americans confidence again about the nation's role in the world economy. The new president did not talk, as President Carter had, of malaise. He talked instead about America standing tall again, as it had throughout most of the 20th century.

Abroad, standing tall meant more spending on the military. As a portion of the national product, defense spending had reached a peak of 9.7 percent in 1968, the height of our involvement in Vietnam. During the 1970s that figure declined steadily, reaching a low of 4.8 percent in 1979.

The Reagan administration was committed to reversing that decline. The administration supported dozens of new weapon systems, from space-based antimissile lasers to more conventional weapons, such as the MX missile, the M1 tank, and the B1 bomber. After adjusting for inflation, the Pentagon's budget swelled from $159 billion dollars in 1980 to $245 billion in 1986—a real increase, unprecedented in peacetime, of 54 percent. As a portion of the national product, military spending turned upward again, peaking at 6.5 percent in 1986.[34]

The military buildup proved to be the easy part of the restoration. The harder part was the effort—ultimately unsuccessful—to lay the foundations for a new period of sustained economic growth and rising standards of living.

THE SUPPLY-SIDE GROWTH STRATEGY

The president, and especially his supporters, did not advocate adjusting the system. Instead, guided by a faith in markets and laissez-faire economics, they viewed themselves as revolutionaries. In February 1981 the Reagan administration presented its growth strategy to Congress. The strategy was based on a simple and—to many Americans—plausible idea, namely, that the key to growth was getting government off our backs. The government was identified with red tape and unproductive bureaucrats. It was the problem, not a part of the solution. The new administration deregulated the financial system. Its solution to the productivity slowdown of the 1970s was to reduce government's role in the economy, especially the environmental and safety and health regulations put in place during earlier administrations. As for poverty, the Reagan administration trimmed back programs helping the indigent, arguing that the programs did not work, that there was little government could do, and that growth was the best answer.

Holding all the pieces of its domestic agenda together was a belief that markets could solve all of our problems. By scaling back government and setting markets free, the Reagan administration felt it could ignite economic growth.

The new strategists criticized income taxes for debasing the American work ethic, sapping incentives to work, save, and invest. If a typical savings account paid 5 percent interest, this was only 2.5 percent for a taxpayer in the 50 percent tax bracket. Cutting the top rate to 30 percent would increase the aftertax benefit of savings so much that people would spend less and save more. A key assumption made by the Reagan administration was that these new savings would be channeled into real productive investments—factories and equipment—and not into financial assets and real estate.

The centerpiece of the administration's tax reform was a 23 percent across-the-board cut in tax rates, phased in over three years. Because the wealthy paid taxes at higher rates, the size of their cuts was larger than the reductions the poorest Americans received. The top rate was scaled back from 70 to 50 percent, effective in 1982, while the bottom rate fell only from 13.5 to 11 percent. In another move that benefited the wealthy, the capital gains tax was reduced from 28 to 20 percent.[35]

The amounts involved in these tax cuts were substantial. The Commerce Department estimated that these reforms lowered tax revenues from individuals by $32 billion in 1982, by $75 billion in 1983, and by even larger amounts in later years.[36]

STANDING TALL AGAIN?

The striking feature of the American economy in the 1980s was the continuation of the downward trends that began in the 1970s. Instead of reversing our economic decline, old problems intensified, new ones erupted, and the failures of some parts of the system aggravated the performance of other sectors.

The promised supply-side boom was not as great as had been hoped for; nor was it sustainable. American households actually saved a smaller share of their aftertax incomes in the 1980s than they had in the 1970s. Personal savings fell from 7.8 percent in the 1973-79 business cycle to 6.6 percent in the 1979-89 cycle. As Chart 2.6 shows, the savings rate for all sectors in the economy—households, businesses, and government—fell from 17.2 percent for 1973 through 1979 to 15.6 percent in the 1979-89 period.[37]

A concomitant policy was the deregulation of the financial industry to stimulate the economy. One result of deregulation was a much weaker financial sector. First, the thrifts had the most costly financial crisis in history. Then the commercial banks ran into difficulties. Weakened by Third World debts,

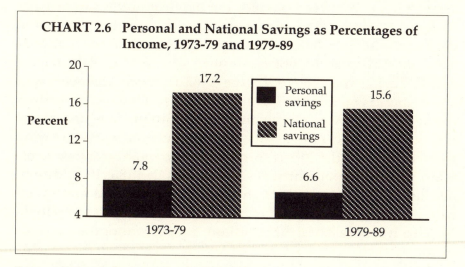

CHART 2.6   Personal and National Savings as Percentages of Income, 1973-79 and 1979-89

Source: *Economic Report of the President*, 1992

the large commercial banks struggled to remain profitable. Many committed large sums of federally insured deposits to highly leveraged transactions and real estate developments. When the real estate boom ended in the late 1980s, the banks found themselves in trouble again.

Investment, hindered by high interest rates and a weak financial sector, did not increase. As we saw in Chapter 1, growth in the 1980s was no better than the 2.8 percent the economy had achieved during the 1970s. Productivity growth continued to stagnate.

THE TWIN DEFICITS

One of the most visible legacies of the 1980s is the staggering national debt. Two types of debt have received attention: the amount owed by the federal government and the amount that Americans owe the rest of the world.

Federal deficits were a direct result of the administration's fiscal policy. Not surprisingly the tax cuts and the arms buildup led to tremendous increases in the federal deficit. In 1979 the deficit was $40 billion—a sum that seemed huge then, though it amounted to only 1.6 percent of the national product. In 1982, after the tax cuts were passed, the defense budget increased, and the economy had plunged into a severe recession, the deficit climbed to $128 billion, or 4 percent of the national product. This should not have been unexpected. What happened during the recovery from 1983 to 1986, however, was surprising. Typically the government's fiscal balance improves during a recovery as tax revenues rise with income, and social welfare spending falls as unemployment diminishes. During the recovery of the 1980s, high unemployment persisted, remaining over 7 percent from 1980 through 1986. In addition, because of additional cuts in the income tax and continued increases in military spending, the deficit continued to widen. By 1986 it had reached $221 billion, 5.2 percent of the national product.

While the budget deficits have received the greatest publicity, the trade deficits may prove more significant in the long run. We saw in Chapter 1 that the merchandise trade balance moved from a deficit of a few billion in the 1970s to $160 billion in 1987 before easing downward to a still huge $116 billion in 1989.

One factor at work here was the sudden appreciation of the dollar during the early 1980s. The Federal Reserve's policy of high interest rates attracted investors from all over the world, eager to buy the debts of the U.S. Treasury. By investing in the United States, foreigners bid up the price of the dollar. As the dollar rose, American goods became more expensive in foreign markets, and imported goods became cheaper here. This was only a part of the problem. Our goods were no longer competitive in many markets, even when the dollar was low.

America's loss of competitiveness was caused by a number of homegrown factors, including obsolete managerial strategies, loss of technological leadership, sluggish levels of investment, and declining growth in productivity. These often added up to products whose quality and cost left much to be desired.

The composition of our trade deficit also changed alarmingly during the 1980s. The 1970s had seen influxes of imports in shoes, apparel, textiles, steel, and automobiles. Countless American firms in these industries either went out of business or drastically curtailed their U.S. operations. At the time, many Americans did not worry too much about the fate of these industries. These, after all, were thought to be the "sunset industries" of America's past, not the high-tech industries that would secure tomorrow's prosperity. But in the 1980s imports swept into many high-wage, capital-intensive sectors, including computers, telecommunications equipment, and semiconductors.

The net result of the twin deficits was a dramatic change in America's relationship with the rest of the world. In 1981 we were the world's largest creditor. By 1986 we had become a debtor, and by 1988 we were the world's largest. It was no longer possible for us to undergird global growth. We could no longer be the consumer of last resort. We could not stand tall on bended knees. We lost technological leadership in some important industries. Our financial system was struggling. International policies no longer advanced our economic interests. Social problems were increasingly becoming economic problems. Rising healthcare costs, for example, put pressure on state and local government budgets, forcing them to cut back access to services. Leading companies that wanted to provide their workers with adequate health insurance found themselves at a competitive disadvantage in overseas markets. Business found that a growing number of high school graduates—especially those from the inner cities—did not have the skills required by today's technology.

Ready for Change

Although many citizens were inspired in the early 1980s by a vision of a stronger, more dynamic country, by the end of the decade the American dream remained for many Americans only that—a dream, distant and unattainable.

By the end of the 1980s more and more people had realized that the American system was no longer working for them. They began to ask if the nation was headed in the wrong direction, whether it needed a new course.

As the proponents of the 1980s restoration struggle to respond to these questions, some answers are beginning to emerge. Across the nation, companies now are becoming more competitive, many by encouraging employee participation and commitment. Support for a national technology policy is growing. States are creating programs to help small and medium-size businesses modernize and export. States also are implementing reforms to control medical costs and expand access to care. Inner-city communities are developing innovative reforms of schools. There is active debate of a new foreign policy, one more attuned to our economic interests. Together these changes outline the shape of a new America and the next stage in our economic and social evolution.

In this respect our present situation reminds the Commission of an earlier period in our history. Many of the national policy innovations of the 1930s, reforms such as unemployment insurance and pensions for the aged, were first proposed and, in some cases, enacted by state and local government in the 1910s and 1920s. Sixty years ago it took a depression and a new president to raise these initiatives to the level of national policy. We do not have to wait for another catastrophe. We know the challenges we face: to develop and implement a comprehensive program addressing America's key problems—investment, competitiveness, poverty, healthcare, and foreign relations.

PART II

An Agenda for Change

CHAPTER 3

Investment: The Foundation of Economic Strength

AMERICA is failing to invest. We are neither matching the investments of our competitors nor making the amount of investments we once made.

This investment shortfall extends from factories and equipment to public infrastructure, from work force training to research and development for new products, from bridge maintenance to innovative technologies. If we allow this dangerous "investment gap" to continue, it will undercut the capacity and productivity of our factories and stunt future economic growth.

Since the 1970s, as shown in Chart 1.2, the United States has suffered a 33 percent decrease in net private investment as a share of national product. By some estimates, our industrial rivals now invest twice as much as we do in new plant and equipment.[1] Of the world's richest nations, the United States has ranked last for the past three years in terms of the share of its income devoted to new investment.[2]

Our recent record in public investment is alarming. In the 1980s the proportion of the federal budget spent on public investment fell to half that of the 1970s and one-quarter that of the 1950s and 1960s. While we grapple with overcrowded, often deteriorating roads, bridges, and other public facilities, our industrial competitors are improving and modernizing their infrastructures. France and Japan are building advanced, high-speed rail systems. By 1994, Japan, Germany, and France expect to have fully operational advanced telecommunications networks that carry both voice and data; ours will be less than half completed at that date. Taiwan, a nation approximately the size of Pennsylvania, recently announced a six-year, $600 billion public investment plan.

To fuel a healthy recovery, American business and government must make a new and immediate commitment to increased investment. But investment is not just a device for spurring the economy and creating new jobs. It is also the first step to rebuilding America's economic strength. Investment is nothing less than a commitment, both by business and by government, to the future. For a business, building a technologically advanced factory or training workers to operate new machine tools are strategies to insure that productivity improves steadily. Similarly, a nation must protect its future by developing and improving its basic assets, be they people, nascent technologies, or public transportation systems.

For 50 years America has been preoccupied with increasing its consumption. Our culture, our tax code, and private-sector initiative have all been dedicated to expanding mass consumption so that we could take advantage of our system of mass production. But now the world has changed. We know that to live well, we must produce well, and this will require more investment.

Disinvestment in the 1980s

As our competitors rapidly build the infrastructure of the future, the United States has yet to begin. Indeed, for the past 11 years Washington has barely kept up the nation's existing infrastructure. Between 1980, the last year of the Carter administration, and 1990, federal investments in infrastructure were cut in half. Infrastructure spending fell from roughly 5.0 percent of all federal spending to 2.5 percent.[3]

This was a sharp break with American traditions of government responsibility for building, maintaining, and expanding infrastructure. In the 1820s expenditures on roads, highways, and canals accounted for 11 percent of the federal budget. Later in the 19th century, the federal government vigorously promoted the construction of railroads. Setting a regulatory climate that nurtured private companies, the government supported telephone service, electrification, and modern aqueduct and wastewater systems, all of which encouraged unprecedented growth and industrial development.

In the 20th century the federal government, working with the private sector, launched two major road-building programs. The Public Roads Act of 1916 gave rise to the automobile industry and a host of supporting industries, including steel, rubber, petrochemicals, tourism, and food. During the 1950s President Eisenhower backed legislation establishing the interstate highway system. Federal spending on highways rose from $3.5 billion in 1956 to $13.2 billion in 1960 (in 1990 dollars). In the early 1960s funding for highways and bridges rose steadily, peaking at $17.1 billion in 1965.

Also in this century, Washington created two huge regional power authorities, built rural America's electrical network, and supported water, sewage, and other public works. Annual federal spending on sewage treatment tripled during the 1960s. Expenditures for fresh water programs also rose.

Throughout the 1960s and 1970s political leaders emphasized the importance of roads, bridges, telecommunications, and airports in sustaining a competitive economy. Because such investments clearly advanced national interests, the public gladly gave its support to these major investment programs.

Coupled with high levels of business investment and a skilled, motivated labor force, public investment programs fostered America's exceptional economic growth during the postwar period. Modern transportation facilities helped to boost productivity growth. Rising productivity meant growing profits, which helped sustain high private investment levels. With strong public and private investment, the economy grew at levels healthy enough to improve the incomes and living standards of most Americans.

Government's infrastructure investment slowed in the 1970s as Washington assigned less importance to new infrastructure and more to maintenance. Federal investments in infrastructure, which peaked at 5.5 percent of federal spending in 1965, hovered at around 4 percent during the early 1970s. (See Chart 3.1.) In the late 1970s, however, the Carter administration substantially increased federal aid for wastewater treatment plants, and the portion of government spending devoted to infrastructure rose again.[4] As recently as 1980, investments in all forms of infrastructure totaled $17.3 billion, 4.7 percent of all federal spending.

Federal officials in the 1980s portrayed nonmilitary federal programs as wasteful—an unproductive drain on the economy. By the end of the 1980s public investment as a percentage of the federal budget had fallen by a third. Washington's lack of commitment to the nation's future was dramatically illustrated by cuts in spending for education and training, which, according to some estimates, were reduced by half.[5] These cuts weakened the ability of states and localities to shoulder their own infrastructure responsibilities.

The Case for Public Investment

Investment is critical to long-term economic strength. No economy or business can sustain growth unless it devotes

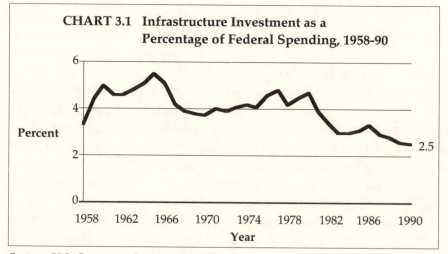

CHART 3.1 Infrastructure Investment as a Percentage of Federal Spending, 1958-90

Source: U.S. Congress, Congressional Budget Office

current resources to expanding the supply of assets used to produce wealth—be they tools, technologies, factories, schools, or workers' knowledge. When companies invest in products, plants, technology, and worker training, they produce more and better goods, increase their productivity, and become more profitable.

Public-sector investments in infrastructure, such as roads and schools, fuel economic growth. Better schools enhance the nation's quality of life, enabling young people to nurture their talents and later earn high wages in productive employment. New roads, combined with improved public transportation, can save millions of hours that workers delivering products might have lost in traffic jams and accidents. In addition, former Secretary of Transportation Samuel Skinner estimated that for every $1 billion invested in transportation infrastructure, between 30,000 and 50,000 new jobs are created.[6]

Consider the case of a hypothetical computer factory. Silicon chips and other parts travel to the plant over networks of rail lines, highways, and airports—the same networks that connect the plant with customers hundreds or thousands of miles away. Potholes and traffic delays mean damaged products, reduced profits, and lost time or accidents for workers traveling to and from work. To communicate with buyers, sellers, and supporting technicians, the factory's managers and engineers need reliable telephone systems and computer networks. The factory also needs access both to clean water and to facilities for disposing of wastewater.

Public investment stimulates private investment. Communication lines, transportation networks, and water and wastewater systems—all are integral to the profitability of industry. Supported by a good infrastructure, owners of profitable factories are more likely to invest and expand production, thus raising productivity and stimulating national economic growth. The fortunes of all of us—consumers, workers, managers, and investors alike—depend on high levels of productivity, investment, and growth.

The research of economists David Aschauer and Alicia

Munnell confirms that public infrastructure investment supports private investment and productivity growth. Aschauer's work indicates that, if the nation's investments in roads, bridges, water and sewer systems, airports, and mass transit had stayed at the level of the 1960s, productivity growth in the 1970s and 1980s would have been significantly higher. According to this research, had infrastructure investment been increased by just 1 percent (of the national product) between 1970 and 1988, productivity growth would have averaged 2.1 percent annually instead of the actual 1.4 percent.[7]

This should not be surprising. As Alan S. Blinder has written, "Just as a truck driver can produce more work per hour if his truck is bigger and more reliable, so can he be more productive if the roads are smoother and less congested—not to mention passable."[8] Good roads are the result of government decisions to invest in construction and maintenance. Thus greater public spending on infrastructure leads to higher productivity across the economy.

Poor infrastructure makes it impossible for industry to implement innovative techniques like just-in-time inventory management. With just-in-time, retailers, rather than accumulating inventory, use modern telecommunications networks to track their sales and to order from manufacturers only those products that customers are currently demanding. They send the electronic orders to manufacturers, who quickly transport the goods to the retailers. Similar systems connect manufacturers with their suppliers. Industries practicing just-in-time inventory management can rapidly improve quality and productivity, thus insuring their future competitiveness in international markets. But without reliable telecommunications and transportation networks, U.S. companies will not be able to use just-in-time techniques. The dependence of private investment, productivity gains, and economic growth on public investment provides the foundation of the case for increasing public investment.

Public investment will stimulate immediate growth more effectively than tax cuts. Consumers may or may not spend a tax cut, and if they spend, they may buy imports. But almost every dollar spent on infrastructure goes directly into the U.S. economy. Direct public investment creates jobs and income while bettering the investment climate in the United States.

Substantial new investments in key infrastructure networks—transportation, water and wastewater, and tele-communications—are one linchpin of a national pro-growth economic agenda. With the nation confronting a huge deficit plus many unmet needs other than infrastructure, we cannot justify the extra $100 billion or more needed each year to meet all our infrastructure needs. On the other hand, more easily financed increases of $10 to $20 billion per year would not stem this decline of our infrastructure.

We recommend that the federal government raise infrastructure investment by $50 billion next year and by $65 billion in 1994 and maintain that level of commitment for nine years. This amount combined with other public investments—in R&D and educa-tion and training—would make up a total investment program of $100 billion per year, a level that strikes a balance between the nation's competing needs.

In Chapter 9 the Commission explains how it would finance this trillion-dollar public investment program. We believe Americans will gladly pay for improved infrastructure—but only if assured that the money is well spent. One way to regain public confidence is to create an investment trust fund that would receive money from a variety of sources, including the peace dividend.[9] The trust fund would issue bonds to finance new public investments. Institutional investors, like pension funds, would find these bonds attractive.

Our proposed increase in infrastructure spending would not meet all of the nation's needs. But it would reverse much of the deterioration and start the process of building the infra-structure of the 21st century. Below are the specific elements of our program.

RENEWING OUR TRANSPORTATION SYSTEM
The 1991 federal transportation plan is inadequate. It will

provide only $150 billion of new investment over five years. Because the United States has neither maintained its current transportation systems nor kept up with new demand, the investment gap in transportation is now huge.

Further neglect would damage U.S. competitiveness. Every year highway congestion in America's largest cities costs the nation more than $30 billion. Travelers, commuters, truckers, and business people lose 2 billion hours annually to transportation congestion. Traffic congestion increased an average of 17 percent a year between 1982 and 1987. If highways are not improved substantially or if viable mass transportation alternatives are not constructed, total waste may soon climb to 4 billion hours per year. In addition, the U.S. Department of Transportation has estimated that about 135,000 bridges are structurally deficient.[10]

Precise estimates for the cost of repairing and modernizing various transportation systems are difficult to obtain. Highway use, for example, depends on energy prices, population growth, the growth rate of the economy, and the development of alternative means of transportation, such as mass transit. Given these uncertainties, former Secretary of Transportation Samuel Skinner estimated that needed capital investments in transportation will cost a minimum of $38 billion per year and may reach as much as $83 billion per year.[11] Other estimates suggest that Skinner may have underestimated the magnitude of the problem. The Federal Highway Authority's calculations indicate that reducing congestion on the existing highway system could take $74.9 billion per year in state and federal money.[12]

The nation's airways and airports cannot safely and swiftly handle current and future demand. According to recent estimates, 25 percent of air traffic delays can be attributed to the inadequate capacity of airports and air traffic control systems. These delays cost air carriers as much as $5 billion in lost time and money. Already 25 large commercial airports are operating beyond their capacity. The Federal Aviation Administration forecasts that, without new investment, 17 more airports will be working beyond capacity by 1997. The air traffic control system is also sorely in need of renovation.[13] According to state transportation officials, the aviation infrastructure requires at least $8 billion per year.[14]

With mass transit and rail added, the cost of maintaining the existing infrastructure reaches over $100 billion per year, as Table 3.1 shows.

TABLE 3.1. Annual Spending and Estimated Needs for the Transportation Infrastructure (over the next ten years)

Network	Current spending	Estimated needs
Highways and bridges	17.0	74.9
Aviation	2.4	8.0
Mass transit	2.4	16.0
Rail	—	1.9
Total (billion dollars)	21.8	100.8

Sources: Congressional Budget Office, Federal Highway Authority, American Public Transit Association, and the Urban Mass Transit Administration

Maintaining and modernizing the current transportation networks should not be America's sole focus. National interest demands that we also invest in the new transportation technologies: high-speed rail and "smart" highways.

High-speed railroads offer great potential for reducing travel time. The Japanese bullet train and the French high-speed train move millions of riders rapidly and comfortably, reducing congestion in badly overcrowded highways and air lanes. While the high-speed French and German trains travel at 150 to 180 miles per hour, Amtrak's premier Metroliner averages only 110 miles per hour, about the same speed as the fastest trains in 1893.

Many observers believe that the future of transportation belongs with a new technology called magnetic levitation—"maglev"—which uses magnetism to lift and propel a vehicle along a guideway at speeds up to 300 miles per hour. Though maglev was invented by two American scientists at Brookhaven National Laboratories in 1960, the United States invested only $3 million in research between 1966 and 1975, then abandoned the effort. Meanwhile, Japan invested $1 billion and tested a model at 320 miles per hour in 1979.[15] Demonstration maglev trains are already operating in Germany and Japan.

In March 1992 the federal government at last created a new $700 million research fund for maglev. A two-way maglev system on an existing interstate right-of-way could easily carry 100,000 passengers per day at speeds of 200 to 300 miles per hour. If it is designed to carry freight also, the revenues of a maglev train are expected to cover its operating costs. But the start-up costs will be large, with several of the key technologies needing further development. The initial costs of building the lines are variously estimated between $8 million and $63 million per mile.[16]

The task force recommends that the federal government play a major role in supporting maglev trains. It can support future R&D, work with industry to develop standards for maglev design and construction, and include high-speed railroads in national transportation plans. It should consider establishing a billion-dollar revolving loan fund to help states finance maglev projects between cities.

Some state governments and the governments of our strongest competitors—but not the U.S. federal government—have shown a keen interest in developing smart cars and highways. In West Berlin the LISB network provides 250 infrared roadside beacons that transmit route-guidance information to help reduce traffic congestion. Sponsored by the German Ministry of Research and Technology, the Berlin Senate, and the private firms of Siemens and Bosch, LISB is a government-business partnership that seeks to improve both German industrial competitiveness and the quality of life in Berlin. Japan also has a smart-highway project under way, and the European Community is subsidizing two different developmental partnerships for smart highways between business and governments.

In the United States, the state of California and several local governments have established the Smart Corridor project. Smart Corridor provides drivers on a 12-mile stretch of the Santa Monica Freeway and its neighboring arterial streets with traffic information. It uses several media: highway-advisory radio broadcasts, signs with changeable messages, menu-driven telephone information systems, and videotext. Another California project is a feasibility study of cars that drive themselves using automated control and roadway electrification systems.[17]

The federal government should help businesses and local governments develop common standards and fund research for these new transportation technologies. We propose that the federal government provide approximately $200 million to support such research.

CLEAN WATER AND WASTEWATER

Maintaining America's water resources is a high priority for the 1990s. Consumers, industry, agriculture, and wildlife depend on abundant supplies of clean water. Cities and regions that can supply adequate quantities of water while disposing of sewage safely and efficiently are more likely to attract industrial investment.

America's water infrastructure is a vast network connecting nearly 60,000 water supply systems to myriad household and industrial users, who are in turn linked to wastewater treatment facilities. The system includes dams, canals, pumping stations, and pipes, as well as sewers, wastewater treatment plants, and septic tanks.

While the nation's sewage treatment plants are all publicly owned, water supply systems are owned and operated by both public and private utilities. Except for a few important federal projects, the overwhelming majority of public water systems are owned and operated by states and localities. The federal government's responsibilities have traditionally included the regulation of water and wastewater quality, and the provision of funds for capital projects, operation, and maintenance.

Water supply experts have recently recognized that proper management and conservation are decidedly more economical than investment in new capital projects.[18] In the mid-1970s, for example, the cost of providing for the future water needs of Washington, D.C., was estimated at between $250 million and $1 billion. But conservation, skillful water management, and one small reservoir sufficed to maintain the capital's water supply.[19]

To avoid unneeded and costly new infrastructure projects, the federal government should more actively manage and conserve the nation's water resources.

Many utilities do not now charge users the full cost of their water supply, thus encouraging waste and discouraging the use of basic conservation techniques. Federal, state, and local water managers should institute timetables for full-cost water pricing. If, by the year 2000, all water users pay the true costs of maintaining their clean water supplies, the nation will have been spared the expense of many unneeded capital projects.

Because conservation projects can eliminate the need for capital projects, investments in conservation should be considered investments in infrastructure. The task force recommends that the federal government support the development and diffusion of water conservation technologies.

Even simple conservation techniques can be extremely effective, especially in urban and suburban areas. For example, Massachusetts requires that new and replacement toilets use no more than 1.6 gallons per flush (compared with 3.5 gallons per standard flush). It is estimated that each household will save between 9,400 and 25,700 gallons annually from this basic measure.[20] The federal government can support similar efforts on a national scale by imposing comparable conservation guidelines in safe drinking water legislation, and by supporting state and local efforts to develop new technologies and to educate the public on the need for conservation.

Even with more conservation, the nation's wastewater system will require significant federal support both for new capital projects and to insure that water supplies meet the standards of the Clean Water Act.

Federal support for wastewater treatment plants should increase significantly. Using projections from Apogee Research, the task force estimates that we must invest $17.9 billion annually in wastewater treatment to meet our needs through the year 2000.[21]

Together, these programs will renew our transportation and water systems. They will improve the quality of our lives and those of future generations. They will promote private investment. The time is ripe for an investment-led recovery program that attacks the roots of our current economic stagnation. The end of the Cold War allows us to shift from the old imperative of defense to the new imperative of economic growth.

TABLE 3.2 Annual Spending and Estimated Needs for the Clean Water and Wastewater Infrastructure

Network	Current spending	Estimated needs
Clean water	4.8	7.0
Wastewater treatment	2.4	17.9
Total (billion dollars)	7.2	24.9

Sources: Apogee Research, the Environmental Protection Agency

Investing in Telecommunications

Public investment in infrastructure stimulates private investment. The government can also foster private investment in the industries it regulates. Today the U.S. telecommunications industry is ineffectively regulated by a quilt of authorities, including state public service commissions, the Federal Communications Commission, Congress, the State Department, the U.S. Trade Representative, and the Departments of Defense and Commerce. Because we lack a national vision for this critical industry, the United States is in danger of losing its international competitive advantage.

Telecommunications may be the single most important

technology of the next century. Modern telecommunications are creating global information highways. Businesses will be able to transmit vast quantities of data and voice information to anywhere in the world in an instant. Nations that build modern telecommunications networks will attract business investment and maintain important employment opportunities. Telecommunications is a composite of local and long-distance carrier services, wireless services like cellular phones, satellite-based communications, equipment ranging from telephones to fax machines, and services like computerized databases. The telecommunications industry is linked to a chain of other industries—computers, television, and more. But this is not all. Telecommunications networks promise to give rise to a host of new industries, from high-definition television to on-line libraries and banks.

The United States is home to the world's largest telecommunications industry and one of the world's largest telecommunications markets. Yet during the last decade we have lost some of our competitive advantage in this vital industry. We have gone from a trade surplus of nearly $12 billion in 1981 to a 1987 deficit of nearly $3 billion. Today the United States is the world's largest *importer* of telecommunications equipment.[22] The principal factor in this dramatic decline has been the equipment manufacturing industry's steady loss of market share.

In part the decline is the legacy of the 1984 breakup of AT&T. It is also the result of a failure to invest. U.S. telecommunications investment fell an average of 8.1 percent a year between 1980 and 1989. Predictably, other industrial nations are now modernizing their communications networks at much faster rates than ours. Germany, for instance, invested $238 for each telephone line in 1989, while the United States spent an average of $88 per phone line. That number places us last among the advanced industrial nations.[23]

During the next decade, technologies such as integrated services data networks (ISDN) are expected to transform the telephone system into the equivalent of one massive computer and cable network. Building such advanced systems involves replacing copper wires and older switches with high-capacity fiber-optic cables and digital switching equipment. Since an ISDN is integrated, it demands uniform standards, and a national ISDN will require national standards.

A number of countries, including Japan, France, and Singapore, have undertaken ambitious plans to develop standardized telecommunications networks. The Japanese telephone company and Japan's Ministry of International Trade and Industry—with the help of such giant firms as NEC, Fujitsu, Hitachi, and Oki—are the driving forces in that nation's effort to produce a national network. Since 1986 the European Community countries have contributed $1.2 billion to pooled research and development for a transnational network. In 1988 the four largest European telecommunications administrations set uniform standards.

Meanwhile, the development of telecommunications in the United States remains mired in regulatory disputes between the Federal Communications Commission and a U.S. district court, and between the Commission and the regulatory agencies of the states. By its nature ISDN should be created on a broad scale. But because of the regulatory disputes, regional holding companies are launching separate ISDN efforts— projects that may prove to be incompatible with each other and which will prevent the emergence of a national network.

Another critical industry, high-definition television (HDTV), depends on the creation of an ISDN. HDTV is linked to major electronics industries, including personal computers, semiconductors, and video cassette recorders. According to some estimates, lack of a competitive HDTV industry could cost America 750,000 jobs in 2010.[24]

Americans need a national strategy for the telecommunications industry. The nation needs to invest in this industry in much the same way as it invested in rail transportation, highways, air travel, and the space program. The task force offers two recommendations:

1. *The federal government should amend the Communications Act of 1934 to create a coherent, consistent framework for regulating*

the telecommunications industry. As it stands, the Communications Act is ambiguous. Regulatory jurisdictions overlap, and the industry finds it impossible to satisfy the requirements of all regulators.

At the national level, a single agency should be assigned prime responsibility for the development of a competitive telecommunications industry. One of the first tasks of this agency would be to develop a plan that would eliminate existing obstacles to a national telecommunications network. Representatives of business, labor, and government would compose the telecommunications infrastructure board charged with carrying out this plan. The Civilian Aeronautics and Aviation Board, which coordinated the successful development of the U.S. commercial aviation industry during the 1920s, provides a precedent for this approach.

2. *Regulators should encourage communications companies to invest in new telecommunications infrastructure.* Current regulations do not offer enough incentives for companies to invest in new technologies or to enlarge fiber-optic networks. The United States should offer financial incentives for telephone companies to lay fiber-optic cables and install digital switches. More liberal depreciation allowances on such infrastructure investment is one possible strategy.

Incentives for Private Investment

While government can invest directly in infrastructure and training, and strongly influence investment behavior in regulated industries, other private investment is less subject to government influence. Most private investment depends upon the independent decisions of companies and individuals. Their decisions reflect their perception of the business climate, which is only partially shaped by government policy.

Government can and should provide incentives that encourage real productive investment. Americans should not find their government supporting programs that encourage speculative financial transactions or investments that move U.S. jobs overseas, especially to low-wage countries.

Presently the Commerce Department sponsors conferences in which government experts provide U.S. business representatives with advice on starting up foreign assembly operations. The government also offers to insure investments made overseas. Using taxpayers' dollars to subsidize the export of jobs is a disservice to the public. It is a practice that should cease.

Perhaps the chief factor determining investment is the most intangible one: confidence. Business people invest only when they expect growing markets and future profits. Recessions and idle factories erode confidence and discourage investment. Stagnant incomes and crumbling infrastructure do not boost confidence either.

Most decisions to invest are predicated on long-term thinking: spending in the present to realize gains in the future. If owners and managers concentrate only on the next quarter's results, or on next year's, they may compromise their future market share and profits by failing to make the necessary long-term investments.

America's approach to corporate governance is partly responsible for the short-term focus of many U.S. corporations. Because they do not focus on the long term, many companies are not making the investments needed to be competitive in the future. In the 1980s too many firms relied upon short-term financial strategies, often entailing risky debts from highly leveraged transactions.

The federal government can enact policies that encourage long-term thinking and investment. The task force suggests three basic measures to stimulate *new and productive* long-term investment: enacting a net investment tax credit for new investments in equipment and workers, reforming the capital gains tax, and increasing the R&D tax credit. Our proposals do not give windfalls on old investments; they reward new, productive investments in capital goods and R&D. In the future we should also consider other measures for influencing investment, such as liberalizing depreciation schedules. Shorter depreciation schedules encourage firms to upgrade their plant and machinery, thus facilitating the introduction of new technologies.

This is by no means a complete list of policies to promote investment. Elsewhere in this book we offer more extensive proposals for macroeconomic policies (Chapter 9), for promoting commercial research and development and investment in new technologies (Chapter 4), and for training American workers (Chapter 5).

1. *Net Investment Tax Credit*

One way to help insure that businesses and working Americans have modern equipment and factories is to provide an incentive—a net investment tax credit—for new investments in plant and equipment and in new training for current workers.

The core of this proposal is a credit of at least 10 percent for investment in productive machinery, pollution control equipment, and training programs. The credit would apply to new, productive investments that give businesses state-of-the-art technology. Such an incentive helps stimulate short-run demand while raising long-run productivity and output.

The net investment tax credit is efficient. It does not reward investments that companies would have made anyway. The short-term cost of the credit would be offset by its long-term benefit. If Washington implements a 10 percent credit, every dollar of tax credit will mean $10 of new investment. As the initial cost rises, growth and productivity will pick up, so that government's future revenues will also rise.

2. *Capital Gains Tax Reform*

The administration's current plan to cut capital gains taxes across the board will not orient businesses toward long-term investments; it mainly provides windfall profits on *old* investments. If a stock is bought one day and sold the next for a higher price, the investor earns a capital gain, but that investor's action has done nothing to provide the company with sources of patient financial capital.

The United States needs to reform the capital gains tax so that short-term gains are taxed at a higher rate than long-term gains. Such a proposal is consistent with long-standing tax policy. From 1920 until the 1986 Tax Reform Act, federal law taxed long-term capital gains at a lower rate than short-term gains.

Our reformed capital gains tax would range from 38 percent on short-term investment gains to 10 percent or even zero on gains resulting from investments that extend for seven years or more. The low rate would apply only to new and productive investments—not to investments in land, art, and collectibles.

3. *Research and Development Tax Credit*
The 1986 Tax Reform Act reduced the R&D tax credit from 25 percent to 20 percent. Research and development activities help companies create and apply new technical knowledge to their operations. They can then produce new products and produce old products more efficiently. Since R&D programs generate benefits throughout the economy, the R&D tax credit should be raised permanently to 30 percent.

Revitalizing the Financial Sector

For any investment program to succeed, investors must have access to a plentiful supply of capital at affordable interest rates. Unfortunately, the American banking system stands today at its lowest ebb since the Great Depression. Nearly 600 of the nation's 4,000 thrifts failed between 1980 and 1986; more than 400 commercial banks closed in the following two years. In 1989 another 200 commercial banks closed because of financial difficulties. The enormous losses of commercial banks threaten the solvency of the Federal Deposit Insurance Corporation, which at the end of 1991 had a deficit of $7 billion.[25]

The situation is compounded by the unprecedented vulnerability of most of our largest banks. Because many of them embarked on high-risk lending operations in the 1980s, some are in danger of insolvency and others are too weak to support new lending. The failure of large banks would deplete the resources of the Federal Deposit Insurance Corporation.

The problem is rooted in financial sector changes that started in the late 1970s. Pressed by strong competition from firms offering banklike services, commercial banks and savings and loans sought to maintain profitability by investing heavily in real estate, junk bonds, and other risky ventures. The banks' participation in these transactions is directly attributable to deregulation and reduced federal enforcement. For almost 50 years after the enactment of the Banking Act of 1933, thrifts and commercial banks followed strict government regulations for their operations. In the late 1970s and early 1980s, however, Congress passed two deregulation bills allowing banks and thrifts to engage in higher-risk activities. In theory, the institutions could earn higher profits, thus growing or earning their way out of their problems. Instead the deregulated industry generated a new and more dangerous set of problems. In 1988 savings and loans owned junk bonds valued at $14.4 billion, while commercial banks typically provided more than 85 percent of the funds for corporate takeovers and leveraged buyouts.[26]

In their current distressed situation, the banks are understandably reluctant to lend. The constraint imposed by too many bad loans on their books has been intensified by new bank capital requirements. In the 1980s U.S. regulators required that all banks maintain "total capital"—shareholders' equity, subordinated debt, and loan loss reserves—equal to at least 6 percent of their assets. (Banks' assets are their loans; to the extent that capital-to-loan ratios are regulated, banks are inhibited from lending more.) The United States and 11 other industrial countries then negotiated the Basel standards (named after the Swiss city where the negotiations took place), which will require that total capital equals 8 percent of assets by 1993. The many banks that now do not have adequate capital are trying to raise capital, reduce their assets (that is, their loans), or both.

The victims of our weakened banking system are small and

medium-size companies that have no alternative sources of capital. Without credit from banks, these businesses cannot invest. Their failure to grow will in turn seriously slow the national economy.

The task force proposes that the Federal Reserve (or another federal agency) inject capital into the banks so that they can extend more credit to private firms. This federal investment would be contingent upon the banks' lending to small and medium-size companies. The task force estimates that $20 billion in capital could support at least $100 billion in new lending.

This proposal does not imply a bailout of failing banks; only banks with reasonable long-term prospects would be eligible to receive the infusion of capital. The program is consistent with the Federal Reserve's role of supporting the banking system.

The federal government also needs to consider financial-sector reforms that promote long-term, stable relationships between banks and industries. American companies now compete against firms in Western Europe and Japan that have stable links to their sources of capital. In exchange for steady, reliable capital, these firms give their banks a voice in management. As a consequence, both lending institutions and industrial firms look to long-term profitability rather than to short-term gain.

With a stronger financial system, public investment, and government-spurred private investment, we lay the foundation for economic renewal in America. But the competitiveness battle will be won or lost in the American workplace. To meet the challenge of global competition, we must address issues of workplace organization, corporate governance, and relationships between companies. Public and private investments must be complemented by fundamental changes in the way American enterprises work.

CHAPTER 4

Industrial Preeminence

Competitiveness: The Unfinished Agenda

AMERICANS are increasingly aware that to live well, we must produce well. It is that simple—and that difficult. Unless our industries efficiently produce well-designed, high-quality goods, our standard of living will inevitably decline.

Many American companies have put the improvement of production at the top of their corporate agendas. They have implemented strategies to cut costs, eliminate management layers, and compete on quality. Numerous companies are becoming more competitive by sharing decision making through employee participation programs and by sharing "a piece of the action" through employee stock ownership plans (ESOPs). Today over 20 percent of the work force benefits from share ownership.[1] These efforts are starting to show results. Manufacturing productivity growth has rebounded from its dismal performance in the 1970s. Improved products and a lower-valued dollar have helped U.S. exports to boom, with aircraft, industrial machinery, and scientific equipment all more than doubling their overseas sales between 1986 and 1991.[2]

Clearly there are some reasons for optimism regarding the future competitiveness of American industry. Yet we must be realistic about how far we still have to go to finish the agenda and regain our leadership in manufacturing and technology. Some of the productivity improvements of the 1980s came from shutting down outmoded factories, a tactic that cannot sustain productivity growth over the long run. And the companies innovating their production techniques remain a minority, outnumbered by those clinging to obsolete strategies.

Many companies are content to rely on macroeconomic factors, such as the lower value of the dollar and stagnating U.S. wages, to compete in international markets. Between 1985 and 1990, the dollar dropped 45 percent against the German mark and 40 percent against the French franc and the Japanese yen.[3] This was equivalent to a 40 percent fall in the price of American products—and labor—compared with their overseas counterparts. Over this same period, U.S. manufacturing wages were rising by less than 3 percent a year, while German, French, and Japanese businesses had to cope with wage increases averaging 4 percent a year. Consequently the cost of American labor, which in 1986 was already below the dollar cost of labor in Germany and other European countries, dropped even lower by 1990 (the most recent year for which data are available). Average wages were then one-third *higher* in Germany and Norway, at $21.53 and $21.86, respectively, compared to $14.77 in the United States. Swedish and Danish workers presently enjoy average hourly wages of $20.93 and $17.85, respectively.[4]

Lower wages and a weak dollar are not permanent sources of competitive advantage. Industries in other advanced countries do not depend on such macroeconomic factors to give them a competitive edge. Instead they seek advantages by continuously improving product quality, innovating production, cutting costs, and by seeking the cooperation of their governments in broader technological endeavors. They also cultivate long-term partnerships with their employees, suppliers, and financial institutions. Business leaders recognize that equitably distributing risks and rewards is a critical strategy for economic success in the global economy. Our industrial competitors also understand that certain economic interests are shared nationally, and that everyone carries a responsibility to advance them. We can learn from their success.

PRIVATE-SECTOR LEADERSHIP

The primary responsibility for determining how America competes with other nations rests with the managers and owners of industry. They decide whether to implement new production strategies and training policies, to invest in new equipment, to launch research projects, or introduce new products. Their decisions, which cannot be dictated from Washington, will shape the competitiveness of industry—and, ultimately, the standard of living of American workers.

The commitment of American business to national economic health depends on the quality of the leadership of America's corporate managers. A national commitment requires a broad perspective. Corporate strategies thus need to serve shareholders *and* other stakeholders: employees, suppliers, customers, and communities. Leadership also requires a long-term vision capable of aligning personal interests with both corporate success and the national economic interest.

GOVERNMENT'S ROLE IN CREATING A FAVORABLE CLIMATE

Private-sector leaders are greatly influenced by the climate government creates. For example, investment decisions are influenced by macroeconomic policies that affect interest rates, inflation, and the value of the dollar.

In most other industrialized countries, governments do not restrict themselves to macroeconomic initiatives. In countries such as Germany and Japan, governments influence the microeconomic environment as well. They work with the private sector to develop key industries and to support economic adjustment programs that cushion the impact of competition. Their strategies include measures to protect the home market, to provide patient capital to regulate competition, to share national research among firms, to train employees, to restrict foreign investment, and to assist companies trying to open export markets.

The U.S. government, by contrast, has generally refused to assign much importance to industries not involved in defense-related production. This indifference has cost us our leadership in many industries. One example is particularly telling: in 1980 American firms produced 85 percent of the world's memory chips for computers; by 1988 Japan held 75 percent of the market, and our share had shrunk to 15 percent.[5] America used to be the undisputed leader in electronics; now we have to work hard to catch up.

The aerospace industry offers more warnings. If the United States does not support this key industry, then we risk losing it to the industrial policies of our competitors. Most of the world's civilian jet aircraft are made in the United States. But in the 1970s government-backed companies from Germany, France, Spain, and the United Kingdom decided to support a new aerospace consortium, Airbus. They have invested more than $7 billion over a 21-year period.[6] Airbus has succeeded: last year Airbus held more than 30 percent of the world aircraft market, second only to Boeing and well ahead of McDonnell Douglas.[7] Its rise to prominence has cost the United States 50,000 jobs and $4 billion in exports in 1989.[8]

A company partially owned by the government of Taiwan recently announced its intention to acquire part of McDonnell Douglas, one of our largest aerospace companies. Taiwan's long-term economic strategy is to establish itself as a power in the aircraft industry. U.S. policymakers should of course make sure that such a deal does not harm American interests—high-wage jobs and critical technologies must remain at home. But the United States, unlike most nations, does not promote strategic domestic industries by regulating foreign direct investment. Instead various groups are pressuring Congress to block the sale. Ad hoc responses to systematic problems—in this case, the targeting of key U.S. industries by foreign competitors—cannot for long protect our national interests.

The McDonnell Douglas case illustrates how American companies are affected by the policies of the federal government. The government has the ability to influence the strategic choices made by American firms. The challenge is to use this influence so that business strategies both enhance the competitiveness of firms and advance the nation's prosperity.

The signals Washington now sends to U.S. producers are not encouraging. Policymakers have yet to agree on a national technology policy to shift federal investment in research and development (R&D) from military to civilian purposes. Nor has the federal government developed a constructive human resource strategy. On the contrary, federal labor policies and cutbacks in worker training programs have discouraged companies from pursuing competitiveness strategies that require increased employee participation.

In addition, Washington has not provided sufficient leadership on the issue of corporate governance. With some exceptions, the federal government has ignored this critical challenge: how to help shareholders, managers, and other stakeholders work together to improve corporate performance. As a result of federal inaction, managers are still focused on the latest swings of financial markets and not on the long-term interests of their companies, employees, suppliers, customers, and communities. Most of the institutional investors that own parts of large companies still do not take active roles in corporate governance. And some of these investors focus on short-term changes in share prices, thus discouraging companies from pursuing long-term strategies to improve productivity and quality.

Precedents exist for federal initiatives to promote industrial competitiveness. The United States has a long history of supporting the development of important industries. From research subsidies to an extension service that spread new technologies and best practices, the federal government has worked to make American agriculture the most productive in the world. A federal agency, the National Advisory Committee on Aeronautics, financed much of the early research on airframes and engines between 1920 and 1935. It made the first wind tunnels and testing facilities available to the industry. Later, during World War II, Pentagon spending played a critical role in the industry's development. The jet engine, an innovation that greatly expanded commercial air travel in the late 1950s, was developed to meet air force requirements during World War II.[9]

Today the federal government tends to limit its support to basic research—research that does not have direct commercial applications. But in its early years, the National Advisory Committee on Aeronautics did not so confine itself; instead it focused on designing useful products that the government and others could buy. At the same time, military orders for new aircraft helped develop important technical skills and knowledge later used by manufacturers in commercial aircraft. Throughout the aviation industry's development, government influenced both the supply and the demand for innovation.

Other industries, most notably those connected with our national security, have enjoyed similar success. As a result of the Cold War, the U.S. Defense Department accounts for the bulk of the federal government's R&D spending. (See Chart 4.1.) In 1991 the Pentagon, the National Aeronautics and Space Administration (NASA), and the Department of Energy (the agency that oversees the development of nuclear power) accounted for 73 percent of all federal research funds provided to industrial firms.[10] Since 1955 the government has spent more than $1 trillion on the research and development of nuclear arms and weapons, representing 62 percent of all federal research spending.

Out of this research and development came an abundance of new weapons—and some products used by ordinary Ameri-

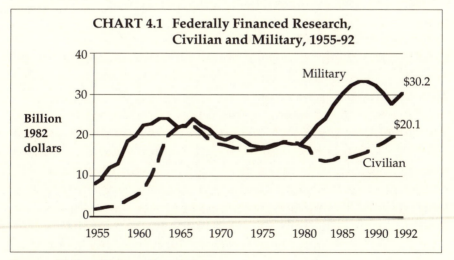

CHART 4.1 Federally Financed Research, Civilian and Military, 1955-92

Source: National Science Foundation

cans each day. The military hardware—the hydrogen bomb, laser weapons, spy satellites, intercontinental rockets, nuclear-powered ships and submarines, the stealth bomber and fighter planes—has revolutionized the way that wars are fought. Teflon, television, passenger jets, weather satellites, computer chips, and microwave ovens are by-products of Pentagon spending that have changed our everyday lives.

Now, with the Cold War's end, national security has become more a matter of economic strength than military might. Therefore it is appropriate to shift our resources and talents from military security to economic security and embark on a program to match the productivity and quality of our international competition.

Competing on Quality, Productivity, and Innovation

American industry can respond to international competition by taking either the high road or the low road. The low road emphasizes cutting the costs of production. The high road focuses on policies that raise quality, productivity, and innovation—making possible a society with both competitive industries *and* rising living standards. The high road requires a new way of thinking about how work is organized.

THE ORGANIZATION OF WORK

Current American thinking about work organization is the legacy of the manufacturing system made famous in the early 20th century by Henry Ford.

Ford based his system on the ideas of Frederick Taylor, who had developed a strategy for efficiently organizing mass production. Taylor broke complex production operations down into myriad simple tasks that workers would repeat with machinelike efficiency. Workers would supply the physical labor needed to operate machines; engineers and supervisors would plan production and solve problems. An extensive hierarchy allowed managers to control a large number of production workers. Under this system, most workers did not need to be skilled—only reliable, steady, and willing to follow directions.

Now, almost a century after Ford popularized it, this form of work organization has become inappropriate for producing high-value-added goods in advanced industrialized countries.

Leading industrial powers can raise their living standards only by maintaining high wages. High wages, in turn, are only possible if nations produce higher-quality products, provide customers with greater product variety, introduce new products more frequently, and create production systems more sophisticated than those that are cheaply operated in low-wage countries. These high-road requirements increase the complexity of production. Today a group of supervisors at the center of production can no longer easily or effectively control the business operation through normal administrative procedures. Under the Taylor model, more products mean more product developers; production innovation means a new layer of employees charged with innovation; higher quality means more inspectors checking the checkers already in place. An increase in the number of steps in production means more managers and more steps where things can go wrong—and they do. The proliferation of support staff and procedures in the mass production system results in more mistakes and more costs.

Companies have another choice. Across the United States and throughout the advanced countries, many companies have adopted a new style of work. The guiding principle of this new organizational form is participation. Bureaucracy and managerial layers can be stripped away if workers have the authority to take over a variety of tasks once performed by others. Giving greater autonomy to workers will require a major cultural change in American management.[11]

THE HIGH ROAD TO COMPETITIVENESS
Companies pursuing high-road strategies build partnerships with their employees and suppliers—partnerships to improve continuously the quality of their products. High-road companies treat employees as valuable assets and as stakeholders.

Compensation and reward systems strive for internal equity and are tightly linked to the performance of the firm. Such a compensation system reinforces the sense that all members of the company, from the chief executive to production workers, share an interest in the long-term success of the company. These companies combine investments in technology with investments in training. Since many investments, especially in training, take time to yield benefits, high-road companies need long-term horizons. If they do not see beyond next quarter's profits, companies will not spend the money needed to develop a new product or process.

"Quality" is the continuing ability to anticipate, meet, and exceed the needs of customers. Since Congress enacted the Malcolm Baldrige award in 1987, many American businesses have undertaken aggressive initiatives to improve quality. In the course of the American struggle to maintain competitiveness, quality has recently become a national preoccupation. This is ironic since the current quality movement, a reaction to Japan's success at improving quality, is rooted in the work done four decades ago by Americans W. Edwards Deming, Joseph M. Juran, and Armand Feigenbaum.

The most successful methods for achieving quality have been cooperative partnerships between departments of the same company and between suppliers and customers. Experts in quality stress the need for management to make a greater commitment to front-line workers, giving them job security, high wages, and extensive training. The reason is simple: they are best situated to maintain and improve product and process quality. Employee participation and employee ownership plans inspire greater employee commitment and provide a way of tapping worker knowledge and expertise.

Many U.S. firms have pioneered high-road strategies. One well-known case is that of Xerox, which was able, in the late 1970s, to meet a challenge from the Japanese copier industry using employee participation to refocus on quality.[12] Other companies have tapped the profits of participation. IBM's circuit board factory in Austin, Texas—also faced with strong foreign competition—could have saved $60 million by closing down and buying the circuit boards elsewhere. Instead IBM taught its workers new skills and changed the work organization. The Austin plant became competitive by improving productivity more than 200 percent.[13] Corporations such as Motorola, Federal Express, and Ford Motor Company have also made major changes in their organization structures and in the way their employees work.

Unfortunately many other companies remain on the low road. The low road follows the familiar pattern of replacing higher-paid workers with lower-paid workers or closing down plants and producing goods in low-wage countries. But computers, modern machinery, rapidly evolving products and production methods, and growing international competition are making this model obsolete. The gains of low-road strategies come at the cost of national economic strength.

EMPLOYEE PARTICIPATION
Virtually every quality initiative centers on eliciting greater employee participation. Shop-floor workers know how to maintain and improve quality: the challenge is to gain their long-term commitment to the firm's health.

One of the most celebrated models of worker participation is the "NUMMI" joint venture between GM and Toyota in Fremont, California. Toyota management and unionized American workers redesigned the work process, reducing the number of job descriptions from one hundred to four. For greater flexibility employees worked in teams, and each employee was trained to perform all of the tasks of the team. Soon the Fremont plant was producing cars at nearly the same low cost as were Japanese factories.[14]

Faced with competition from both Japanese and American manufacturers, A. O. Smith, a major manufacturer of auto parts, decentralized its decision-making hierarchy and instituted joint labor-management committees to solve operating problems. In a major shift, shop-floor workers were given responsibility for quality control, just as in Japan. The company invested heavily in training, teaching workers new skills for insuring quality. Building quality control into the shop floor eliminated much of the bureaucracy and yielded dramatic quality improvements. With the old system, rework was needed in 1,600 out of 5,000 parts; now rework has been virtually eliminated.[15]

Many large and small companies have solved their operating problems with "study-action teams" of engineers, managers, and hourly employees, which spend several months full-time on a particular problem. Through a process of competitive benchmarking—comparing production quality and cost to the best in the world—workers and managers in many plants have developed strategies to remain competitive. At Xerox's Webster, New York, subcomponent plant, for example, the first study-action team found ways to save jobs by saving costs.[16]

The experience of American companies suggests there are three keys to making participation work. First, participation strategies must focus on the work actually done on the shop floor. Second, they must include substantive decision-making rights for workers, rather than mere consultation. Finally, such strategies only make sense in an environment of employment security, which leads to strong employee commitment and to employee-management trust.[17]

EMPLOYEE OWNERSHIP
Employee ownership can increase productivity and help workers earn higher salaries. By giving workers a stake in the success of the firm, employee ownership helps create common interests between labor and management.

The most successful programs are Employee Stock Ownership Plans (ESOPs) which combine share ownership through employee trust funds with employee participation programs. By 1990 more than 11 million workers were beneficiaries in ESOPs, as Chart 4.2 shows. However, only a portion of companies with plans have them combined with employee participation.

AMERICAN-STYLE *KEIRETSU*

By developing closely knit families of companies—a system known as *keiretsu*—Japanese corporations have enhanced their ability to compete. Firms in a *keiretsu* are connected through cross-shareholding, time-honored buyer-supplier arrangements, shared directors, and the exchange of personnel.

A small but growing number of U.S. firms have developed an American version of *keiretsu*. Perhaps the best-known example of collaboration was the recent agreement between IBM and Apple to jointly develop personal computers and software. Collaborative efforts are a response to some of the challenges facing business today. Another forum of collaboration, research consortia, such as Sematech and the Microelectronics and Computer Technology Corporation, share technology with member companies, making their industries more competitive.

Though collaboration might seem alien to the American style of business, it actually dates back to the early days of Henry Ford's automotive factory. In the beginning Ford relied on closely linked supply companies for all auto parts except bodies and wheels. Ford's vertical integration did not occur until the 1930s. Today Ford is returning to the practice, establishing close relationships with such suppliers as Cummins

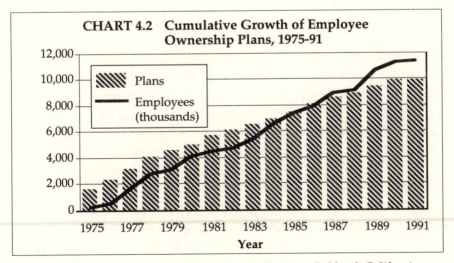

CHART 4.2 Cumulative Growth of Employee Ownership Plans, 1975-91

Source: National Center for Employee Ownership, Inc., Oakland, California

103

Engine Company for diesel engines and Excel Industries for 70 percent of its windows. Ford's deal with Excel followed a failed attempt to manufacture windows in-house. The link saved Ford millions and enabled Excel to spend $4 million on better manufacturing systems.

Keiretsu-style relationships between suppliers and large manufacturers are spreading because they are mutually beneficial. Traditionally, big companies have dealt with suppliers in an almost adversarial manner, often playing them against each other to get lower prices. When companies instead develop long-term, cooperative relationships with suppliers, they receive better quality and service.

Long-term relationships enable the suppliers to modernize and become more productive. IBM has assisted troubled suppliers with strategic partnerships and advance payments. Harley Davidson trains its suppliers in just-in-time inventory management. The upshot: both manufacturer and supplier share the advantages of better competitiveness.[18]

AN AGENDA FOR QUALITY

Government can assist industry in its pursuit of quality. The task force recommends that the federal government implement the following measures:

1. *A National Certification Program for Quality in Manufacturing*
Manufacturers such as Ford, GM, IBM, Xerox, and Digital have adopted a variety of quality certification programs, each with different standards and administrative requirements. Their basic goals are virtually identical, but in practice these programs are idiosyncratic and redundant. Quality programs have become time-consuming for large companies and a nightmare for their suppliers. Instead the United States needs uniform national standards for manufacturing.

Building on the success of the Malcolm Baldrige award, we propose a national manufacturing quality certification program. The federal government should organize firms to develop uniform industry standards for quality. Supplier firms meeting these standards will be certified as qualified vendors by their buyers or by outside experts. A standard certification process will simplify matters for supplier firms, since they will have to meet only one set of requirements. Once a firm is certified, it will have a marketing edge that it can use to expand its business.

To encourage companies to participate in such a program, federal and state procurement practices should be amended to adopt these quality standards and practices.

2. *Industrial Extension Services*
The federal government needs to help smaller manufacturers meet national industry standards for quality. It can do this by supporting state and regional quality efforts already under way.

A number of states—including Michigan, New York, and Pennsylvania—now have manufacturing modernization services. These state economic development programs are modeled on the agricultural extension services. Though each state effort is organized differently, all help small businesses upgrade and modernize their operations. The federal government can and should expand these services by funding them, by linking them to colleges and universities, and by making them part of the extension service system.

3. *A National Center for Employee Participation and Ownership*
Policies to promote employee ownership and participation are a vital part of our effort to create a new, more participatory type of American capitalism.

A number of states have programs to promote company ownership by employees.[19] The federal government should establish a national center for employee ownership and participation, modeled along the lines of New York State's initiative. Such a center would help interested companies study the feasibility of employee ownership, facilitate training in employee participation, and promote pay-for-productivity systems such as profit sharing and other forms of gainsharing.

A STRATEGIC INVESTMENT IN TRAINING

The U.S. government must help its workers adjust to the ever-changing requirements of the workplace. Worker training is often the key to producing high-quality goods in the modern workplace, and federal assistance is crucial for training programs.

Because modern, world-class production places greater demands than ever on the abilities of workers, our time has been called the "era of human capital."[20] New ways of organizing work, such as flexible manufacturing systems and just-in-time inventory, depend upon a front-line work force that is both technologically sophisticated and able to assume much more responsibility for planning and coordinating the flow of work. And to implement modern quality techniques, workers need to learn new skills continually.

As a nation the United States continues to invest little in its workers and their training. The Commission on the Skills of the American Workforce pointed out that as long as companies stick to low-road strategies, we will continue not to invest in training. The commission concluded by declaring: "The choice we have is to become a nation of high skills or low wages."[21]

Other advanced industrial nations spend generously on worker training. Germany, Japan, Sweden, and Denmark maintain coordinated, fully funded labor market services that encompass training, placement, labor market information, and retraining for displaced workers. While the United States allocates just 0.6 percent of its gross domestic product to employment and training programs, Germany spends 2.4 percent; Denmark, 4.8 percent; and Sweden, 2.3 percent. Large German companies provide free courses, while small firms pool their resources and train through industry associations or chambers of commerce. In Denmark, where small businesses predominate, the government sponsors free training.[22] And the Japanese system of lifetime employment includes extensive in-house training and job rotation systems.

Because U.S. policy lacks a commitment to full employment, it effectively *encourages* the low-road approach. Companies find it easier and cheaper to hire temporary workers and lay them off—or to move factories to low-wage countries. Rather than train employees to produce quality products, firms opt for quick, and temporary, profits by slashing their labor costs.

A few large American companies have invested in successful training programs. These enterprises are thriving. When General Electric faced international competitors that made inexpensive refrigerator compressors by paying low wages, the corporation decided not to buy the compressors offshore but to invest $120 million in technology and training. With the help of the state of Tennessee, General Electric retrained its unskilled workers to use new technology, work in teams, and take responsibility for work flow and quality.[23]

American companies spend $30 billion a year on training, but $27 billion of that amount comes from 0.5 percent of the companies. Fewer than 200 firms spend more than 2 percent of their payrolls on training. Most of the funding is for training managers; only one-third of the total goes to front-line workers.[24]

Meanwhile government training efforts remain uncoordinated. Together, federal and state programs have created a bewildering array of training services and training providers, which are generally not responsive to labor market conditions. Federal agencies use seven different classification systems for jobs; in addition, some 500 private groups set job standards. In New York $725 million in training funds support 85 different programs administered by 19 state departments and numerous local providers.[25]

To maintain its high-wage economy, the United States must begin to invest substantially in its work force. Continuous improvement is the standard for world-class firms; continuous improvement of workers' skills must again become standard practice for U.S. firms and for the federal government.

Part of the nation's training effort should be directed to mature markets where workers face long-term decline in employment. American workers and their communities bear too much of the burden of such structural dislocation. Germany has used transitional vouchers to subsidize the wages of displaced workers and to pay for retraining.[26] When its Ministry of Technology decided to close smaller steel plants and focus on larger ones, the government offered incentives for other industries to open plants near the closing steel mills.[27]

Not only are adjustment policies compassionate and fair, but they make competitive sense. Workers require support and assistance to learn new skills and change careers, especially in today's rapidly evolving technological environment. Unless the United States commits itself to training and reemploying dislocated workers, they will continue to resist trade liberalization measures, such as the proposed trade treaty with Mexico.

To meet the challenges of the 1990s and the next century, we need a coordinated national system for training the American work force. The task force recommends that such a system encompass: basic literacy and computational skills; federal support for apprenticeship programs for young people not going to college; continuous training to upgrade the skills of all employees; and retraining for workers who have been laid off.

To fund the system, we propose that *all employers contribute at least 1 percent of their payroll to the education and training of their workers.* Employers not wishing to contribute would pay a tax of 1 percent of their payroll to finance general training programs, run by the states, to upgrade worker skills.

We also call on the federal and state governments to establish a system of employment and training panels. These panels would consist of representatives of business, labor, professional associations, and government, and would be responsible for administering government-sponsored training and retraining programs for regional work forces. The panels would also develop and diffuse information on expected trends in the supply and demand of jobs.

Retraining laid-off workers and helping them attain the skills needed to shift into new careers is a key to competitiveness. Under our current system, state unemployment insurance dispenses money to laid-off workers, but only if the workers actively continue to look for work and only if they remain in the state. Many laid-off workers need new skills, placement assistance, and, in some cases, assistance in moving out of state to better job markets.

Reforming the Governance of the Corporation

In America corporate governance tends to ignore the interests of long-term stakeholders in the corporation. As Figure 4.1 illustrates, U.S. corporate governance has evolved from a model in which owners (one group of stakeholders) were managers to a different model that separates ownership and management. Other groups of long-term stakeholders, such as employees and their communities, are even more isolated from corporate decision making today. Since the voices of long-term stakeholders are diminished in the prevailing model of corporate governance, American corporations are less likely to pursue strategies that advance the interests of all the stakeholders.

Germany and Japan, with their distinct types of capitalism, have different approaches to corporate governance, approaches that enhance their competitiveness. Their rules for governing the corporation have resulted in more partnerships between the corporation and its key stakeholders: employees, owners, financial institutions, and the government. In Germany factory-level work councils bring labor and management together to discuss issues such as new equipment. In Japan employees are viewed as valued assets with long and secure futures in the corporation, and the human resources department strongly influences company strategy.

In the United States corporate management can and does insulate itself from shareholder-owners. Proxy campaigns, which allow shareholders to vote (usually by proxy) on motions proposed by other shareholders, are one of the few ways that shareholders can collectively initiate changes in corporate policy. Yet federal regulations that date from the mid-1950s require Securities and Exchange Commission (SEC) approval for all information that participants present in a proxy cam-

Figure 4.1

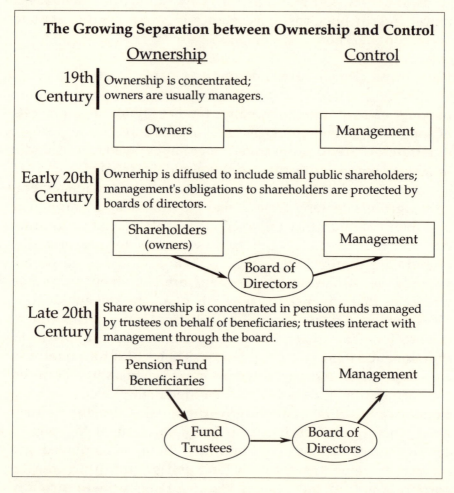

The Growing Separation between Ownership and Control

Ownership   Control

19th Century | Ownership is concentrated; owners are usually managers.

Owners — Management

Early 20th Century | Ownerhip is diffused to include small public shareholders; management's obligations to shareholders are protected by boards of directors.

Shareholders (owners) → Board of Directors → Management

Late 20th Century | Share ownership is concentrated in pension funds managed by trustees on behalf of beneficiaries; trustees interact with management through the board.

Pension Fund Beneficiaries → Fund Trustees → Board of Directors → Management

paign. In the past the SEC's rules have discouraged proxy votes on such important issues as executive compensation. SEC approval is also required for shareholder meetings or conversations. Thus shareholders effectively are barred from collective action.

Many who have studied this issue recommend dismantling these SEC restraints. A recent study by Michael T. Jacobs of Harvard Business School calls our system of corporate governance "dysfunctional" and endorses rewriting the SEC's proxy rules to allow shareholders to talk among themselves and increase their power to change boards of directors.[28]

Executive compensation, currently a controversial topic, illustrates how corporate managers have been able to advance their own interests, often without advancing those of other corporate stakeholders. Typically corporate management chooses and dominates corporate boards of directors. These boards, in turn, set executive compensation. Thus management is in effect accountable to no one—a situation that lends itself to abuse.

Critics point to the fact that often the amount paid to a chief executive officer (CEO) bears no relation to the company's performance or to the returns to other stakeholders. CEO salaries have been rising while workers' real incomes have declined. Executive compensation in the United States is about three times that of British executives, four times that of German and French bosses, and six times that of Japanese CEOs.[29]

Meanwhile the voices of shareholders are growing louder. After the United Shareholders' Association and the California pension fund protested, ITT announced it would link its executive compensation more closely with corporate performance.[30]

For decades shares of America's public corporations were held by millions of relatively anonymous individual investors. But today most stock in public corporations is held by huge institutional investors, such as pension funds, insurers, and mutual funds. Together they hold assets worth $6 trillion, approximately 45 percent of American corporate equity.[31] In the past, though they owned significant stakes in many firms, their participation in corporate governance was limited to selling their stocks when disappointed with a company's financial performance. They left decisions on corporate strategy to management.

Institutional investors can improve the conduct and operation of boards of directors. Many experts are urging institutional investors to assume stronger roles in corporate decision making. Recent studies have focused on the involvement of institutional investors in four ways: monitoring the corporation's performance; establishing a dialogue with management; voting proxies and participating in proxies; and being accountable to beneficiaries (such as pensioners) by disclosing how their votes are being used.[32]

Measures should be taken to encourage institutional investors to become more active owners and to exert influence on boards of directors. Corporate rules should be reformed to make boards of directors more effective at focusing management on long-term performance, while at the same time basing management rewards on company performance.

We propose the following changes in corporate governance as steps in the right direction:

- *To give stakeholders more of a voice in the governance of the corporation, the SEC should assure that they are fairly represented on the committee that nominates outside directors (directors that are not part of corporate management).* The stakeholders include employees, institutional investors, major customers and suppliers, and representatives of communities in which the corporation has large operations. If the company has an employee stock ownership plan, then there should be mandatory representation of the employees' trust on the committee that nominates outside directors. This reform would be consistent with the traditional role of outside directors, who are supposed to represent constituencies other than the present management. Such a reform would encourage managers to develop longer time horizons.

- *The federal government, in cooperation with the private sector, should expand the supply of independent outside directors.* The SEC should foster the development of an independent institution that trains more people to serve as outside directors.

- *Federal and state laws and regulations should be modified to encourage institutional investors to exercise their ownership rights.* Institutional investors should be encouraged to work together to monitor and influence boards of directors and top management.

• *The SEC and the private sector should consider steps to better align the compensation of directors and senior management with the long-term performance of the firm.* Outside directors have to take the lead in setting compensation for all directors and senior managers. Compensation packages should contain stock options and other features connected to the company's long-term performance.

Using the Best Technologies

In addition to skilled workers, the high-road workplace takes full advantage of modern technologies. For most of its history the United States has possessed a mix of public and private institutions that proved uniquely favorable to invention. Research departments of firms, labor markets, professional associations, technical journals, government agencies and procurement policies—all have interacted to make the U.S. economy one of the most technologically dynamic of capitalist history. The list of American successes is long: from machine tools, electric motors, and the telephone to the airplane, the computer and semiconductors. With the nation's technological lead eroding in industry after industry, it is time to revamp the public-private partnerships that worked in the past.

A crucial part of the inventive process is the commercialization of new products. Until recently our businesses excelled at commercializing technologies, marketing them both at home and abroad. No longer. Our industries now suffer from the consequences of "persistent failures to convert technologies into products."[33]

America's neglect of manufacturing technologies is hurting the nation's competitiveness. Despite outstanding success in basic research in recent years, American industry has failed to follow through consistently with product development and manufacturing. MIT's Commission on Industrial Productivity has noted a "long-term devaluation of production-related functions and skills."[34] Small and medium-size firms have been slow to modernize, in part because they are virtually unaided by government or larger firms. In contrast, Japanese and European competitors expend considerable money and effort to help smaller firms modernize.

What a country produces matters as much as its rate of production. Along with most industrial experts, this task force rejects the notion that all goods and services contribute equally to the nation's economic well-being. Recently one Washington official is reported to have quipped, "What's the difference between exporting computer chips and wood chips? They're all chips."[35] We disagree. Some sectors of the economy provide crucial benefits to many others. The advantages of these key sectors do not stop at the narrowly economic; rather they spread throughout communities and entire regions. That is why our industrial competitors have worked so hard to nurture them.

Computers and microelectronics, for example, are indispensable components of countless new products and processes—from high-definition television to high-speed trains. Countries that lead in computers and microelectronics are therefore likely to lead in many other strategic industries. Leading sectors will earn greater profits, they will invest more, and they will move on to newer technologies first. Computers, microelectronics, and related industries thus have the potential to revolutionize production across the national economy. As the MIT commission noted, manufacturing firms account for virtually all of the research and development done by American industry. "They thus generate most of the technological innovations adopted both inside and outside their own industry."[36]

We do not suggest that Washington bureaucrats pick the next century's winners and losers. We do recommend that the government act on what is now common knowledge. Experts in business and academia, in the United States and abroad, have identified many key technologies and sectors. Compare the lists of the different nations: they are virtually identical. If we fail to secure leading positions in these sectors, we will squander America's greatest tradition: prosperity.

Let us take a closer look at some of the factors that contribute to technological preeminence: research and development, commercialization, and diffusion of manufacturing technologies.

R&D: NEW PRODUCTS AND TECHNOLOGIES

Both here and abroad, governments are coming to understand the importance of supporting R&D in strategic technologies. Recently the independent national Council on Competitiveness released a report calling for substantial efforts to assist American industry in bringing certain critical generic technologies to the marketplace.[37] Soon afterward came the announcement of the first awards from the Commerce Department's Advanced Technology Program and the White House's own listing of 22 critical technologies. Overseas our foreign competitors are accelerating their technology development. The European Community spends more than $1.1 billion a year on inter-European cooperative projects in information technology, industrial technologies, and telecommunications networks. This is in addition to extensive national and private-sector efforts. Bull, ICL, and Siemens, for example, recently collaborated in a joint research laboratory.[38]

1. *Organizing Our Technology Policy*

The United States needs a concerted effort to regain its competitive position in critical technologies. At present federal technology efforts are spread out among Defense, Commerce, NASA, and many other agencies. We should reorganize federal technology policy, increase support for critical technologies, help industry commercialize technology, and support efforts to diffuse process and product technology within specific industries.

The White House should take the lead in generating technology policies. At the top of the agenda should be the creation of a strategic plan for critical product and process technologies. (This could be a role for an Economic Security Council, which we discuss in Chapter 7.)

Currently the federal government pays for about 44 percent of U.S. R&D spending—but more than half of the federal expenditure still goes to defense projects.[39] The 700 federal laboratories do not contribute significantly to the technology needs of our commercial industry. During the Cold War, the Pentagon's Defense Advanced Research Projects Agency oversaw the development of many technologies. The agency maintained a policy of scientific excellence, which attracted gifted researchers. In the 1990s the nation needs a similar organization that will coordinate the evolution of strategic technologies—for the commercial, civilian industries that will confer economic leadership in the post–Cold War era.

2. Increasing Support for Critical Technologies
The federal government should develop a plan to increase R&D in critical technologies. The Commerce Department's Advanced Technology Program should be expanded to become the center for this effort.

3. Strengthening Industry's Ability to Commercialize Technology
Though the United States is still a leading inventor, it has become less successful at commercializing technologies.

Industry consortia can be instrumental in technology commercialization. Sematech and the Microelectronics and Computer Technology Corporation are good examples. The government should support these cooperative efforts and pay particular attention to smaller firms. Other incipient local and regional networks have been led by industry associations, research facilities, and networks of small, independent manufacturers. These, too, are promising vehicles for transferring technologies and deserve government support.

Congress should therefore direct cabinet agencies such as Defense and Commerce to use industry consortia to pursue their research agendas. To further encourage industry consortia, the federal government should direct the Commerce Department's National Institute of Standards and Technology to support these efforts.

Another problem in commercialization is the failure of most American companies to keep up with foreign technological developments. Other countries systematically use their intelligence-gathering resources to monitor technological developments in the United States. We, too, must find ways to stay current with international technological developments. The Department of Commerce could convene government-industry boards to tap our overseas intelligence-gathering expertise. The federal government could also provide startup funds to help professional societies or industry associations establish offices in Europe and Japan to monitor technological developments there. Finally government should help fund efforts of R&D consortia to license foreign technologies.

DIFFUSING MANUFACTURING TECHNOLOGIES
While many of America's large, sophisticated corporations use the newest technologies, diffusion of manufacturing technologies has essentially stopped there. Our smaller companies—having neither the time, money, nor expertise to modernize their operations—are being left behind.

In the past, federal and state governments have helped diffuse technological advances throughout research communities composed of universities, national laboratories, and major corporate research institutions. But these institutions are not offering small firms much help, since they are more interested in high-profile research than in manufacturing technologies. Washington's commitment is weak. The federal government spends just 0.8 percent of its R&D budget on technology transfer, and much of that is for product technology, not manufacturing process technology.[40] The result is that our technology transfer programs are inadequate. Typically they are after-thoughts tacked on to the R&D efforts of national laboratories or the Defense Department.

Most of the technical help for smaller firms comes from the

states. State extension programs, modeled on the agricultural extension programs, offer technical assistance to smaller companies. These efforts are underfunded, and federal support is low and unbalanced. Agricultural services to farms, which produce about 2 percent of the national product, are allocated $1.1 billion; manufacturing contributes some 20 percent of the national product and receives just $22 million.[41]

The task force recommends that large, federally funded research laboratories share technologies with industry. This can be accomplished in part by having federal agencies such as Commerce, Energy, and NASA establish partnerships between major research laboratories and industry consortia. Also, manufacturing extension services (discussed in our quality proposal) can act as agents for diffusing advanced manufacturing technologies to small and middle-size companies.

Coping with Change: Adjustment Policies

The dramatic reduction in defense spending projected over the next several years will place many defense-dependent companies and workers at risk. International trade will continue to dislocate yet more companies and their employees. In both cases, economic forces will push companies to find new lines of business—and workers to find new skills and jobs. For many of them, the transition will not be easy.

The Congressional Budget Office predicts that over 600,000 defense-related jobs will be eliminated by 1995. If defense cuts are larger than currently planned, defense industries could lose up to 1.4 million jobs.[42] At the same time, a trade treaty with Mexico could mean greater relocation of industry and a loss of 550,000 jobs in the United States.[43] The nonstop inflows of automobiles, apparel, computers, and other products continue to threaten jobs in manufacturing. The European Community is requiring that products made in Europe contain a high portion of European inputs. Responding to this requirement, American corporations have moved production from the United States to Europe. These changes leave behind jobless workers not only in the companies that move, but also in their suppliers and communities.

A national initiative to help these businesses and workers find new work is essential to U.S. economic development. We propose two measures—one designed to help workers directly and another targeted at companies.

1. *New training systems must include separate provisions for aiding workers dislocated by imports, investment overseas, and defense cutbacks.* Many of those who have lost their jobs as the result of declining defense procurement or rising trade competition are highly educated, with years of training and experience. The United States cannot afford to squander the skills and creative abilities of hundreds of thousands of hardworking Americans. As a nation we must provide alternatives to unemployment or low-paying, low-skill work. Economic common sense requires that America invest in adjustment programs that put the talents of these Americans back to work in enterprises that restore our industrial health.

How an adjustment program is structured is very important. An effective trade adjustment program must be linked to labor market institutions, as is the case in other nations. Adjustment programs should be administered by the employment and training panels that would administer the task force's proposed training system.

2. *Washington should give grants to the states to establish industrial innovation programs.* State industrial assistance programs, already in place and operational, offer the most effective way to deliver immediate adjustment assistance to defense-dependent firms. These state programs are tailored to serve each state's unique industrial base, work force, and education and science infrastructures.

Producing for a World Market

Historically American industry could almost entirely depend on its domestic market. Today, however, as the U.S. market matures and foreign markets develop, American firms have to become better positioned in markets abroad.

Unfortunately the nation still lacks policies that encourage the export efforts of small and medium-size companies. Despite the internationalization of markets, few American manufacturing companies export. Even U.S. firms that do not compete in the world market will sooner or later face strong competition from foreign firms at home. Companies that want to flourish have little choice but to challenge their international competitors.

In other industrialized nations, governments and corporations do much more to promote exports. Japan has more trade assistance personnel working in America *alone* than we have throughout the world.[44]

A serious national effort requires aggressive measures to open foreign markets, provide competitive financing, and encourage the export efforts of small and medium-size firms.

The task force recommends the following:

- *Government and industry must jointly gather, organize, and disseminate market intelligence and trade expertise to small manufacturers.* Federal resources should be expanded at the regional level and better coordinated with state efforts, industry organizations, and other local resources.

- *Tax incentives or low-interest loans should be offered to small and medium-size firms to support the initial years of their export efforts.* Incentives might be offered for redesigning products for foreign markets, investing in warehouses or inventory, applying engineering work, and for advertising and promoting. The benefits should gradually disappear as the firms gain export experience.

- *The Department of Commerce and the Export-Import Bank should develop export-financing strategies oriented toward small and medium-size firms.*

Forging a State-Federal Partnership

The circumstances of our global economic position will ultimately force the federal government to embrace more active and comprehensive ways to restore American industry's health. Washington has much to learn from another part of American government: state government.

With little or no federal support, the states have had to respond to local conditions such as factory shutdowns and economic stagnation. A number of states have already launched many of the initiatives we recommend in this chapter: retraining displaced and disadvantaged workers, financing business startups and "incubating" small businesses, helping manufacturing firms modernize, supporting technological innovation, and encouraging employee ownership. In drafting national policies, the federal government can benefit from the experiences of these states.

The earliest state programs were characterized as "smokestack chasing," granting tax and other concessions to firms so they would locate in particular areas. Since then, however, many states have recognized that today's companies look for other kinds of incentives, including an educated work force and strong research institutions. Several states have attempted to stimulate technological innovation by encouraging interaction between businesses and university researchers. One of the best examples was the Ben Franklin Partnership in Pennsylvania, which offered grants for university-based applied research that was funded by business. The Ben Franklin Partnership also funded training programs, including a center to train people in computer-aided design.[45]

Other successful state initiatives include extension programs that provide hands-on technical assistance for modernizing manufacturing. Michigan's Technology Deployment Service, for instance, employed a small group of consultants who advised firms on installing computer-based production technologies. The program also funded training through the state's community colleges. New York's Center for Employee Ownership and Participation conducts feasibility studies for companies interested in employee buyouts. And New York and New Jersey's Port Authority has launched the nation's first publicly sponsored export-trading company.

State programs have in the past served as models for federal programs. In the 1930s, state programs prefigured the initiatives that became President Franklin Roosevelt's New Deal. Rather than dismantle the state programs, the Commission believes that the federal government can provide coordination, support, and financial incentives such as matching funds. State efforts are often fragmentary and vulnerable to changes in political climate. Recently a new administration in Michigan, for example, slashed the funding of that state's economic development programs.

The federal government should encourage states to sustain economic development efforts. Yet it must also assume responsibility for national issues—international trade, technology policy, industry-wide development and adjustment programs—and support for specific industries and applied research projects.

Because the states have laid the foundation, national commitment to industrial preeminence need not be built from scratch. What is needed now is the will to enact appropriate government policies, giving all Americans an incentive to participate in the process. The struggle to regain our industrial preeminence will not succeed unless workers have the proper economic incentives, rights, responsibilities, and—most of all—opportunity. Achieving this level of economic participation will be impossible if we focus just on the current work force and ignore the millions of poor people, most of them children, who have the potential to contribute to our economy but so far have not had the chance to develop adequate skills. The concentrated poverty of the inner city epitomizes the problem of exclusion. If we address this problem, all of us will gain. If we ignore it, the nation is not likely to regain its economic leadership. Nor will our country preserve its social stability and quality of life.

CHAPTER 5

Economic Inclusion:
The Challenge of Inner-City Poverty

A Problem for All Americans

IF the past decade has taught us any lesson, it is this: we cannot prosper as a nation unless the majority of Americans prosper, and the majority cannot prosper if the most disadvantaged are excluded. Inclusion, on the other hand, makes good economic sense: distributing employment opportunities as widely as possible builds a broad and stable base for consumption. Growing markets in turn attract investment and propel faster economic growth.

Our nation needs a new agenda to achieve an old-fashioned goal—prosperity created by and for all Americans. The new agenda should rely on traditional values—opportunity for all, reward for hard work, concern for family and community, and commitment to helping the disadvantaged.

At the top of that agenda must be urban poverty. America's inner cities are in a state of crisis—a crisis that needs to be addressed if our nation is to renew its economic strength in the 1990s. The recent riot in Los Angeles is only the most visible indicator of the crisis. Far from the television cameras and newspaper reporters, poverty blights the lives of millions of city residents. Compared with other classes in society, the poor are more likely to be homeless, to be out of work, to die prematurely from sickness, to be victims of crime, or to commit crimes. Although these problems are most evident in our large metropolitan areas—New York, Los Angeles, Chicago, Detroit, Atlanta, and Washington, D.C.—no city is immune. The

124

economic *and* social costs of this tragedy make it one of the nation's most pressing domestic concerns.

The deepening crisis of our urban areas has created a distinct subculture of inner-city poor whose alienated behavior imposes huge costs on themselves and on society as a whole. Chronic urban poverty weakens the norms that are the foundations of civic life for the poor and not poor alike: tolerance, respect for others and the law, support for public education, and a willingness to work together to build and maintain the urban community. Just as important, poverty creates a drag on the nation's economy in terms of wasted human resources, lost productivity, higher social service expenses, and impaired competitiveness.

Despite the obvious deterioration of our inner cities, our country has yet to mobilize an effective response. Why? There are several reasons. First, although most people are aware of the problem, few seem to appreciate its seriousness or its connection to other national concerns, such as education, rising healthcare costs, and the quality of the work force. Second, some Americans apparently believe that the plight of the inner-city poor is not their problem. These people assume that they can somehow insulate themselves from the spreading effects of urban decline. Third, still others, who accept the need for fundamental change, nevertheless throw up their hands in despair. Urban poverty is too intractable a problem, they say. All efforts to ameliorate it are futile. Finally, some members of the public, apparently believing that the problems of the poor are largely self-inflicted, hold that nothing should be done for people unwilling to help themselves.

Although all of these viewpoints are based on false or misleading assumptions, none can be summarily dismissed. Each raises important questions about the root causes of urban poverty and the likely efficacy of efforts to improve inner-city conditions. We disagree wholeheartedly, however, with those who would ignore the problem or who would counsel passive acceptance of the supposedly inevitable. We believe that the grip of poverty on our inner cities can be broken. Workable strategies exist for helping the children of today's urban poor escape the binds of poverty and become tomorrow's active, productive citizens. Making relatively modest investments now in selected self-help programs—for basic healthcare, infant and child nutrition, and improved learning environments—can save society far greater expenses in the future.

Social-Economic Roots of the Crisis

Inner-city poverty is an example of what happens when social structures and the economic system no longer fit together. For many generations, young people growing up in America's poor urban neighborhoods could hope that, with access to education and jobs, they could escape the grim realities of their environments and improve their lots in life. Social institutions such as churches and schools played an important role in helping them achieve their goals. People from widely different economic backgrounds could find in these institutions expressions of their shared values and collective pride. Children, in particular, benefited. Leading figures in these institutions—teachers, clergy, community activists, businesspeople, successful middle-class neighbors—often served as role models for these children. These institutions also provided mechanisms for obtaining regular information about available social services, job openings, and other economic opportunities.[1]

In the 1960s and 1970s, the institutional structure of the inner city began breaking down as blue-collar manufacturing jobs vanished and an increasing number of working- and middle-class families moved out of the cities. As late as 1974, for example, roughly half of all African-American males worked in decent-paying semiskilled jobs, many of which were located in the major urban areas. By 1986 only one-fourth of young black males held such positions.[2] Not only were blue-collar jobs becoming scarcer, but more and more of them were migrating from urban areas—especially from cities in the Northeast and the Midwest—to the suburbs. This impelled many working-class families with sufficient means to abandon their inner-city homes in search of new employment opportunities. For the inner-city community, the net effect of this job flight was to exacerbate the already high levels of unemployment and to create severe economic dislocations.[3]

This trend continued in the 1980s. Between 1982 and 1987, for example, the biggest manufacturing job losses occurred in the cities. (See Table 5.1.) Virtually all the recent growth in entry-level and low-skill jobs, in fact, has taken place in suburbs and rural areas. The cities, in contrast, have emerged as centers for high-skills employment.[4] The result, for the poor, has been devastating. Too many workers remaining in today's inner cities lack the qualifications demanded by the growing high-skills, high-performance marketplace. A laid-off semiskilled worker cannot easily start a new career as a computer programmer.

TABLE 5.1. Changes in Manufacturing Employment, Eight Cities and the United States, 1982-87

	Change (in thousands)	Percent
New York	-92.9	-17.6
Buffalo	-2.0	-5.4
Chicago	-56.4	-20.4
Detroit	-3.5	-3.3
Newark	-7.5	-21.9
Cleveland	-16.9	-18.3
Philadelphia	-29.1	-23.3
Pittsburgh	-21.5	-41.1
United States	243.0	1.3

Source: U.S. Bureau of the Census, *Census of Manufacturers*, 1982 and 1987

With the exodus of middle-class families, the fragile economic-social system of inner-city communities began to deteriorate. Once-thriving neighborhoods were left with "a much higher concentration of the most disadvantaged segments of the [minority] urban population."[5] Poor children lost their routine contacts with middle-class role models who exemplified the rewards of education, hard work, and family stability. By default, adults in their lives were too often ill-educated, unemployed, and suffering the consequences of chronic poverty. Inner-city job seekers also found themselves with fewer and fewer ties to individuals and institutions that could help them improve their employment prospects in the urban economy.

Moreover, as the density of poverty increased, so did the burden on inner-city institutions. Churches, schools, and other service-providing organizations found it harder to function effectively. A school class containing only a few disadvantaged students might still be a viable forum for learning. But a class composed almost entirely of disadvantaged children presented a far more difficult challenge, one requiring a much different approach to teaching.

Gradually a distinct population, which we have come to call the inner-city poor, emerged. This group is distinguished by its social isolation—its detachment from the institutions that have historically equipped poor people with the skills and values necessary to gain entry into mainstream society.[6] As one expert has commented, the inner-city poor is a group that "feels excluded from society, rejects commonly accepted values, [and] suffers from behavioral as well as income deficiencies."[7] In recent years the increasing concentration of urban poverty has produced a dramatic intensification of these behavioral problems. This is apparent in the rising numbers of inner-city dropouts, drug addicts, people with AIDS, welfare recipients, and homeless people. And along with these escalating problems have come ever higher social and economic costs—costs that we, as a nation, can no longer ignore.

A Costly Neglect

America's failure to address the crisis of its inner cities has carried an expensive price tag. In 1987 the United States spent more than $19 billion for income maintenance, healthcare, and nutrition to support families headed by teenagers.[8] The burdens on the criminal justice system are also enormous. In 1989 nearly four times as many African-American men were behind bars in Washington, D.C., jails as had graduated that year from the district's public schools.[9] In New York it now costs $80,000 to build a prison cell and $23,000 per year to maintain a prison inmate.[10] A male high school dropout earns $260,000 less over his lifetime than does a high school graduate, and he pays $78,000 less in taxes. A female dropout earns $200,000 less and pays $60,000 less in taxes.[11]

To meet the challenge of global competition and to provide a rising standard of living for its people, America must produce better-educated, more highly skilled workers—individuals capable of communicating well, exercising initiative, and working efficiently in teams.[12] As *The Cuomo Commission Report* argued in 1988: "As long as a significant portion of our population remains uneducated and unskilled, American society will pay a huge price to sustain those who lack the skills to contribute. The persistence of inner-city poverty puts us at a continuing competitive disadvantage with other major industrialized nations."[13] Reports by other groups have taken similar positions.[14]

A quarter century ago, President Lyndon Johnson warned that poverty posed the ultimate challenge to the well-being of our democracy. "If we stand passively by," he said, "while the center of each city becomes a hive of deprivation, crime, and hopelessness . . . if we become two peoples, the suburban affluent and the urban poor, each filled with mistrust and fear for the other . . . then we shall effectively cripple each generation to come."[15]

That threat looms even larger today. Poverty and its associated problems are creating deep social, economic, and racial cleavages within America—divisions that are eroding the bonds of mutuality upon which all democratic governance is based. Drugs, crime, urban blight, AIDS, and homelessness can no longer be dismissed as "someone else's" problems. They diminish the quality of life for all city dwellers and serve as a continuing reproach to American ideals.

Crime takes an especially devastating toll on inner-city life. All children need to grow up in peaceful, physically secure environments. The signals they receive about the safety of the outer world should reinforce the love and support they get from their parents and other family members. But residents of the inner cities have always been at greater risk of victimization from crime, and over the past two decades the level of violence has escalated.[16] Innocent children and teenagers are now frequent victims of random gunfire. Quarrels between drug dealers are turning parts of our inner cities into combat zones.

Our inner cities are fast becoming killing fields. The national homicide rate in 1989 was one out of every 11,500 Americans. (See Table 5.2.) But in Detroit, it was seven times higher (one out of every 1,700 citizens), and in Washington, D.C., it was eight times higher (one out of every 1,400). Although the murder rates in other major cities were lower, they were still well above the national average. Furthermore, while the national murder rate declined during the 1980s, the rate in many urban areas rose.

A disproportionate number of murder victims are African-American males. While this group makes up only 5.8 percent of the United States population, it accounts for 37.7 percent of its homicide victims.[17] In fact, murder is now the leading cause of death among young African-American males.

The face of today's poor is less likely to be old and wizened, like the wintry faces in a Walker Evans photograph, than it is to be young and bewildered. One out of seven Americans—34 million people—currently lives below the poverty line. Among the nation's poor, children now constitute the neediest and fastest-growing segment. Twenty percent of all American children under the age of six currently live in poverty. One in seven children depends on the government for cash relief. Close to 30 percent of American children lack basic immunization protection against such preventable childhood diseases as measles, mumps, and rubella.[18]

TABLE 5.2. Murders per 100,000 Population, Seven Large Cities and the United States, 1980 and 1989

| | Murder Rate | | |
	1980	1989	Change
Detroit	45.7	60.0	14.3
Dallas	35.4	35.2	-0.2
Washington	31.5	71.9	40.4
Chicago	28.9	24.8	-4.1
Baltimore	27.5	34.3	6.8
Philadelphia	25.9	28.7	2.8
New York	25.8	25.8	0.0
United States	10.7	8.7	-2.0

Source: U.S. Department of Commerce, *Statistical Abstract of the United States*, 1982 and 1991

From Awareness to Action

Our strategy to address the crisis of the inner city emphasizes human development. It is a community-supported strategy because we all need the support of our families, schools, local healthcare providers, and other community institutions. It is a self-help strategy in which society helps individuals acquire the knowledge and skills to earn a decent living. And it emphasizes the need for positive norms, such as the determination to work hard in exchange for rewards, respect for others and the law, and the importance of individual responsibility.

Although past antipoverty efforts have stressed skills and opportunity, the social isolation of the urban poor and the need to develop positive behavioral norms have not received adequate attention.

The members of the task force believe that behavior patterns among the poor that are destructive to themselves and their communities are a central factor in the urban crisis. People who drop out of high school, who rarely have a job, who commit crimes, or who have children when they are still children themselves have far less chance to lift themselves out of poverty.

The destructive behavior patterns that characterize some of the urban poor have many causes. The loss of economic opportunities in the inner city, the consequent increase in the social isolation of the urban poor, the absence of social services, and the effects on children of their parents' diminished aspirations—all are primary causes of this problem. We will leave it for others to debate the relative weight of these factors. Our focus is on the measures that can help inner-city children develop the behavioral norms needed to succeed.

Many inner-city residents have come from groups (such as American Indians, Latinos, African Americans) that have had traumatic experiences within American society. In these communities, especially when jobs are scarce, it has been difficult to maintain faith in mainstream norms. Antisocial behaviors, from drug taking to violent crime, are exactly that: behaviors governed by a sense of alienation from a society that has apparently rejected people who in turn reject society. As James Comer, of Yale University has pointed out, those on the margins of the economy who have defensively rejected mainstream society have done so in order to preserve a sense of self.[19]

The rejection of mainstream society has troubling implications for the education of inner-city children. In spite of their alienation, many inner-city residents still see school as the only hope for their children. At the same time, they often expect schools to fail their children, just as other mainstream institutions have.

Traditional inner-city schools have found it difficult to provide poor minority children with the skills and experiences that will enable them to succeed. Staff people often place blame on the students, the parents, and their communities. Parents take difficulties at school as further evidence of being rejected by mainstream society. Ashamed of their own lack of education or their inability to hold a job, some parents simply avoid contact with the school staff.

The resultant climate of mutual distrust between home and school makes it difficult for inner-city children to learn skills and absorb mainstream norms. A child's healthy development requires emotional bonding with competent caretakers. If parents, teachers, and children are all alienated from one another, children do not have the nurturing bonds that support development and learning. When, at approximately eight years old, inner-city children begin to see academic success as unattainable, they may protect themselves by deciding that school does not matter. They may seek a sense of self-worth in groups that do not value academic achievement, and thus they become at risk for dropping out, teenage pregnancy, and crime.

We support the conclusions of many previous studies, which have demonstrated that civil rights enforcement, new economic initiatives, and welfare reform must be part of any comprehensive attack on poverty. The development of positive behavioral norms is influenced by, but cannot be reduced to, the availability of economic opportunities. Absence of mainstream norms is both a consequence of urban poverty and a factor that helps perpetuate it.

New economic and social initiatives are vital, but they are not sufficient in themselves to solve the problem. These efforts must now be complemented by a focus on human development, starting at the earliest possible age.

Human Development Programs: A Track Record of Success

Children everywhere share the same basic developmental needs: good healthcare, a nutritious diet, a supportive family, excellent schools, positive role models, and the opportunity to make the most of their skills and talents.

BEATING THE ODDS

Children of the inner-city poor face daunting barriers all along their developmental paths. Problems begin, quite literally, from the moment of conception. Poor mothers often do not receive prenatal care. Their children are also less likely to

133

receive essential preventive medical treatment, such as routine "well-baby" checkups and immunizations. Poor children often lack nutritious food and roofs over their heads. They are more likely to be the victims of violent crime. They frequently attend schools that do little to promote their social and psychological growth. And they have too few mentors outside the family who are interested in steering them out of harm's way.

According to some commentators, it is the combination of these risk factors that keeps inner-city children from developing into productive citizens—a view we accept.[20] Yet despite these formidable challenges, developmental strategies exist that can change the odds and break the cycle of urban poverty.

The idea that children develop skills in stages is not new.[21] Yet up until now, developmental programs have generally been regarded as discrete solutions to specific problems rather than as a continuum of services stretching from the prenatal period through early adulthood. Our strategy is to link the most effective child development programs in a self-help lifeline for the disadvantaged. (See Figure 5.1.)

We believe that such a strategy can exert a positive influence on a child's behavior. As one prominent educator has observed, "a child develops a strong emotional bond to competent caretakers (usually parents) that enables them to help the child develop."[22] If the adults with whom children bond rise early and work hard, then the children are likely to accept these habits as normal. On the other hand, if families cannot provide their children with the material and emotional support they need, then their children will suffer.

Policymakers need to consider where in the process of attitude formation government and the private sector can successfully intervene. The transmission of values from parents to children takes place primarily in private, in the home. However, one public institution, the school, plays a vital role in the socialization of youth. We should use our schools, therefore, to maximum advantage: to increase the exposure of at-risk children to mentoring figures, and to help these students clarify their

Figure 5.1

Stages in the Development of Productive Citizens

STAGE:	Fetus	Infant and Pre-School	Grade School	Adolescence	High School
NEEDS:	Prenatal Care	Preventive Care	Basic Medical Care and Education	Developmentally Appropriate Education	High Skills Education and Occupational Training

Fetus / Prenatal Care
- Screening mother and fetus for problems
- Regular physical examinations
- Health/pregnancy information and counseling
- Educational and social counseling

Infant and Pre-School / Preventive Care
- Physical exams
- Immunizations
- Required intake of milk, vitamins, and other nutrients
- Healthy and safe living conditions

Grade School / Basic Medical Care and Education
- Education
- Medical care and healthy meals
- Guidance counseling
- Parental participation in school

Adolescence / Developmentally Appropriate Education
- Role models and mentors
- High expectations

High School / High Skills Education and Occupational Training
- Proficiency in reading and math skills
- Basic work skills
- Exposure to working world
- Apprenticeships, vocational training, internships, co-op programs, etc.

135

personal and social choices concerning sex, parenting, education, crime, and work.

RAISING HEALTHIER BABIES

A successful human development strategy must begin by providing access to good prenatal care. Low birthweight is the single factor most associated with high rates of infant mortality. About one in fourteen babies born in the United States has a dangerously low birthweight (less than 5.5 pounds). The figure rises to a startling one in four, however, for babies born to unwed mothers.[23] Babies who weigh less than 5.5 pounds at birth are 20 times more likely to die in their first year of life than are babies who weigh over that amount. If they survive, there is a high likelihood they will suffer recurring illnesses, learning disabilities, behavior problems, and psychiatric disorders.[24]

Many pregnant woman do not seek prenatal care because they are not aware of its importance or its availability. Some pregnant teenage girls try to keep their weight down in the belief that a smaller baby is easier to deliver.[25] Others are not aware that consuming alcoholic beverages and using drugs (prescription and nonprescription) can retard the development of the fetus, resulting in a low-birthweight child, central nervous system damage, or mental handicaps. Nationwide, more than 10 percent of pregnant women abuse drugs, and one in six infants exposed to drugs exhibits symptoms of drug dependence.[26] As a result, it has become even more imperative to integrate prenatal medical services with other services, such as substance-abuse counseling. Pregnant women at Boston City Hospital, for example, curbed their heavy drinking when a team of physicians counseled them on the threat alcohol posed to the health of their babies. The doctors concluded that "providers who are knowledgeable, interested, and accepting can successfully treat pregnant patients at risk from alcohol" and thereby improve pregnancy outcomes.[27]

Prenatal care is cost-effective. A dollar spent on prenatal care can save $3.38 in later medical bills.[28] Employer-provided insurance, however, covers a smaller portion of the work force than it did in the past. Approximately 26 percent of all women between the ages of 15 and 44 currently lack insurance for maternity care.[29] Nearly half a million pregnant women are uninsured, increasing the likelihood that their pregnancies will not be carefully monitored, and that, as a result, they will give birth prematurely.[30]

After children are born, their need for quality medical care continues. Less than half of all poor and minority children under four years of age are fully vaccinated against preventable childhood diseases such as rubella, mumps, measles, polio, diphtheria, tetanus, and whooping cough. According to the report of the1990 Report of the House of Representatives' Select Committee on Children, Youth, and Families, a dollar spent on childhood immunization saves ten dollars in later medical costs.[31] In addition to immunizations, preschool children should receive yearly physical examinations. Many of these children also need access to quality day care. The task force believes that needs of children at this stage can be addressed through a program of immunizations, through linkages between medical and social services, through high-quality day care, and through measures to educate parents, such as the Birth Start program being developed by the Carnegie Corporation of New York.

A HEAD START ON LEARNING

Children who grow up amid defeat, despair, and chaotic living conditions are less likely to develop analytic skills or to gain confidence in the efficacy of their actions. In homes where economic and social stresses are severe and the educational level of parents is low, young children are less likely to be read to or to have conversations with adults that stimulate the development of language. By the time they are two or three, such children often lag noticeably behind their middle-class counterparts in intellectual development.

Preschool programs combining education, counseling, and healthcare provide critical benefits to poor and disadvantaged children. According to the Select Committee, prudent investments in quality preschool education will reduce the probability that an at-risk child will later require special education, collect public assistance, or be arrested for a crime. A mere fraction of 1 percent of our national education budget currently goes into preschool education. For want of adequate funding, Head Start reaches less than one out five eligible children. This is penny-wise and pound-foolish. A dollar spent on programs like Head Start can save society six dollars in the long run.[32]

The Perry preschool program in Ypsilanti, Michigan, for example, has provided minority children from disadvantaged families with a solid educational foundation that has served them well in later life. A longitudinal study of the Perry program has shown that by the time the graduates were 19 years old, they were twice as likely as members of a control group to be working, attending college, or receiving further training. Their arrest rate and teenage pregnancy rate were 40 percent and 42 percent lower, respectively, while their high school graduation rate was one third higher.[33] By the same token, 21-year-old graduates of an integrated preschool program in East Harlem in New York City were twice as likely to be employed, one third more likely to have received a high school diploma, and 30 percent more likely to have gone on to college or to have received vocational training than members of a control group.[34]

Our competitors abroad recognize the importance of preschool education. In France, for example, such schooling is provided free to all children between the ages of three and five, and virtually all of the country's children attend. *We cannot afford to do less.*

TEACHING THE WHOLE CHILD:
BUILDING ON THE COMER MODEL

Our public schools promise to provide children with the education they need to enter into the prized circle of social and economic opportunity. But in communities across America— not merely those in the inner cities—schools are breaking that promise. As a 1988 study by the Departments of Education, Labor, and Commerce concluded: "The basic skills gap between what business needs, and the qualifications of the entry-level workers available to business, is wide. This gap is particularly acute in the technical fields, which rely heavily on math and science skills."

If American public schools were issued a report card today, the grades would hardly be flattering. One out of five students who have passed through their hallways cannot read beyond an eighth-grade level. Nearly half of all high school graduates cannot perform basic arithmetic skills. In standardized tests of math and science achievement, American schoolchildren consistently place near the bottom of the list of industrial nations.

All American public schools are in need of reform. Most experts agree, for example, that the school year should be lengthened and that there must be a new national focus on excellence and achievement.

For America's inner-city schools, though, the obstacles to reform are enormous. Too many inner-city schools are not child oriented. Students are counted, lectured at, tested, reprimanded, passed to the next grade, and marched out. Teachers and staff often have low expectations of students' performance—and these low expectations become self-fulfilling.

An inadequate grade school education produces predictable results in high school: poor academic performance, truancy, misbehavior, and failure to master essential skills. Grade school performance, in fact, is a reliable indicator of future dropout rates, juvenile delinquency, and early childbearing.[35]

The cycle can be interrupted by restructuring the governance and management of schools. Two decades ago, Dr. James P. Comer, a child psychiatrist at Yale University, revolutionized inner-city grade school education in New Haven by bringing together families, educators, and social service providers in troubled schools. The Comer model attempts to sensitize teachers and school staff to the problems of poor minority children. This method helps educators to recognize that the academic and behavioral problems of their students may be due to the social gap between home and school.

Ethnic groups that have been systematically alienated from American society, such as Native Americans, Latinos, and

African Americans, seem to have the greatest problems adapting to school. The Comer model and similar programs seek to bridge the gap by involving parents or guardians in the life of the school. Schools shape the social development of students. In Comer's words, schools "don't have their effect through the specific skills they transmit alone, but through their values, climate, quality of relationships . . . . Children learn by internalizing the attitudes, values, and ways of meaningful others. And then, whatever content you expose children to, they learn it."[36]

Parents benefit from this participation as well. Some join with teachers and administrators on the school's governance committees. These committees try to solve problems, not fix blame, and arrive at their decisions through consensus rather than by formal vote. Other parents help out in the classrooms as assistants, tutors, or aides. Every parent who wishes has a positive role to play. The program helps develop the pride of the parents in their children. In addition, it exposes the parents to the possibilities of life outside the ghetto.

The Comer program has been extremely successful. In 1968, two years before the project began, the two schools selected for experimentation ranked last and next to last in reading and math scores among New Haven's 33 elementary schools. Disorganization and lack of classroom discipline had made learning impossible. In 1985, fifteen years after the program was inaugurated, Comer's demonstration schools ranked third and fifth among New Haven schools in composite fourth grade test scores—without any change in the basic socioeconomic composition of the student population. Measures of achievement continued to rise. In 1986 graduates of one of the schools ranked significantly higher than a control group from an unreconstructed school in language, math, "school competence," and "perceived total competence." Moreover, neither of the Comer schools has had any serious behavior or attendance problems since the program began to take hold.[37]

Other cities have successfully adapted the Comer method. In Benton Harbor, Michigan, suspensions dropped 8 percent in schools following the introduction of the Comer program, while they rose 34 percent in the district as a whole.[38] In the Comer-based schools of Prince Georges County, Maryland, preliminary results indicate that disciplinary problems have dropped sharply, while tests scores have gone up. At the Green Valley school, for example, children exceeded the national average on standardized achievement tests for the first time anyone can remember.

Similar educational reform efforts have enjoyed analogous success. In the 1987-88 school year, the Success for All program was introduced in grades prekindergarten through three at the Abbotston Elementary School in Baltimore, Maryland. Unlike the Comer approach, Success for All puts its primary emphasis on instructional intervention. If a first grader is having difficulty reading, he or she is assigned a tutor who works one-on-one with that student every day. A family-support team, consisting of two social workers, a parent liaison, and a public health nurse, helps students respond to problems at home. The results? Abbotston students perform at or above grade level in all grades, while a comparable population of students lags six months behind grade level in the first grade, seven months behind in the second, and eight months behind in the third.

Another educational success story that has attracted national attention is the Central Park East (C.P.E.) Elementary School in East Harlem, New York, a district in which half the families fall below the poverty line. In 1974, when educator Deborah Meier took charge of the school, it had the worst attendance rate, the highest suspension rate, and the lowest reading and math scores of 32 school districts in New York. Like Comer, Meier opted for a truly "open classroom" approach. Doors were flung wide for parents to join teachers as active contributors to their children's education. C.P.E. made extensive use of art and music in its curriculum (it was the only public elementary school in New York City to offer its students regular in-school violin instruction). Children learned to write before they could read. Once they learned how to read, they read constantly. Through this intensive focus on self-expression and language skills, Meier sought to strengthen children's self-confidence and sense of self-worth. Soon C.P.E. became a model, not only of an outstanding inner-city school, but also of the kind of public school that works for all children.

Six years after the first 32 students graduated from Central Park East, 29 had completed high school and 2 were still in school, planning to graduate. This contrasts sharply with the districtwide dropout rate of 78 percent for blacks and 72 percent for Hispanics. Between 1979 and 1985, three-fourths of the school's sixth graders scored above average on standardized reading tests; as second graders, only 40 percent of these students had been reading at grade average. An evaluation report commissioned by New York's Community Trust concluded, "Many C.P.E. students 'caught up' and surpassed national norms during their years in school," compared with the usual pattern for disadvantaged children, who tend to fall farther and farther behind with each passing year.[39]

EARLY ADOLESCENCE: PROVIDING POSITIVE ROLE MODELS

Adolescence is a time of transition and vulnerability. Teenagers are confronted with difficult choices to make about sex, drugs, and other types of risky behavior. Children without ambition or hope, who have no one to look up to, are more likely to make unwise decisions that result in addiction, imprisonment, self-injury, sexually transmitted illnesses, or the birth of unwanted children.

The family is unquestionably the best source of role models, but too many urban families have been fragmented by poverty. Schools, churches, and other community organizations, which have historically provided mentoring figures for troubled youth, have also lost their moral authority over inner-city teenagers.

Some middle schools have made deliberate efforts to address this void. Their strategies have included reducing the average class size, creating special teacher-student teams, and assigning an adult adviser to each student. The Shoreham-Wading River Middle School on Long Island, for example, has sought to bridge the gap between the adult and adolescent worlds through an advisory system.[40] Each adviser supervises a group of under ten students, with whom he or she regularly meets to discuss their academic progress, complaints about school, problems at home, or anything else that might concern them.

At the Jackie Robinson Middle School in New Haven, a Comer-model school, a school planning and management team sets goals for each student's academic and social development. This helps teachers to guide students toward making better personal choices about their lives. Rates of teenage pregnancy, for example, have dropped dramatically. Similarly, the Human Biology Program at Stanford University counsels students on adolescent development—in particular, on the relationships between the reproductive system, sexual behavior, and health.[41]

FROM SCHOOL TO WORK: EXPANDING APPRENTICESHIP
In today's global economy, young job seekers can only hope to land good positions that pay well if they can offer prospective employers valuable skills and a demonstrated capacity to think and act intelligently. Recognizing that fact, many of our international competitors have established comprehensive programs to help their non-college-bound youth acquire essential vocational and job-related skills. Yet few American high schools have forged similar links to the world of work.

Never have we been more in need of such bridge-building programs. Nationally, only half of all 16- to 19-year-olds are working or looking for work. In New York City only one out of five working-age teenagers is in the labor market.[42] About a quarter of all 18-year-olds and almost half of inner-city students drop out of high school, often because they do not see any advantage in staying in school. And too many of those who do graduate leave without the skills necessary to obtain jobs at decent wages with opportunities for advancement.

Fifteen percent of employers report difficulty in finding workers with specific technical skills. Many employers, including large manufacturers, financial service firms, and communication firms, say that advances in technology are obliging them to look for workers with enhanced educational skills. Managers are distressed by the prevalence of illiteracy and innumeracy in the work force. By one calculation, U.S. firms spend as much as $30 billion annually to train and retrain their employees. Even so, the major portion of that money goes into training the college educated, rather than frontline employees.

Workers today not only must read job orders and calibrate equipment, they must also possess a strong work ethic and good social skills.[43] The capacity to solve problems, to work well in teams, and to reach accommodation with others is fast becoming a sine qua non of the emerging American workplace.[44] Good social skills are also vitally important for aspiring entrepreneurs.[45]

Roughly half of all 18-year-olds do not go on to college. Most of these teenagers usually make their first job contacts through family members, friends, or neighbors.[46] In many inner-city neighborhoods, however, the young do not have any realistic job contacts. As William Julius Wilson, author of *The Truly Disadvantaged*, has pointed out, the increasing social isolation of the inner-city poor during the 1970s and 1980s narrowed their exposure to mainstream norms associated with the world of work. In fact, few inner-city families today have a steadily employed breadwinner. Too many inner-city youths now find their role models in gang members and drug peddlers.

The divide separating inner-city schools and the modern workplace must be bridged if disadvantaged teenagers are to enjoy job opportunities that can draw them into mainstream society.

We believe that any successful reform must do the following: transform workplaces and community settings into learning environments; link educational and occupational goals; give youths responsibilities; and foster close relationships between young people and adult mentors.

A number of European countries, most notably Germany and Sweden, have national apprenticeship programs to help young people make the transition from school to work, and to create large pools of skilled, highly paid workers.[47] Local employers visit schools and teach students about occupations in the seventh grade. After completing compulsory school at age 15 or 16, the majority of young people enter two- to four-year professional programs. Apprentices attend school on a part-time basis to learn the theoretical principles of their trades. They also work on a part-time basis, receiving on-the-job training from business-run organizations. By the time students have completed their training, they are certified as journeymen and have developed the contacts and ties in the business community that can lead to productive careers. None of these programs is so rigidly determined, though, that a student who elects to pursue a totally different career cannot continue on to some form of higher education.

The German model cannot be imported wholesale to the United States. Important differences exist between our respective economies and educational systems.[48] Nonetheless, the European programs provide useful examples of successful systems designed to create a skilled labor force. If the United States develops its own approach, it could offer to all young people an attractive alternative to the dead-end choices of unfinished schooling, premature parenthood, crime, and drugs. America should build on the success of apprenticeship in the construction trades. It should link its vocational education system to employers and the labor market.

Opportunity to Advance:
Federal and State Economic Policies

Programs to enhance the work and social skills of the urban poor must be complemented with new federal efforts to expand economic opportunity. Washington needs to coordinate a pro-growth macroeconomic policy with new economic development initiatives aimed at creating urban jobs. In addition, our government should institute a national public employment program.

NATIONAL MACROECONOMIC POLICY

The health of our nation's cities is inextricably linked to the strength of the national economy. When Washington sets in motion the levers of fiscal and monetary policy to speed up or slow down the national economy, inner-city neighborhoods feel the effects. During periods of healthy economic growth, real wages, hours of work, and labor-force participation of the poor all increase.[49] The inner-city poor were particularly hard struck by the recessions of the early 1980s. If America is to give the inner-city poor the opportunity to help themselves, it must pursue a pro-growth macroeconomic policy.

CIVIL RIGHTS ENFORCEMENT

Even when the economy is booming, the inner-city poor must overcome formidable barriers to prosperity. Discrimination in the labor market causes disproportionate injury to the inner-city poor, a majority of whom are black or Latino.[50] We believe that more effective enforcement of the civil rights laws is necessary. But with urban poverty having so many deep-rooted causes, that enforcement alone is not sufficient to solve the problem. In smaller cities, 28 percent of the inner-city poor are white, indicating that, although racism has contributed to the formation of inner-city poverty, other factors have also been at work.[51]

NEW ECONOMIC DEVELOPMENT POLICIES

City governments, aided by states and the federal government, must redouble their efforts to control crime, improve schools, and provide a well-functioning transportation infrastructure. Taking such steps would enhance the quality of urban life for all city residents. This, in turn, would attract more people and business to the city, which, in its turn, would directly benefit the urban poor.[52] To the extent that education reforms succeed, cities will become relatively more attractive to business—and opportunities will grow.

States can also play an important role in maintaining the

competitiveness of the factories that remain in cities. Among other measures, state and local governments might work together to create special industrial extension services that would help manufacturers introduce state-of-the-art technologies and improve their quality-control procedures. Although such services would help all industrial regions within a given state, the large urban areas, which still compose the major manufacturing centers, would be primary beneficiaries. (For a more extensive discussion of the Commission's recommendations on industrial competitiveness, see Chapter 4.)

PUBLIC EMPLOYMENT PROGRAMS

Public employment programs have been used periodically to help create jobs during times of chronic unemployment. The most famous programs were those created during the Great Depression—the Civilian Conservation Corps and the Work Projects Administration. The Kennedy, Nixon, Ford, and Carter administrations all authorized different types of public employment measures. Even President Reagan, while opposing the concept, approved the Emergency Jobs Act in 1983.

In the United States, properly designed jobs programs have proved effective in cutting welfare costs and providing valuable public goods during cyclical downturns.[53] In other countries, such as Sweden, public employment programs exist on a permanent basis and are expanded during cyclical downturns.[54] The responsiveness of training programs to local labor market conditions is a key to success. The same is true of public employment programs. One way of making these programs responsive would be to have the federal government disburse the money to local employment training panels, which would evaluate employment proposals of different local governments, provide the funds, and evaluate the programs.

A good program would need to provide wages high enough to convince potential participants that work is more rewarding than welfare. In some states, welfare benefits plus in-kind assistance, such as medical care and day care, exceed the minimum wage. To reduce dependency on welfare, a jobs program

needs to pay more than the minimum wage. The need to provide incentives for work must be balanced against the fact that
the higher the wage, the fewer the jobs that can be created with
a given amount of money. Weighing both of these factors, we
believe that a jobs program should pay at least 20 percent more
than the minimum wage. At this wage level, a $3 billion pro-
gram could create over 230,000 jobs.[55]

With the unemployment rate at its highest level in three
years, a public jobs program would be particularly helpful now.
Such a program would help people escape from poverty and
unemployment. In fact, without public employment jobs, it
may be impossible for many of those now on welfare to meet the
work requirements mandated by recent welfare reforms.

Needed: An Integrated Strategy

Many people in the inner city, trapped by poverty and social
isolation, are unlikely to become productive without a helping
hand from the community. We recommend that the public and
private sectors provide that helping hand by implementing a
community-based self-help strategy. We see this plan as a systematic effort to reconnect the inner city with mainstream society.
It offers measures for providing expectant mothers with quality
prenatal care, for reforming grade schools so that students and
teachers build respect for one another, and for helping high
school students develop skills that prepare them for the workplace. All of these efforts will help inner city youth to overcome
their sense of social isolation.

This report and its recommendations do not address other
measures also needed to improve conditions in the inner city.
For example, we have not reviewed the new policies to promote
work by welfare recipients. Also outside our scope are issues
such as homelessness, inadequate housing, crime, and drugs.
Working- and middle-class families are indispensable to the
health of institutions such as churches and schools, yet without
safe and affordable housing, they are likely to continue their
exodus, leaving our cities with higher concentrations of the

poor. We do not have recommendations for addressing these problems, but we recognize their seriousness.

A successful attack on inner-city poverty cannot be mounted in a piecemeal fashion because, as we have shown, its interrelated problems manifest themselves in all of the critical stages of human development. Government programs have typically been designed to respond to isolated needs, providing specific services to narrowly defined groups of recipients. If adolescents in inner-city communities lack certain skills, government creates a training program designed to improve those skills. If these adolescents do not know how to look for a job, how to prepare a resume, or how to act in a job interview, government creates another narrowly targeted program to answer those needs, administered by a different group of people. The result is a proliferation of highly specialized but unconnected programs that cannot effectively meet the interdependent needs of the poor.

An effective development strategy must be built on linkages between service providers. Such linkages increase the likelihood that the children of the urban poor will receive the healthcare and education they need to develop into productive citizens. Without such linkages, service-providing agencies will continue to operate in isolation, forcing their intended clients to navigate a bewildering maze of bureaucracies to obtain the necessary services.

The United States needs to reorganize its welfare, social services, and education systems in order to integrate the delivery of proven programs. The nation must concentrate on applying the new strategy in the most disadvantaged neighborhoods. And government needs to enlist the aid of the private sector in implementing these changes.

Many of these programs should take place in a school setting, which is generally the most efficient place to deliver services to children. Many urban schools have instituted human development programs and have enjoyed great success. The task force recommends building on these programs.

Below we have summarized the human development

reforms needed to reduce inner-city poverty. Together, the recommendations represent a comprehensive approach to the development of productive citizens. (See Figure 5.2.)

1. *Access to Prenatal Care*

Government at all levels must act to increase usage of existing prenatal care services. States must spread the word to expectant mothers that these services are available, and that if they fail to take advantage of them, they are putting their babies at risk. In those urban areas where prenatal care is not now available, private providers and the appropriate governmental agencies must coordinate efforts to make sure that care becomes available at neighborhood centers.

2. *Immunization Programs for Young Children*

Working with the private sector and local government, states should increase the proportion of three- and four-year-olds who are immunized against measles and other preventable diseases. This and other efforts to increase the availability of preventive and primary medical care for young children should be coordinated with preschool programs.

3. *Preschool Programs and the Special Supplemental Food Program for Women, Infants, and Children (WIC)*

In 1990 the Congressional Budget Office estimated that only 55 percent of the eligible children and women were receiving WIC benefits. Washington needs to simplify the registration process and make WIC available where women and children receive primary medical care. Washington also needs to reduce the regulatory barriers that prevent the effective utilization of Head Start. Since Head Start provides many more benefits than traditional day care does, children should be eligible for two prekindergarten years, including a full-day program. Income eligibility should also be broadened, so that parents moving into the work force would still be eligible, even as their incomes rise above the poverty level. The Family Support Act provides a precedent for such transitional funding. The Act provides

Figure 5.2

Policies for the Development of Productive Citizens

STAGE:	Fetus	Infant and Pre-School	Grade School	Adolescence	High School
POLICIES:	Prenatal Care	Preventive Care	Basic Medical Care and Education	Developmentally Appropriate Education	High Skills Education and Occupational Training
	• Increase the utilization of current prenatal care services. • Establish neighborhood centers to provide counseling, health education, and social services.	• Expand immunization. • Increase the availability of preschool programs, such as Head Start.	• Support the Comer model and other forms of school-based management. • Coordinate the delivery of education, social, and health services by expanding the Community Schools Program.	• Increase support for teacher training, especially in inner cities. • Expand mentoring programs in schools. • Support Regents' plan for restructuring mid-level education.	• Establish state-wide academic standards for high school students. • Provide youth centers for at-risk students and for dropouts to help them attain these standards. • Expand cooperative education, apprenticeship, and other school-to-work programs. • Grant industry-accepted technical certificates to students.

151

Medicaid and child care for a year after women leave the Aid to Families with Dependent Children program.

4. *Developmentally Appropriate School Reforms: The Comer Model*
The Comer and related reform models have demonstrated that inner-city schools can be transformed into exciting learning environments in which poor minority children develop the educational and social skills they need. The next step is to encourage schools in the inner cities to adopt these models, which increase parental involvement and train teachers to become more sensitive to students' developmental issues.

The federal government also needs to reconsider its role in education. Currently it is considering initiatives to create national standards and to expand choice between private and public schools. The process of establishing standards does not help disadvantaged children attain them. Washington's primary effort to help communities with the education of disadvantaged children is commonly known as Chapter I. Unfortunately the regulations for spending this money are inflexible. Schools with large portions of disadvantaged children need to be allowed to use Chapter I funds to provide integrated services, such as counseling and healthcare. Such flexibility will make it easier for local schools to implement the Comer model.

5. *School-Based Clinics*
States and the federal government should support the establishment of more school-based clinics to deliver health services, including mental health treatment, to poor children. Private, not-for-profit hospitals should be encouraged to adopt schools throughout the city, helping them start new clinics.

Federal policies should support the development of school-based clinics, which would be part of a network of primary care providers. At the junior and senior high school level, these clinics would pay particular attention to mental health, substance abuse, nutrition, and physical fitness. Pregnant students without major health problems would receive prenatal care in these facilities. It would be appropriate to grant Medicaid waivers, so that a school serving a population with 50 percent or more Medicaid-eligible students would be allowed to bill for all students without checking their Medicaid status.

6. *Middle School Reform*

The directions reform must take are clear: mentoring programs to increase the availability of adult role models, smaller learning environments, grouping teachers and students into teams, and bringing quality health and social services into the schools.

Mentoring programs offer an excellent opportunity to provide at-risk youths in both middle school and high school with positive role models. These programs need much more support, especially from the private sector.

7. *Linking Schools to the Labor Market*

Too many high school graduates do not measure up to the demands of today's labor market. States should establish uniform educational standards that all students should meet by age 16. National standards would be desirable, but we cannot wait for Washington to act. Therefore we propose that the individual states establish uniform performance standards keyed to the highest international achievement levels. Students who achieve those levels would receive "certificates of initial mastery," which would qualify them to continue on to college, to technical and professional education, or to the work world.

We hasten to add that the mere act of setting standards will accomplish nothing in the absence of fundamental reforms. For disadvantaged students, especially, such standards may come to represent yet another obstacle for them to overcome. America's commitment to standards must be matched by an equal commitment to the students. The nation needs to establish youth centers for struggling high school students and dropouts as well as second-chance centers for adults who require additional help to gain their diplomas. If children are not succeeding, we must ask ourselves: "How have *we* failed *them*?"

Establish a comprehensive system of professional certification for non-college-bound students and workers. Most workers have jobs that do not require a college education. Yet present policies do little to help the young who are not college-bound to gain the skills, credentials, and connections they need.

Expand apprenticeship programs that combine academic courses with on-the-job training. The academic content of the program should not be limited solely to trade-related subjects but should also provide a well-rounded education. A certificate would signify successful completion of a program of workplace-based instruction in a trade or skill.

Apprenticeship programs should be expanded beyond those serving the building trades—the most common type of apprenticeship program in the United States today. There should be programs for the service sectors, including the banking and hotel industries, which have generated much of the job growth in our cities.

Apprenticeship programs could be organized on a variety of bases: single-employer, single-industry, or through a consortium of employers sharing needs for workers with similar skills. Unions can play pivotal roles as initiators, organizers, and program-delivery agencies.

8. *Mobilize Private-Sector Support*

Government efforts to address the problems of the inner city can be greatly aided by private-sector involvement. In fact, some of the projects that have succeeded, such as the Comer model, have their origin in private-public partnerships.

We recommend the formation of new private-public advisory committees to support the implementation of the human development strategy. The advisory committee and other private-sector leaders can play a number of effective roles.

First, they can advocate. Private-sector leaders can help make urban poverty policies a political priority—an issue by which elected officials are judged. Building support will require extensive public education campaigns to change the view that urban poverty is a hopeless cause and to show the public that comprehensive programs do work.

Second, they can fund demonstration programs and special services. Community and philanthropic organizations should expand support for these programs. For example, philanthropic organizations could work with state and local governments to implement the Comer or similar models.

Third, they can participate in school governance. Private citizens should play an increased role in the education of children and the governance of local schools, particularly those with school-based management programs.

Fourth, they can serve as mentors. Responsible adults should commit part of their time to mentoring programs.

Fifth, they can offer jobs. Companies and unions should play an active role in helping high school students make the transition to the world of work.

9. *Federal Leadership and Resources in the War against Drugs*
The federal response to the crack crisis has been to fund small demonstration projects. These reach only a small portion of addicts and leave service providers without funds at the end of the demonstration. A better approach would be to fund programs at all primary care providers in areas with high concentrations of substance abusers.

10. A *New National Public Employment Program*
The program should be designed to emphasize service and labor-intensive projects. With proper safeguards against substitution of existing workers, and carefully drawn eligibility policies, such a program would be well worth the costs.

Better Cities for All of Us

Our nation faces a crisis in its inner cities. Economic self-interest requires the nation to address this crisis—it is central to the economic challenge facing America. We can no longer afford the cost of welfare payments, prison expenses, lost productivity and taxes, lagging competitiveness, and an eroded sense of community. A start can be made by framing the issue as one of human development in the inner city.

Our strategies are designed to build on the successes and avoid the failures of earlier efforts. Economic opportunity is vital, but racial barriers and a lack of technical skills are not the only obstacles that prevent the urban poor from escaping from the ghetto. In many cases, the children of the urban poor suffer from problems in physical and social development. Programs that take a developmental approach, such as Head Start and Comer's school development program, have shown that we can change the odds and break the cycle of urban poverty. The key to a successful strategy is recognizing that because *all* children share common developmental needs, under our democracy *all* should enjoy an equal opportunity to live with dignity and to develop their skills to the utmost.

Opportunity, skills, and positive norms are the ingredients for success. The process of expanding opportunities will require macroeconomic policies that promote growth and rising wages—variables that cannot be controlled at the state level alone. Washington must articulate a vision, exercise leadership, and commit the needed resources. If our agenda is carried out, our competitiveness will improve, and our nation's cities will be better places for us all.

CHAPTER 6

Restructuring the Healthcare System

AMERICA'S healthcare system is ailing and in urgent need of reform. The system is failing to deliver quality care at affordable prices to our citizens. Past efforts to solve these problems through piecemeal reforms have proven unsuccessful. The costs of medical care are escalating at an alarming rate, while access to basic services is declining. The spiraling costs of an inefficient system are taking a toll on America's competitiveness and on its standard of living.

Not one key player—the medical community, business, labor, senior citizens lobbies, insurers, or even government—has yet been able to define a workable agenda for change. So far they have all based their reforms on incremental approaches. Inevitably, one party or another has perceived threats to its interests and has acted swiftly to defend its prerogatives, thereby thwarting chances for significant progress. The task force believes that comprehensive reforms can halt the cycle of soaring costs and shrinking protection.

Spiraling Costs

Few national issues touch Americans as directly as skyrocketing healthcare costs. The nation will spend a total of $817 billion on medical services in 1992, an increase of 12 percent from the previous year's total.[1] That staggering sum is equivalent to an outlay of more than $2.2 billion a day.

All told, healthcare spending now accounts for 14 percent of our national income—up from 5.9 percent in 1965. According to one estimate, the total national bill for medical care is likely to grow by 12 to 15 percent annually over the next five years and could reach $1.3 trillion by 1995.[2] If this trend continues, by the year 2000, one out of every five dollars spent in the United States will go to healthcare. (See Chart 6.1.) Inevitably, increases of this magnitude mean that the nation will continue to curtail investments—in child nutrition, education, housing, research, and infrastructure—needed to reestablish America's economic leadership.

Other industrialized nations have managed to provide comparable (and often superior) quality healthcare to a larger portion of their citizenry at much lower per-capita costs. Using two commonly accepted indicators of overall public health—infant mortality and life expectancy—the United States ranks behind Canada and other industrialized nations. In 1990 U.S. per-capita spending was 131 percent greater than Japan's, 99 percent greater than West Germany's, and 43 percent greater than Canada's. Further, the costs of individual procedures are often much lower in other countries. For example, a 1986 study

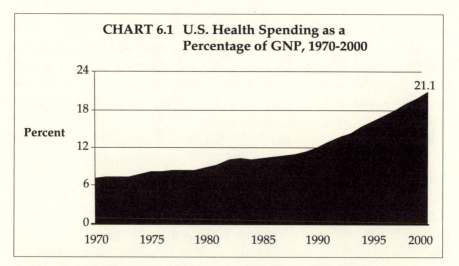

CHART 6.1 U.S. Health Spending as a Percentage of GNP, 1970-2000

Source: U.S. Health Care Financing Administration for 1970-89 data and Karen Davis, Johns Hopkins University for projections for 1990, 1995 and 2000
Note: Data for years between 1990 and 1995 and between 1995 and 2000 are interpolated.

of Canadian rates found that charges for coronary bypass operations and cataract removals were one-quarter of the standard prices charged by physicians in the United States.[3] If the United States could reduce its per-capita healthcare expenditures to the level of Germany's or Japan's, we could conceivably save $300 billion per year—a healthcare dividend that would exceed the peace dividend.[4]

STRAINED FAMILIES

The rising cost of healthcare has put a severe strain on the financial resources of American families. During the 1980s, when family income grew by 88 percent—barely keeping pace with inflation—healthcare costs rose by 147 percent.[5] Today the direct and indirect costs (including taxes) amount to $8,000 per family, or 19 cents of every dollar earned by the average family.[6] Unchecked healthcare costs contributed to the stagnation of American family incomes over the past two decades. Unless this juggernaut can be slowed down, Americans can expect to be paying as much as one-third of their earnings for health insurance and medical bills two decades hence.

LESS COMPETITIVE BUSINESSES

For corporate America, the healthcare crisis has reached epidemic proportions as well. Roughly seven out of ten working-age Americans receive their health insurance coverage through employer-provided plans.[7] A major factor in the runaway inflation of the system has been the spiraling costs of employer-paid insurance premiums. Faced with the prospect of even stiffer rate increases in the future, many corporations have been eliminating or reducing employee medical benefits, raising prices, cutting wages, or, in extreme cases, laying off workers.

Underlying these disconcerting trends is a growing fear within the business community that America cannot support a healthy industrial base if it maintains an unaffordable healthcare system. To some corporations the burden of carrying ever costlier health plans now spells the difference between profit and loss, or between international competitiveness and fading dominance.

Corporate spending on medical plans has jumped in recent years to 25 percent of corporate profits.[8] General Motors, for example, spent more than $3 billion to maintain health benefits for its employees, dependents, and retirees in 1990.[9] According to some estimates, international differences in the costs of care for employees and retirees give foreign automobile makers a de facto subsidy of $300 to $500 per car.[10] Thus one hidden effect of the healthcare crisis on U.S. businesses has been to raise the production costs of American goods, making them less competitive both here and abroad. Another has been to absorb valuable corporate resources that might otherwise have been invested in research and development, worker retraining programs, or new plant and equipment.

FISCALLY STRAPPED GOVERNMENT

As both a large-scale employer and an insurer of last resort, government has not been exempt from the mushrooming costs of healthcare services. Tens of millions of Americans who do not receive health insurance on the job or who cannot afford to buy it directly from an insurer are entitled to coverage through various publicly financed programs, such as Medicare, Medicaid, and Champus (the Department of Defense's medical plan for military personnel and their families).

Despite the fact that the U.S. government is the single largest purchaser of medical services in the country and has set limits on what doctors can charge Medicare and Medicaid patients, its total medical bills have been growing by more than 8 percent annually—faster than the rate of inflation. In 1980 one out of every nine dollars spent by the federal government went to healthcare; by 1996 that share could virtually double to one out of every five dollars.

Part of the reason healthcare is taking a larger and larger bite out of the federal budget is the ballooning expenses of Medicare and Medicaid, two programs that expanded access without imposing firm constraints on costs. Medicare, the insurance system that provides the elderly and disabled with acute care, is mandated and financed entirely by the federal government, predominantly through payroll taxes on worker earnings. Medicaid, the jointly financed federal-state program, provides coverage for more than 27 million of the nation's poor citizens, including senior citizens needing long-term care. Medicare, currently costs in excess of $100 billion a year. Medicaid, with a 1991 budget of $158 billion, is the fastest-growing spending program in the United States. It now costs nearly 70 times what it did in 1967, when the program was launched.[11]

State governments, collectively the nation's second-largest consumer of health services, already spend one-fifth of their budgets on medical care. Their share of the Medicaid bill alone claims 14 percent of overall state expenditures. (States presently pay up to half of the system's tab.) It is projected that, if costs continue to climb at current rates, Medicaid will account for 28 percent of state budgetary expenses by 1995.[12] (See Chart 6.2.) In addition to Medicaid, most states also offer general assistance programs to provide some care for poor people who do not meet Medicaid's eligibility requirements. Costs for these programs are also rising rapidly.

The result could be disastrous for the fiscally strapped states. The ability of many states to provide services has been hurt by the current recession and more than a decade of federal

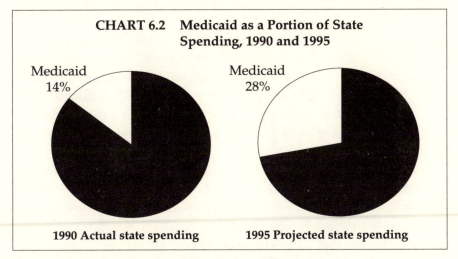

CHART 6.2   Medicaid as a Portion of State Spending, 1990 and 1995

Medicaid 14%

Medicaid 28%

1990 Actual state spending

1995 Projected state spending

Source: National Association of State Budget Officers

cutbacks. If the states must struggle now to raise revenues for essential public services, how will they fare in the future when their healthcare expenditures grow proportionately larger? As a recent report by the National Governors' Association has warned, "If steps are not taken now to build a real healthcare system, too many children will continue to come to school unprepared to learn, too many adolescents will continue to face serious but preventable health problems, and too many adults will be prevented from leading full and productive lives."[13]

Declining Access

Between the 1940s and the 1970s, the American healthcare system witnessed phenomenal growth. The idea of a work-place-based system of social insurance first took root during the New Deal. In time, workers, vested with new collective bargaining rights began winning management's acceptance of health insurance as a routine job benefit. The postwar boom in the U.S. economy put medical policies within the reach of even those Americans who were not covered at work. In 1940, 12 million Americans had private coverage; by 1975 the number had multiplied to 178 million. With the introduction of Medicare and Medicaid in 1965, tens of millions of additional Americans, who might otherwise have slipped through the cracks of the system, became eligible for publicly financed health protection.[14]

Since the 1970s, however, as our system has grown more costly, access to basic services has declined.[15] For all the hundreds of billions of dollars Americans lavish on medical care, we have not managed to purchase a system that guarantees us greater peace of mind. Why?

For one thing, the employer-based system does not cover the entire working population. More than half of all small businesses—firms that create the bulk of new jobs in the economy—offer no health benefits to their employees.[16] For another, the system as a whole is becoming less and less inclusive, providing fewer and fewer protections. In the 1970s, for example, Medicaid was able to enroll 65 percent of the eligible poor; today it only covers 40 percent. A similar winnowing process is occurring in the workplace. Faced with escalating insurance costs, many large companies that historically assumed the burden of insuring working America are terminating plans, cutting back on benefits, or requiring their employees to pay a larger percentage of policy costs. This has forced many employees to make the no-win choice between absorbing the additional costs and forgoing protection for their loved ones.

With more jobs being stripped of medical benefits and with access to public programs narrowing, the number of Americans exposed to health risks has soared. In 1978, 12.3 percent of the total population lacked medical insurance coverage; by 1989, the figure had risen to 14.9 percent. Today, as Chart 6.3 shows, an estimated 34.7 million Americans have no health insurance whatsoever.[17] The majority of these people—members of the working poor and middle class—are self-supporting Americans who now find themselves caught in a terrible bind.[18] They earn too much money to qualify for Medicaid, yet not enough

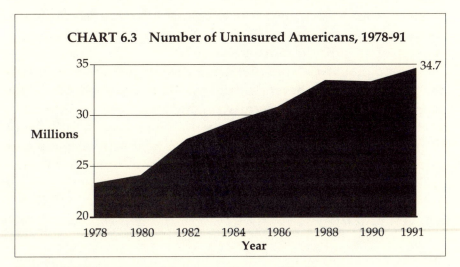

CHART 6.3   Number of Uninsured Americans, 1978-91

Source: U.S. Department of Commerce, Bureau of the Census

to pay for no-frills private coverage. All of them live in fear that one debilitating illness could wipe out their life savings.

These trends have other alarming ramifications. As the system excludes an increasing number of workers and poverty-stricken adults, fewer of their dependents enjoy coverage. Among the growing ranks of the uninsured are 500,000 pregnant women. Without adequate health coverage, these expectant mothers are less likely to get the prenatal care they need to help them deliver healthy babies, at full term, free of birth defects. Also among the uninsured are approximately 8 million children, whose chances of developing into healthy, alert, and productive adults are significantly lowered if they do not receive early and ongoing medical attention during their formative years.[19]

The bitter irony is that our system gains little by restricting access to basic care in the name of cost containment. Quite the contrary: it virtually guarantees that society as a whole will pay a higher price tomorrow for failing to detect and treat the preventable medical problems of its citizens today.

Finally, even those who formally have access may not get the services they need. Although the total number of physicians practicing medicine in the United States has increased from 1.6 per thousand to 2.4 per thousand in the last 20 years, many communities—most notably the inner cities and rural areas—suffer from a chronic shortage of family doctors.[20] Such shortages mean that at-risk people do not receive needed preventive and primary care. Other industrial countries have a much higher proportion of doctors in family practice. In Canada 50 percent of all doctors are practicing family doctors, as opposed to only 10 percent in the United States.[21] Our healthcare system, as currently structured, offers no meaningful remedy for this problem.

Uneven Quality

Just as our system lacks safeguards to insure that everyone who needs care will get care, it also lacks effective quality-control mechanisms to insure that all who receive care will be well served. The task force defines quality care as treatment that is appropriate, timely, and effective—by which we mean treatment that involves no extraneous procedures, that focuses on early detection and prevention, and that is performed well and has the desired outcome.

Unfortunately the evidence is mounting that, under these criteria, many Americans are not getting the best care money can buy. Some patients receive treatments that are known to be ineffective, while other patients receive care whose effectiveness has not yet been established. Because physicians are not in agreement about how to treat effectively many conditions, wide variations in practice exist.

Examples abound. According to one study, tonsillectomies were performed ten times as often, on a per-capita basis, in one Vermont town as in a neighboring town. Another study documented that the frequency of coronary bypass operations in New Haven was twice that in Boston. A third report, comparing hospitals in Harrisburg, Pennsylvania, found that postoperative death rates for coronary bypass patients varied by as much as 200 percent from one hospital to the next and that the hospital with the worst record was the one charging the highest prices! A former editor of the *New England Journal of Medicine* has estimated that at least 20 to 30 percent of the care provided by well-meaning physicians in good hospitals is either inappropriate, ineffective, or unnecessary.[22]

Malpractice suits result from poor practice. Patients who suffer from malpractice deserve to be compensated. At the same time, the fear of malpractice lawsuits is driving doctors and hospitals to order costly, unneeded tests and to conduct unwarranted surgery, simply to protect themselves against possible charges of negligence. The American Medical Association has calculated, for example, that such defensive practices may add as much as $21 billion annually to the total U.S. medical bill.[23]

As it presently operates, our healthcare system places a disproportionate emphasis on healing patients after they become sick rather than on preventing them from becoming ill in the first place. The widespread availability of miraculous new treatments and technologies—CAT scans, MRIs, dialysis machines, organ transplants—merely accentuates this systemic bias. Preventive medicine enjoys a far less exalted status in the system than does the delivery of acute care services—that is, the provision of institutional and specialized services for treating illness. For care to be both timely and effective, our system must redirect its energies toward preventive and primary care at the community level.

Most lapses in quality care are not the result of unskilled or careless providers, but rather of faulty work organization and poor understanding of standard practices and norms. This is mainly due to the fact that our disorganized system has no institutionalized mechanisms for assuring continuous quality improvement. Isolated providers can make improvements in their own delivery of care, but they cannot control other aspects of the system that lower overall quality.

Of course, quality-of-care issues cannot be divorced from questions of cost and access. A system with insufficient safeguards against malpractice, operating in a society in which legions of lawyers stand ready to litigate, creates incentives to propel costs ever higher. Anxious about the risks of malpractice litigation, physicians are understandably inclined to order batteries of tests that may or may not be useful, to hospitalize patients unnecessarily, and to prescribe drugs that may not be needed. All of these factors add to the cost of care, driving insurance premiums higher and forcing more and more Americans to go underinsured or uninsured.

Underlying Causes

Any realistic approach to the healthcare crisis must take into account the underlying problems that drive up costs, limit access, and lower quality.

A SYSTEM THAT GENERATES RISING COSTS
The present structure of our healthcare financing system is an

uncoordinated mix of private and public payers, reflecting a fundamental American ambivalence about how to balance government involvement and market-based financing. The federal government has assumed responsibility for purchasing medical care for the elderly and the poor, thus making it the single largest purchaser of medical services. When the costs of those services have risen prohibitively Washington has asserted its authority—and its considerable market clout—to control the prices of the services that it pays for. But it has not been able to broker fair prices for all; nor has it asserted such a prerogative. As a result, our system remains unbounded: federal efforts to cap costs at one end are more than easily offset by price increases passed along to the private sector at the other end. Because the U.S. healthcare system lacks any mechanism for global budgeting—that is, any way rationally to constrain costs on a systemwide basis—spiraling costs are among its defining features. Spending caps are needed because restrictions on prices are not sufficient to hold down spending, since providers often increase the volume of services they provide in order to offset price decreases.[24]

A PASS-THE-COSTS SYSTEM

How do costs get shifted? In several ways. When the federal government fixes limits on Medicaid fees for example, many hospitals and doctors wind up treating these patients at lower than customary rates. Providers also have to compensate for the costs of those who receive care but have no coverage at all. (See Chart 6.4.) Care providers try to compensate for their losses by charging higher prices to the privately insured. Then insurance companies pass these inflated costs along to employers, who, in turn, shift them on to workers, either by imposing ever higher cost-sharing requirements or by canceling their employee health plans altogether. Uninsured workers add to the pool of Americans who must, in times of desperation, throw themselves on the mercy of public and private nonprofit hospitals. This sets in motion another relentless round of price hikes aimed at making those who carry coverage pay for the failure of the system to provide universal care. Like a dog chasing its tail, such a mad pursuit leads nowhere.

Increasingly restrictive insurance industry practices also impose hidden costs on the system. Recently insurers have begun raising their rates for employers with high-risk employees—workers who have been ill or whose medical profiles suggest they might become ill. This practice, called experience rating (distinguishable from the more traditional community rating, which spreads risk across a wide population), can result in prohibitive rate increases, especially for small employers. The effect on startup companies can be both sudden and devastating. A six-person firm, for example, in which one worker has a long and costly bout with cancer may find its premiums increasing so astronomically that it either has to shun or fire high-risk employees or terminate health benefits. In either case, the firm can lose its competitive edge overnight. For those on the losing end of the cost-shifting game—workers and firms that cannot shift costs to someone else—the ultimate price of our present healthcare system can be bankruptcy.

These practices take another economic toll. Each year an estimated 20 million Americans switch jobs. Under current

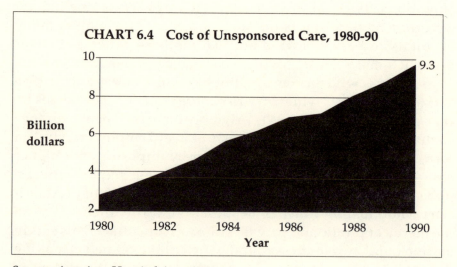

CHART 6.4   Cost of Unsponsored Care, 1980-90

Source: American Hospital Association

arrangements, employees covered by their present employers must change insurance plans when they take a new job. If a wage earner or dependent has a preexisting medical condition, however, he or she may think twice about making a move if there is a chance that the condition will not be covered under a prospective employer's health plan. For many in the work force such uncertainty presents an unacceptable risk. Its net effect is to deprive millions of Americans of their historic mobility to seek better employment opportunities. For the business community, it also means that access to the best work-force talent may now be foreclosed, in certain instances, entirely by insurance considerations.

AN UNFAIR SYSTEM
With no in-built mechanisms or incentives for deploying services rationally, the U.S. healthcare system chronically underserves some populations and, arguably, overserves others. As previously noted, primary and preventive care programs are almost nonexistent in many areas of the country. Moreover, health insurance rarely covers the costs of preventive care, the kind of services most needed by the least fortunate members of our society. Within the industry the prevailing view is that premiums would have to climb even higher if preventive services were covered.[25] Consequently the system currently reinforces existing priorities, despite their extremely high cost to society as a whole.

The system is unfair in another, less obvious, way. Poor households spend a disproportionate share of their income on healthcare.[26] Further, many of the working poor, who may not themselves have health benefits, subsidize through their taxes those on Medicaid.

A SYSTEM SNARLED IN RED TAPE
More than 1,500 different health insurers operate in the United States. Each has its own bureaucracy, and each has its own forms and filing procedures. According to one reckoning, the U.S. healthcare system's administrative costs alone amounted

to $200 billion in 1991. In 1987 record-keeping costs totaled 4.9 percent of U.S. healthcare spending, compared with 2.5 percent for Canada and 2.6 percent for Great Britain.[27]

A system awash in red tape is, not surprisingly, a system ripe for fraud. Insurance companies charge that patients, care providers, and outright cheats may be bilking the system for as much as $75 billion per year. Experts add that Medicaid pays out billions in fraudulent claims for fictitious patients each year.

A SYSTEM WITHOUT QUALITY CONTROLS
Our system has no standard mechanisms for monitoring the services provided to determine, over time, which are effective and which are not. With rare exceptions, providers make that determination unilaterally, operating within practice guidelines that are at best inconsistent from one practitioner to another, one clinic to another, one community to another, one state to another. Efforts to limit unnecessary practices and procedures by putting caps on individual services have been thwarted by practitioners who have simply increased the volume of other services they order. The Congressional Budget Office has pointed out that excess capacity resulting from the rapid dissemination of new technologies has encouraged overuse, resulting in potential harm to patients as well as higher costs.[28]

The system should aspire to continuous quality improvement, refining the care-giving process on the basis of data from the processes themselves to better improve patient satisfaction. Assuring quality control does not necessarily mean more government regulation. Rather it should be understood as a process of disseminating information about quality improvements throughout the system.

Incremental or Comprehensive Change

Our nation's reluctance to impose global budgeting plans, or to otherwise contain healthcare expenditures, has led to various uncoordinated, incremental efforts to regulate the delivery of services—often in ways that fail to save money, widen coverage, or improve quality. Advocates of incremental reforms tend to treat matters of access, cost, financing, and quality of care as if they were separable problems. They also seek to maintain the existing separation of private and public responsibilities.[29] Some propose to broaden access by making more people eligible for Medicaid or by expanding the use of tax credits to encourage more employers to offer health insurance. Others seek to clamp down on costs by expanding the use of managed care systems, by eliminating state-mandated coverage inclusions, by reforming group insurance practices, by limiting malpractice lawsuits, or by capping Medicare and Medicaid outlays.

Not one of these approaches simultaneously addresses cost and access. Proposals to put more stringent limits on Medicaid payments, for example, are likely to lead a larger percentage of doctors to refuse to treat Medicaid patients. When the federal government cut back Medicaid funds, the states were unable to maintain reimbursement rates at attractive levels, and the percentage of participating pediatricians dropped from 85 percent in 1978 to 77 percent in 1989.[30] Thus the net effect of attempts to control costs in one sector of the system is to shift them—in this case, into the future, by increasing the odds that poor children will not receive the preventive and acute care they need.

Managed care, another cost-containment strategy, has a positive role to play in the system, but it is not a panacea. It involves the strict management of utilization. Under the broad rubric of managed care falls everything from third-party payer reviews—which can, in effect, veto physicians' decisions by denying reimbursement for certain procedures—to health maintenance organizations, which focus on preventing and treating illnesses before they require costly hospitalization. Some insurance companies seized upon managed care as a way to control their own costs, but the strategy has inherent limitations. Managed care may help an individual insurer or perhaps a group of insurers to contain costs, but it is unlikely to control the costs of the entire existing system.

The alternative to incremental change is comprehensive

reform—an agenda designed to achieve universal access, improved quality, and stabilized costs at the same time. Some critics accuse proponents of comprehensive reform of seeking to replace America's healthcare system with socialized medicine. This characterization is untrue. In fact this approach seeks to preserve and build on the strengths of the existing healthcare delivery system while giving government a more direct and central role in the healthcare financing system.

This task force believes that the time for comprehensive reform has come—for two reasons.

First, we are persuaded that the United States cannot possibly reach the goal of universal access unless costs can be brought under control.

Second, our country has had enough experience with incrementalism to know that such an approach cannot effectively control spending or enhance the quality of healthcare services on a consistent basis nationwide. We believe that restricting ourselves to incremental approaches will only postpone the day when all Americans can have access to quality care.

Our goal is a system that will guarantee health coverage for all Americans, control costs, improve the quality of care, emphasize wellness and prevention, and preserve American traditions of pluralism and freedom of choice. We believe that only a coordinated national system of universal health protection can meet all of these criteria.

While many states have developed innovative approaches to healthcare delivery and financing, states cannot be expected to address the entire range of problems alone. The same is true of those communities where progressive alliances of providers and purchasers have recently been working together to contain costs and enhance quality. In fact a proliferation of state and local reforms that are inevitably inconsistent with one another may actually increase the administrative burdens of businesses that operate in multiple jurisdictions. There is, in short, no escaping the fact that the problems we face are national in scope and require a national response if we are to reach the goal of quality medical care for all Americans at affordable cost.

Other countries with democratic political systems have

demonstrated that it is possible to combine universal access and quality care with effective cost controls. Canada, Germany, France, and Japan have systems that retain private medicine and patient choice. Canada has a single-payer system, while the others have multiple payers, but all four have national budgeting or expenditure targeting and systems for governing provider rates. In particular, most countries have uniform rates for public and private purchasers of care. Furthermore, all four countries have guidelines to control excessive investment in healthcare technologies and other capital expenditures.

Although the United States must develop reforms tailored to the specific needs of our own society, we should pay close attention to strategies that have worked elsewhere. Twenty years ago, when Canada implemented its system, the United States and Canada were spending roughly the same share of their gross national product on healthcare. By 1989 the U.S. share had risen to 11.6 percent, while Canada's was at 8.9 percent. A General Accounting Office study attributed the difference to lower administrative costs and to uniform reimbursement of care providers.[31]

The General Accounting Office studied the healthcare systems of Germany, France, and Japan and found that large savings were also possible under their multipayer, employment-based systems.[32] These similarities suggest that the United States could achieve universal coverage and other major health-financing goals while retaining key features of its current system. These countries have been able to achieve universal access at reasonable costs because they have national policies and institutions that set goals for much or all of healthcare spending and govern provider rate setting.

Just as we can learn from what works in other countries, we can also incorporate some important state-level initiatives in a national program of healthcare reform. For example, New York, Maryland, New Jersey, and Massachusetts have all adopted standardized all-payer reimbursement systems for hospitals. Researchers have found that this approach slows the rate of cost increase.[33]

Support for comprehensive reform is growing rapidly. No

longer insulated from the costs of healthcare, middle-class voters have made healthcare reform a potent political issue. The business community and organized labor are cooperating on this issue because there is a "consensus of frustration," in the words of one U.S. Chamber of Commerce official.[34] The United Steelworkers and Bethlehem Steel have agreed to work together for comprehensive national reforms. The United Auto Workers and the major automakers endorse the same goals. Major corporations, such as Xerox and Safeway, have joined with the unions to endorse the report of the National Leadership Coalition for Healthcare Reform. Together they have called for a "play-or-pay" approach to universal coverage—one in which employers either offer private insurance or contribute to a public plan—coupled with no-loopholes cost containment. Public employers are also joining this trend: the state of Michigan and the Service Employees Union have agreed to work together for national reforms. And the increasing micromanagement of medical practice, largely a result of incrementalist approaches to cost containment, has prompted some groups of healthcare providers, such as the American College of Physicians and the American Medical Association, to endorse comprehensive reform.

With support for comprehensive reform growing among concerned consumers and providers alike, and with a number of reform proposals now pending in Congress, we believe that the United States has a historic opportunity to create a new healthcare system we can all be proud of.

Prescription for Reform

The task force members agree that a comprehensive reform strategy must include the following elements. These elements can be applied now to our system for acute care and they provide a framework for eventually addressing the problem of long-term care.

1. *All Americans must be guaranteed access to a package of basic health benefits.* These basic benefits—whether secured indi-

vidually, from an employer, or through a public plan—should include preventive and primary care, especially prenatal care, well-baby care, physical examinations and tests, mental health services, substance-abuse treatment, hospital services, and allowance for alternatives to hospitalization, such as home care. Healthcare should be obtainable through community-based delivery systems.

Universal access can be implemented in more than one way. A single-payer approach would enroll everyone in a publicly financed plan, eliminating employment-based coverage. The plan proposed by Senator Robert Kerrey, consistent with American traditions of choice, would allow Americans to choose between competing health plans at the state level. Another approach (favored by the National Leadership Coalition for Health Care Reforms, Senators Mitchell and Kennedy, and many members of this task force) builds on the present employment-based system. Employers would have two options: they could provide at least the standard package of benefits to employees and dependents through private health insurance, or they could offer enrollment in a public plan and pay a payroll tax to help cover the cost of the plan. The content of the employer-based plan could be subject to collective bargaining.

Some task force members prefer to reform the existing multiple-payer, employment-based system; others advocate a publicly financed single-payer system; still other task force members favor models such as New York's single-payer authority or Senator Kerrey's proposal. There is strong consensus that the implementation of our package should not be delayed because of the difficulty of choosing a particular financing mechanism. We believe, as do others, that it is possible to enact a comprehensive reform plan without irrevocably committing the nation to one specific financing model. For example, the cost-control measures, proposed by Senators Paul Simon and Brock Adams as an amendment to the Senate leadership proposal, allow the states to choose between two models of financing. This approach would be consistent with our tradition of giving state governments primary responsibility for regulating the health insurance market. Whatever model the states choose, the national goal of providing universal coverage can be accomplished.

Under the National Leadership Coalition proposal, the coverage of part-time workers would be phased in, and employers could choose to provide private coverage to their full-time employees while letting the public plan cover their part-time employees. Under the play-or-pay option, a public plan would cover everyone who is not covered by an employer plan, including the unemployed.

We admit that comprehensive reforms securing universal access will not happen overnight. In the meantime the states may need to pursue more modest measures. For example, access to healthcare could be enhanced at the state level if states adopt—as New York is now adopting—community rating as opposed to experience rating. Experience rating, because it raises the costs for certain populations beyond their ability to pay, has the effect of denying access to Americans who need it the most. The practice of community rating is more consistent with the task force goal of establishing fairness and equity in our healthcare system.

2. *The federal government should establish a national board for the improvement of quality in medical care.* Comprehensive reform must include a mechanism for quality control that does not come at the expense of cost and access. A national board would be able to develop guidelines and help providers implement continuous quality improvement techniques. It would also help medical care providers by assessing the value of new technologies, by gathering and disseminating information on outcomes and on continuous quality improvement techniques, and by developing guidelines for surgical practice.

The board would also fund research and demonstration projects and establish an information clearinghouse to publicize successful quality initiatives. The board's work in the area of new technologies would help practitioners and consumers determine the most appropriate and efficient ways to use such technologies and procedures.

In the absence of procedures to assess practice profiles and patterns of care, insurers and regulators have turned to case-by-case review of medical decision making. For example, one set of New York regulations requires hospitals to report all "untoward incidents" to the Department of Health. Case-by-case review is administratively costly and does not lead to quality improvements in the overall system of healthcare. To improve this situation, hospitals, physicians and the Health Department need to work together to address practitioner profiles and facility service patterns based on commonly recognized standards of care. Achieving this objective will improve quality while winning the confidence of patients, payers, and providers alike.

If states undertake systematic reviews of their existing regulations, they should be able to reduce administrative paperwork and improve the quality of information made available by care providers to regulators and consumers. The members of the Institute for Healthcare Improvement are presently considering how healthcare regulations can be made more proactive, and the New York Health Department should participate in this process.

3. *Federal and state governments should work together to curb malpractice and to reduce the costs of adjudicating malpractice claims.* Measures are needed both to reduce the incidence of malpractice and to limit the burdens of liability insurance. A national board for quality improvement in medical care, as described above, would benefit conscientious practitioners by providing comprehensive information and guidelines on effective procedures. Physicians are generally willing to modify their practice patterns when they are made aware of more effective procedures.[35] Physician retraining and accreditation requirements must also be improved. At the same time, the cost of liability protection could be greatly reduced by relying more on arbitration and less on litigation to resolve malpractice claims. This could provide a more effective way of compensating the victims of malpractice.

4. *Policymakers at the national and state levels must cooperate in setting limits on total healthcare spending.* A board composed of private and public members should propose global spending limits, either as budgets or as expenditure targets, on an annual or multiyear basis. Limits on healthcare spending must be applicable to fee-for-service as well as capitated (fixed fee per-patient) payment systems. Standard sets of negotiated rates, applicable to all payers and providers, would accomplish this goal in fee-for-service systems.

Limits should be set for different types of spending, including capital spending, at levels sufficient to provide for adequate staffing and appropriate compensation consistent with the goal of providing quality care to all. State governments will need to establish mechanisms to insure that the rates paid to providers are consistent with state healthcare expenditure limits, and policymakers at both the state and national levels will have to make explicit trade-offs between healthcare and other priorities.

The National Leadership Coalition and other groups have proposed an all-payer fee schedule as part of a comprehensive package of cost reform. An all-payer fee schedule is a set of prices applicable to all payers, public and private. In addition to preventing cost shifting, an all-payer fee schedule can also be used to pursue other policy goals. For example, fees for primary care services could be raised relative to those for specialties as a means of increasing the nation's supply of primary care practitioners.

In New York State, for example, all-payer fee schedules are currently used for inpatient hospital services. The task force recommends that the all-payer fee schedule be expanded to include outpatient hospital services as well.

5. *Implementation of a process to limit spending must be accompanied by a reduction in the micromanagement of care providers.* Adopting a national package of standard minimum benefits will eliminate the need for conflicting state insurance mandates. Implementing capital spending limits can reduce the need for

capital utilization controls. The task force believes that establishing direct limits on spending offers the only realistic way to reduce micromanagement of healthcare providers by government regulators and insurance companies.

6. *Federal and state governments must work together to reduce administrative overhead.* The task force believes that this can be accomplished either by moving to a single-payer system or by dramatically reforming the present multipayer system. Either approach would save billions of dollars per year.

The simplest, but politically most controversial way of reducing administrative overhead—and containing the growth of total spending on healthcare—would be to implement a single-payer system at the national level. The U.S. General Accounting Office has estimated that moving to a single-payer system would save $34 billion annually in insurance overhead and $33 billion annually in hospital and physician administrative costs—amounts that should more than offset the cost of providing health protection to those who are not now insured as well as the cost of eliminating many of the co-payments and deductibles imposed under current insurance plans.[36]

A number of proposals for single-payer systems would allow private insurers to play different roles in the system. Senator Kerrey's proposal, for example, would let insurance companies operate healthcare plans such as health maintenance organizations. States would have the option of hiring a private company to administer public plans.

We believe that significant administrative savings can also be achieved under a reformed multipayer system. The National Leadership Coalition for Health-Care Reform plan, for example, calls on government to require insurers to use the same forms, offer the same standard benefit package, and pay providers at the same rates.[37]

Another strategy for reducing waste and controlling cost is to make greater use of simplified electronic billing procedures. Consumers could be issued electronic cards, which providers would then use to bill the payer. Centralized computer systems would track spending, providing data that could be used to forecast costs and determine annual healthcare budgets. The same database, which would need built-in safeguards to protect the confidentiality of patient information, could be used to monitor trends in the use of specific procedures and technologies and to compare treatment outcomes within service areas and between comparable areas.

Another alternative—a single-payer authority—would achieve some of the benefits of a single-payer approach within our current multipayer system. A single-payer authority, such as UNY*Care, which is being considered by New York State, would develop uniform billing practices for use throughout the system. Providers would no longer have to deal with myriad health insurers but would simply bill the authority, which would then bill the appropriate healthcare plan.

Although these reforms would require an increase in public spending, they could bring the nation's total health bill under control for the first time. The potential savings to American families and businesses are extremely large. Under current policies, the nation's healthcare bill can be expected to reach $1.9 trillion by the year 2000; in contrast, the public-private plan proposed by the National Leadership Coalition would cost an estimated $1.3 trillion in that year—saving $600 billion.[38]

Fair Financing

Under our present system, Americans pay for medical care in a variety of ways. Insurance premiums, paid largely by employers and to a lesser extent by employees, account for a large portion of the dollars. A second large piece comes out of federal and state taxes. A third source of financing: out-of-pocket expenses that patients pay.

The financing of healthcare should be guided by the principles of fairness and progressiveness. Just as no one should be barred from receiving needed care because of cost, so should everyone pay into any public or public-private plan according to income. In particular, a sound financing strategy should consider the special needs of new and small employers, low-wage workers and their employers, and part-time workers. Under any approach, public financing must be used to cover the out-of-pocket expenses of low-income Americans.

With any comprehensive reform, private insurance premiums will diminish in importance and the public sector will pay more of the bills. The reforms that we recommend can be financed through payroll taxes coupled with a higher ceiling on the amount of income subject to such taxes. Setting the payroll tax at a level low enough to keep labor costs competitive would, of course, be especially important for labor-intensive industries. Financing could be made even more progressive by including revenues from personal and corporate income taxes. Chapter 9, on macroeconomic policies, provides more details on the financing of reform.

Although co-payments and deductibles are featured in the financing of many proposed plans, we believe that they act as barriers to care. They should be minimized—applied primarily to elective procedures and other optional services above and beyond the standard package of benefits—and eliminated outright for low-income families.

While taxes will rise, this increase will largely be a result of the shift in financing from the private sector to the public. As the growth of spending for healthcare slows down, Americans will have larger savings to put to other uses.

Improving our healthcare system is simply one of the reforms needed to better the quality of life in America and to enhance our international competitiveness. As we have seen in earlier chapters, most of the reforms must be carried out within our own borders. These initiatives, however, will not be enough to assure an improvement of America's standard of living. The nation's fortunes are now increasingly linked with those of its trading partners, and an agenda for domestic rebuilding must be complemented by new international strategies.

CHAPTER 7

Economic Imperatives and a New Foreign Policy

Advancing America's Interests

INCREASING public and private investment, regaining industrial preeminence, reducing poverty, and reforming our healthcare system should be the nation's priorities in this decade. Does that mean America should, as some have suggested, assign less importance to international policy? The task force believes the answer is no.

Only with the appropriate international policy will America be able to carry out the comprehensive domestic reforms it needs. The United States has an enormous stake in the shape of the world economy. The United States is increasingly dependent on international markets to sell its products and on international sources of capital to finance its debts. Our quality of life is influenced by global environmental conditions, the movements of emigrants, and international drug trafficking.

Some Americans do not understand the reality of our international ties. Having suffered the consequences of economic decline for well over a decade, they believe that America's domestic problems are so serious that we must retreat from the international arena and concentrate exclusively on the home front. Their frustration is understandable. But the argument for retreat overlooks the extent to which America's health depends on the global economy. Rather than disengaging from the world and relinquishing international leadership to our strongest industrial competitors, we need to fashion a new global strategy.

The old international policies no longer make sense, neither for world peace nor for American prosperity. For the past 45 years, containment of the Soviet Union was the dominant goal of our international policy. That era is now over, and we have entered a world where strength is measured by productivity growth and investment rates, not by missile "throw weights." Instead of an arms race and strategic defense alliances determining the scope and nature of America's foreign commitments, we now have economic, environmental, and social problems that are changing the world and placing new pressures on America's international policy. These changes would dictate a new U.S. international strategy even if the United States did not have competitiveness problems.

We have entered a formative period in world history comparable to the remarkable years immediately following World War II. America will not be able to escape the influences—both direct and indirect—of the economic and social transformations now under way throughout the world.

- Germany and Japan, two of America's closest postwar allies and now its most powerful economic competitors, are taking on new roles that could make them more assertive and less cooperative in the future.

- The republics of the former Soviet Union and the countries of Eastern Europe have witnessed a dramatic fall in production, investment, and trade as they strive to make the transition to market economies. At the same time, these countries are now involved in a concerted effort to expand their exports to the West, thus sharpening the struggle for shares of international markets. Future investment required by the transition will put immense weight on already straining world capital markets. And ethnic turmoil now ravaging the region casts a shadow over plans for economic renewal, while triggering greater emigration to Western Europe.

- The world economy is moving toward the formation of regional trading blocs. While providing some order to a rapidly changing international economy, these blocs could nonetheless reduce America's access to the prosperous markets of Europe and Asia.

- Much of the Third World is going through difficult economic adjustments. The United States has much at stake in their success, for if the next decade brings more economic stagnation, then we can expect further political turmoil, faltering export markets, uncontrolled immigration, worse drug trafficking, and rapid environmental destruction.

- Economic growth in the world's major industrial economies is weak. The advanced economies in Western Europe saw their growth rates fall from 2.9 percent in 1990 to a feeble 1.4 percent in 1991.[1] Even growth in the powerful Japanese economy slowed by a third in 1991. As the world economy cools off, export producers will face stagnant markets, and many producers for the domestic market will confront increased competition from imports. Slow global growth makes it more difficult for the United States to sustain domestic growth and balance its trade account.

These transformations mean that international *economic* policy will become a prime concern of Congress and the president. Fighting the Cold War did not, however, require well-developed decision-making structures for questions of international economics. An important question arises: are U.S. public institutions capable of dealing with these transformations in ways that protect America's long-term economic security?

Proposal: Establish an Economic Security Council

Four decades of Cold War thinking and planning oriented the nation's policymaking apparatus heavily toward political and military issues, obscuring America's national economic interests. When our allies failed to share equitably the enormous military costs of the West's defense, Washington could nevertheless point approvingly to their deference on U.S.-led security initiatives. When the nations of Western Europe erected protective walls around their banking, telecommunications, and aviation industries, competitive American firms lost potential markets. But as long as American industry remained dominant at home, these markets did not matter much. And as long as these countries continued to follow America's lead on issues of global security, Washington raised few objections to their restrictive economic practices.[2] More recently, as Third World countries have adopted development strategies based on increasing their exports, they have found European and Japanese markets relatively closed. The United States has accepted their goods willingly, continuing to play the now costly role of "consumer of last resort." Like Europe and Japan in prior decades, these Third World nations willingly defer to Washington on security matters in exchange for U.S. economic openness.

Now the most pressing national goals include technological leadership, competitive and high-wage industries, full employment, and rising living standards. In addition to these economic concerns, environmental issues, such as global warming and ozone depletion, are forcing themselves onto the agendas of policymakers. While the American government is today well equipped to decide questions of world politics and military security, it lacks an effective mechanism for addressing our economic, social, and environmental concerns in the international arena.

MAKING INTERNATIONAL ECONOMIC POLICY
Alone among national officials, the president is accountable to

185

all the voters of the United States. Only the president represents the entire constituency of America. For leadership in helping our country prosper, Americans must look to the president. Unfortunately, the current process for fashioning international economic policy makes it difficult for the president to exercise effective leadership.

The president's major instrument for formulating foreign economic policy is the Economic Policy Council. This council includes the secretaries of Treasury, Agriculture, State, Commerce, Labor, and Transportation, along with the director of the Office of Management and Budget, the chair of the Council of Economic Advisers, and the U.S. Trade Representative. On the surface, this council looks like a satisfactory forum for making foreign economic policy. The reality is rather different.

In part because the Economic Policy Council is not run by a senior member of the White House staff, it lacks prestige. The influence of the council depends upon the level of interest of the secretary of the Treasury, who acts as chairperson; under Nicholas Brady the council has been largely inactive.[3] Moreover, the council tends to meet at the end of the policymaking process, simply to ratify presidential decisions formulated elsewhere. Policymaking is hindered by the fragmented organization of the current apparatus.

TRADE POLICY
The president and the executive branch negotiate international agreements on trade and offer relief to firms hurt by import competition. As the U.S. trade position has deteriorated over the past 15 years, Congress has delegated new trade responsibilities to the executive branch. In 1988 Congress passed the Omnibus Trade and Competitiveness Act, containing the "Super 301" provision, which required the president to identify trade partners that unfairly closed their markets and to negotiate with these nations to remove such barriers. If no progress were to take place, the president could sanction the offending countries by imposing tariffs on their goods.

The requirement to identify unfair trading nations has

lapsed, but the next president will undoubtedly face similar decisions in the coming decade. He will also face a more active and better informed Congress—particularly if it creates the proposed Congressional Trade Office (a new research institute similar to the Congressional Budget Office).

Within the executive branch, trade issues are divided among several agencies. The U.S. Trade Representative advises the president on trade policy and negotiates agreements with other countries. Consistent with Article XIX of the General Agreement on Tariffs and Trade (GATT), American trade laws offer recourse to firms and workers injured by import competition. The Department of Commerce has jurisdiction over dumping and countervailing duty cases. The U.S. International Trade Commission hears trade cases and determines whether a U.S. firm has been damaged by unfair foreign competition. For example, a countervailing duty can be laid on imports that gain a price advantage from subsidies provided by foreign governments. A similar penalty can be laid on imports "dumped" in the American market—that is, temporarily sold below production costs in order to gain market share.

Such administrative remedies have become more common over the past two decades. They have also become the heated topics of recent battles over trade policy. Complaints about unfair foreign practices forced the president to negotiate "voluntary" limits on imports of automobiles and steel into the United States. Because this is a product-by-product process, driven by the complaints of individual firms, it constrains the president's ability to implement industrywide development and adjustment programs. By its nature the process is adversarial and piecemeal; as a result the outcome may not help the country as a whole.

Developing trade pacts and offering relief from imports are two aspects of a single American trade policy. Yet because the authority is divided between agencies and because the process is partly adversarial and partly driven by negotiations, the president often finds it difficult to integrate trade policy into a comprehensive, long-term economic strategy.

EXCHANGE RATES

The president also needs advice on how domestic policies affect the value of the dollar and the price competitiveness of American goods. Monetary policy—especially the setting of short-term interest rates—is the most important factor in determining the dollar's exchange rate. The Federal Reserve System, which conducts our monetary policy, is free of day-to-day control by the president and Congress. It nevertheless remains responsive to the needs of Washington policymakers. The Governors of the Federal Reserve are appointed by the president and confirmed by the Senate. Further, the chair is required by law to report to Congress about the Fed's assessment of the economy and the implications for monetary policy. The Federal Reserve intervenes in currency markets at the request of the Treasury Department.

Under the present process, the Federal Reserve and the Treasury Department have the greatest control over the value of the dollar. The Agriculture, Labor, and Commerce departments, which represent American producers, have little voice in exchange rate policies.

FOREIGN DIRECT INVESTMENT

Many nations regulate foreign direct investment in order to promote critical industries The United States, however, regulates direct investment only in rare instances. The Omnibus Trade and Competitiveness Act of 1988 includes a provision giving the president power to block foreign acquisition of domestic companies when such actions are deemed a threat to national security, which has been understood as military security. The implementation of this power rests initially with the Committee on Foreign Investment in the United States, an interagency committee chaired by the secretary of the Treasury with representatives from the departments of State, Defense, Commerce, and Justice, the Office of Management and Budget, the U.S. Trade Representative, and the Council of Economic Advisers. The committee investigates proposed investments in sectors related to national security and makes recommendations to the president for or against blocking the transactions. So far the committee has followed the lead of the secretary of the Treasury and seldom recommended that an acquisition be blocked.

The problem with this structure is that the lead agency, Treasury, has duties that can create an institutional conflict of interest. It has responsibilities for the health of the financial sector and for financing the federal budget deficit, which requires selling Treasury bonds to foreign buyers. Consider the hypothetical case where a foreign government supports the efforts of one of its national companies to acquire a U.S. company. If that country is a major supplier of capital to the United States, then Treasury's dependence on foreign financing for the federal deficit may make it reluctant to offend the government by restricting the proposed acquisition. Only the president, through a body whose sole responsibility is to advise the chief executive, can weigh the competing considerations in such cases.

INTEGRATING THE POLICYMAKING PROCESS

The president and Congress need to formulate policies that reflect the new importance of global economic issues. History provides some guidance about the necessary changes.

In 1947 the United States faced a difficult and seemingly permanent challenge to its existence and international standing from the Soviet Union. As we saw in Chapter 2, Congress responded by passing the National Security Act of 1947, which created the National Security Council (NSC). Congress charged the NSC with advising the president on how best to integrate domestic, foreign, and military policies concerning national security. This reform told Americans and the world that the United States was ready to combat the Soviet Union in defense of its national interests.

The forum provided by the NSC has forced agencies and departments concerned with national security to discuss, debate, reach consensus, and cooperate in the policy arena. The NSC also informs the president about what different agencies are doing to implement national policies. Both of these NSC functions have enhanced the president's ability to anticipate problems, see opportunities, manage the national security agencies, and formulate and carry out national security policy.

The task force believes the next president should create an Economic Security Council (ESC) for the same reasons that led to the NSC over 40 years ago. The Economic Security Council would help the president fashion a coherent set of policies to advance the national interest, now defined principally in terms of the economy. The council would advise the president how best to integrate policies for domestic prosperity and improved international competitiveness. Just as the NSC assists the president in defending the nation's security, the ESC would enhance the president's ability to defend our economic interests. Creating the council would also clearly signal America's determination to regain leadership in the new world economy.

The ESC should be headed by an assistant to the president for economic security, a senior official charged with the whole of international economic policy. The Economic Security Council should include the president, the vice president, the secretaries of State, Commerce, Treasury, and Labor, and the administrator of the Environmental Protection Agency. Each member would offer special expertise to the council's deliberations. The Department of the Treasury manages the international financial affairs of the nation. The Department of Commerce represents the concerns of firms competing in international markets. With its global network of diplomats, the Department of State can provide a sense of the nation's role in the world. The Department of Labor can analyze how current and proposed policies affect our standard of living. The Environmental Protection Agency assesses the environmental consequences of economic and technology policies and could help U.S. industry move quickly into the next century's markets for more sustainable technologies and sources of energy. Departments such as Justice, Interior, Energy, and Education could send representatives to ESC meetings when the issues under consideration required their expertise.

The Federal Reserve Board merits special mention. Given the history of the board's independence, the ESC could not expect to direct the board to set monetary policy in tandem with other national economic policies. Representatives from the Fed, however, could attend council meetings and then report on the content and expected consequences of current monetary policy. The Fed's assessment of the state of the economy would be useful to decision making within the ESC.

By integrating the economic policymaking process, the ESC would help develop international strategies that would allow the United States to achieve its domestic agenda. The following is a possible agenda for the Economic Security Council—the most important problems the president should address, as well as the task force's ideas on promising reforms.

A New Trilateral Bargain

Viewed with hindsight, the unwritten bargain between the United States and its allies in the postwar period was inherently unfavorable to America's economic interests: the United States provided military protection and open markets in exchange for European and Japanese deference on foreign policy and security issues. When the U.S. economy began to stumble under the weight of these burdens in the 1970s, the three powers modified the bargain. In order to support the common goal of Soviet containment, Europe and Japan began to pick up more of the defense bills and helped to support the dollar.

With the collapse of the Soviet Union and the full emergence of Japan and Europe—led by Germany—as economic powers, the bargain must be restruck. This time U.S. goals should reflect our economic interests: sharing the burdens of global leadership fairly, encouraging and developing strong multilateral institutions, and establishing mechanisms for growth in the world economy. The overriding purpose of the new bargain should be to establish a workable system of collective management of a growing world economy.

International cooperation may not come so easily, though.

In the post–Cold War world, America can no longer take European and Japanese cooperation for granted. The common alliance against the Soviet Union allowed the United States, Western Europe, and Japan to relegate many of their differences to the sidelines. Now these conflicts, many of them economic, have greater political significance.

In a number of areas, Japan and Germany have interests that differ significantly from those of the United States. As creditor powers, for example, they tend to see monetary and currency questions differently than does the United States, now the world's major international debtor.[4] Both Germany and Japan have begun to discover that they have regional options beyond full-scale cooperation with the United States. For Germany, a greater European community that includes the oil-producing regions of the former Soviet Union promises to provide nearly everything it needs in the way of trade and resources. Japan has begun to see similar possibilities in Asia.

Our traditional levers of power and influence no longer carry the same weight. The U.S. security guarantee, in general— and the ability to project military power, in particular—no longer translates directly into leverage with Bonn and Tokyo. Even the threat of American trade retaliation has become less of a factor in their calculations because they know we depend on them for capital, export markets, and, in some cases, critical technologies.

As U.S. leverage has diminished, and as the regional preoccupations of Germany and Japan have grown, these two nations have become increasingly wary of America's demands for greater burden sharing. They are now more reserved about security demands that have little bearing on their own interests. Germany has even begun to turn the burden-sharing argument around, demanding that America do more to aid the transformation process in the former Soviet empire. In the post–Cold War world we can no longer assume that Germany and Japan will coordinate their monetary and fiscal policies with Washington, help us manage the dollar, or provide the financial wherewithal for American global leadership.

America will consequently need a thoughtful and sophisticated strategy for maintaining trilateral cooperation. To begin with, Washington must better understand the ways in which Germany and Japan still need the United States. Despite a growing awareness of their own clout, both nations continue to look to the United States for cues regarding their own global responsibilities. Both are aware, too, of the deep-rooted suspicion their own actions evoke among other countries in their respective regions. Both look to some form of continued U.S. cooperation to help allay those suspicions. The two countries also know that the United States has better relations with each of them than they have with each other, and that only America can broker international agreements of concern to both of them. In spite of regional preoccupations, Japan and Germany still want greater recognition on the world stage—a greater say in the United Nations, the World Bank, and the International Monetary Fund (IMF). And both know that this will require America's agreement.

The United States will also need to articulate more clearly what it, in turn, wants from Germany and Japan. America's overarching goal should be that Germany and Japan direct their power and influence outward, toward collective global efforts, which will benefit the United States, rather than toward regional empire building, which will not. The United States must find new ways of encouraging Japan and Germany to pursue expansionary, macroeconomic policies and supply capital for Third World development. Washington must also insist that Japan and Germany open their markets wider to imports from developing countries. Another important U.S. objective is to secure the further help of Germany and Japan in managing the dollar. Washington should strive to avoid speculation that could destabilize the dollar and restrict America's access to global capital. Finally, we want both countries' agreement on new rules of world trade and investment, which would generally give us the same opportunities in their markets as they enjoy in ours.

To achieve these goals, the United States should pursue a

strategy of "cooperation, yet competition" with Germany and Japan. This means acting on three fronts. First, we must negotiate new bargains with both Germany and Japan to reflect the changed realities and to share more fairly the burdens of managing the world economy. Second, the United States needs to engage Japan and Germany more actively in collective global institutions—the World Bank and the IMF, for example—while at the same time reforming those bodies to promote stronger and more equitable global growth. Third, we must develop new levers of influence over Japan and Germany to help secure and maintain these new agreements.

The Economic Security Council should consider the following initiatives:

1. *The United States needs to strike a new bargain with Germany and Japan over the power and resources of the world's international financial institutions.* Because the United States has supplied most of the capital of the World Bank and the IMF, it has had an effective veto over their policies. In order to preserve its veto, the United States has repeatedly resisted or diluted proposals to expand the mandate and resources of these institutions. As a result, the ability of these agencies to provide long-term capital assistance to developing countries has not evolved at a pace with the growing demands of the world economy. America should, in exchange for a significant increase in their financial contributions, give Japan and Germany a greater say in the running of the IMF and the World Bank. The benefits that we would derive from better-funded, stronger institutions— especially an expansionary approach to structural adjustment—would clearly outweigh any concerns we have about the loss of the veto.

2. *Washington should place more attention on global burden sharing.* A first step would be for the Group of Seven nations (Canada, France, Germany, Italy, Japan, the United States, and the United Kingdom) to agree to issue annual reports measuring their contributions to international public goods, such as

peacekeeping, development assistance, refugee relief and re-settlement, and environmental protection. Such a reporting system should establish a budgetary target—perhaps 5 percent of GNP. To encourage the use of multilateral institutions, only aid channeled through them would be counted against a country's target. Providing a relatively open market for other countries' products is a measurable international public good and should thus be included in the reports.

3. *To balance Japan's and Germany's greater clout, the United States should begin to establish close working relations with midsize and future midsize powers.* Although we share many global economic interests with Germany and Japan, their regional concerns and strategic goals will in some cases diverge from our own. With greater power and responsibility in the world public institutions, Japan and Germany will find it increasingly useful to work out such differences on a multilateral basis. America should therefore begin to strengthen its bargaining position in the multilateral forums. Russia, the nations of Eastern Europe, and countries such as Sweden and Canada are likely to share America's interest in open markets and stimulative global macroeconomic policies. They, too, want access to Japanese and European Community markets and lower interest rates. This group of nations, especially with farsighted U.S. leadership, would constitute a powerful coalition within the World Bank, the IMF, and the United Nations.

Partnerships for Global Growth

Four years ago the first Cuomo Commission wrote that "America should affirm its faith that global economic growth is both possible and desirable."[5] Today the need for strong growth is even more apparent. In the advanced nations, economic growth is slowing, many Third World economies have yet to rebound from the stagnation of the past decade, and the former Eastern Bloc countries are in a depression.

For decades the United States was in a unique position. It

had by itself the economic strength to supply the capital, the credit, and the open markets necessary to keep the world economy growing at a robust pace. Now the American locomotive can no longer pull the international economic train by itself.

The other economic superpowers are limited in their abilities to promote global growth with national policies. Beset by the enormous costs of reunification and consequent worries about inflation, Germany has decided to pursue more restrictive monetary policies. (To push forward the process of integration under the European Monetary System, the other nations of the European Community must work within the constraints set by Germany's policy. So unless the German measures are countered by stimulative international policy, growth throughout Europe may be dampened.) Stimulative policies in Japan are also unlikely to propel the world onto a strong growth path. Looser monetary and fiscal policies in Japan have little effect on world growth, since Japan's markets are still relatively closed to imports.

Today no country alone can be the locomotive that pulls the train of the global economy. Rather, this responsibility must be shared among all the countries of the world, in accordance with each country's ability and stage of development.[6] Together, Japan, Europe (led by Germany), and the United States can perform the role of the global locomotive. Together they can ensure that international markets are supplied with the needed capital, credit, and buyers if they coordinate their policies.

Three other developments make international cooperation even more necessary. First, the products of recent Japanese and East Asian investments in new industrial capacity will soon sweep into the markets of a stagnant world economy. Second, many developing countries have embarked simultaneously on IMF and World Bank structural adjustment programs. These programs prescribe domestic austerity, liberalization of trade and investment markets, and export promotion. The cumulative effect of such programs is to weaken global aggregate demand while increasing supply in export markets. Finally, both consumption and production in Eastern Europe and the former Soviet Union are falling. For humanitarian, security, and economic reasons, Europe and the United States are going to provide assistance. The situation in the former Eastern Bloc depresses global demand for goods and services while increasing demand for world savings.

Better policy coordination between the United States, Germany, and Japan should be combined with a new effort by world financial institutions to support global economic recovery. The three superpowers should support public initiatives by the World Bank, the IMF, and the European Bank for Reconstruction and Development to foster growth and development in the Third World and Eastern Europe while easing the effects of anticipated capital shortages. Using the international public sector to supply macroeconomic stimulus to depressed regions would be less inflationary and thus less disruptive to sustained economic growth than would relying on separate national policies. (Multilateral institutions can spur global growth without causing trade imbalances that lead to weakened currencies or overheated domestic economies—both sources of inflation.)

Further, a global public-sector strategy would be more effective in helping correct current account imbalances. Such a program would not only help create new markets for U.S. goods but would also relieve pressure on the United States to act as the consumer of last resort. Balanced trade could be achieved through the *expansion* of global markets, rather than through economic *contraction*. More importantly, by directing capital into depressed areas of the world economy that are undergoing painful economic adjustment, a multilateral growth strategy would help relieve some of the potential for political turmoil.

We recommend that the United States pursue the following measures to promote global growth:

1. *The United States, Germany, and Japan should coordinate more stimulative macroeconomic policies.* Working together, the three powers should lower long-term interest rates, manage

exchange rates, and develop strong public investment programs. In the short run, such efforts can lift global growth substantially.

2. *The United States should support a one-time issue of special drawing rights by the IMF.* Such an issue would help alleviate the strain caused by the growing imbalance between world investment needs and savings. Increased reliance on special drawing rights as a world reserve currency would give additional liquidity to the global economy, easing capital shortages without sparking inflation.

3. *The United States should support expanded World Bank lending programs for the development fundamentals—education, healthcare, and environmental conservation.* Projects to improve these crucial preconditions for strong and sustainable growth should be as well funded as more traditional infrastructure projects. Furthermore, to be economically viable in the long run, development projects must be supported by the people they are meant to serve. This means that the World Bank will have to consult, plan, and work with the grass-roots, nongovernmental organizations that represent those most affected by lending projects. The United States should ask for an immediate increase in the World Bank's statutory lending limit, with the explicit understanding that the new money will go to support this new lending.

4. *The United States should support efforts to establish a hard-currency (payments) clearing union for Eastern Europe and the Commonwealth of Independent States.* With the collapse of the Soviet Union, trade between Eastern European States has nearly ceased. These economies now lack the hard currency reserves needed to maintain decades old economic linkages. A payments union would create a multilateral mechanism, so that these countries could use their trade surpluses with one nation

to pay for goods from another. The union would allow Eastern European nations to continue trading among themselves without having to come up with scarce Western currencies. Backed by $25 billion to $30 billion of hard currencies, the union would help to reverse the recent downward spiral of intra-Eastern European trade.

5. *Current debt relief efforts by the United States and others should be expanded to include multilateral debt forgiveness.* For developing countries, debt from multilateral lending institutions has two disadvantages: no rescheduling whatsoever is permitted, and current debt relief programs do not affect it. As a result, most African and Latin American countries are sending more money back to the IMF and World Bank than they are receiving in new loans from these institutions. While a plan is worked out for debt forgiveness for the most hard-pressed countries, the United States should call for the suspension of interest payments on their loans from the World Bank and the IMF. A suspension of interest payments would work as an injection of capital, allowing these countries to increase investment.

6. *The United States should study the feasibility of forming a world central bank.* Such a bank could be an effective mechanism for promoting global growth. The United States should especially consider how an international central bank could inject liquidity into the system, thus easing global capital shortages. A world central bank could also be empowered to buy and sell currencies of the three major blocs and to recycle surpluses from trade surplus countries to deficit countries for adjustment purposes. These measures would insure that imbalances between supply and demand did not undermine market growth, thus lending stability to the world's financial system. Finally, a world central bank could establish a well-funded facility for providing long-term development capital and currency support to developing nations.

Reciprocity in Trade and Investment

The debate on trade policy has been constricted by a narrow, often ideological, focus on rules of trade rather than on the results for the United States. An ideal set of "free trade" rules guarantees neither trade balance for the United States nor prosperity for the world.

Trade policy will not solve America's serious competitiveness problems—such deep-seated ailments cannot be cured simply with new trade laws or protectionist measures. Nor is trade policy a substitute for the industrial competitiveness strategies outlined in Chapter 4.

Trade policy does, however, have a role to play in restoring our economic strength. We need only look overseas to understand the importance of trade policy. In Europe and Japan, trade policies are closely linked to industrial policies that foster the development of strategic, high-wage industries. In the next century the nations that produce knowledge-intensive, high-value-added goods will succeed. These dynamic industries provide high-wage jobs that support rising living standards. America's experience during the 1980s demonstrated that our trade policy is a critical tool for insuring that these key U.S. industries encounter open markets overseas and are not hurt by unfair foreign competition at home.

Trade policy will become even more important in the near future, as economic competition between Europe, Japan, and the United States intensifies. The world is moving into a post-GATT era of partially managed trade and loose trade blocs. Most trade, particularly in high-tech products, is not "free." National competitive advantage in these strategic industries is *created* by a combination of private investment and public policy—not endowed by nature. Recognizing the important social and economic benefits stemming from these sectors, our industrial competitors have implemented a wide range of government policies to foster long-run competitiveness in high-tech industries. In the face of Japan's and Germany's successful industrial policies, U.S. efforts to operate strictly according to free trade principles have instead reduced our technological leadership.

Trade with Japan exemplifies the limits of free trade. Many important barriers to the Japanese market are structural, rooted in the character of Japanese businesses and their distinct relationship with each other and with the Japanese government. The Japanese *keiretsu* organization is a good example of such a barrier. As we described in Chapter 4, *keiretsu* are composed of firms that have long-standing business relations among their members. These firms are connected through cross-shareholdings, time-honored buyer-supplier arrangements, shared directors, and the interchange of personnel. Furthermore, *keiretsu* often enjoy privileged relationships with government agencies, enabling member firms to secure crucial procurement contracts. This industrial structure makes it very difficult for American and other foreign firms to enter Japanese markets.[7] Although such differences deny opportunities to American producers, GATT's remedies do not apply to these barriers. Therefore, to address America's trade interests with Japan, our policymakers must begin to look at new ways of conducting trade policy.

Historically the United States has been most concerned with establishing multilateral rules for trade—that is, with process and not with results. GATT, for example, does not set any figures for trade volumes or market shares. Rather it establishes the basic ground rules by which trading partners agree to play. The results have been left up to market forces.

Because formal barriers—the tariffs, subsidies, and quotas that GATT addresses—have become less important and structural barriers have become more significant, this traditional American focus needs to change. Our trade policy should be guided by the need for reciprocity: American firms in foreign countries should have the same *real* opportunities—not just formal access—that companies from those nations enjoy in U.S. markets. Rules are still important—but they may not be enough to insure reciprocity.

When a country organizes its productive economy in a

dramatically different manner than does the United States, requesting that country to change its economic blueprint will lead to failed negotiations. When our trade negotiators fail, competitive American firms are the losers. When another country has a radically different system, the surest way to establish trade reciprocity is to set specific results—minimum market shares for foreign firms, for example—leaving authorities in that country with the responsibility of enforcing the agreement.

Our ultimate goals remain the same—more trade, more competition, more access for U.S. producers. The only difference is how we get there.

America should propose a new international framework to regulate trade and investment flows. Of course, until an international mechanism for enforcement is put in place, we will have to rely on bilateral trade and investment agreements. The U.S. trade strategy, therefore, needs to follow two interrelated tracks: short-term measures to safeguard U.S. interests and a longer-term program for institutional reform. As Laura Tyson, a professor of economics, has observed, "The challenge is how to fashion national policy to defend one's own national economic interests without unduly jeopardizing the chances for deeper integration over the longer run."[8]

In the short run, the United States should negotiate agreements that increase American producers' access to foreign markets. Such agreements will not, however, satisfy all domestic producers. Some companies face unfair competition within our borders, and others are struggling to regain both their international competitiveness and their domestic market shares. Both kinds of firms are likely to confront Washington with requests for restrictions on imports.

In the cases of strategic industries that should have viable futures in the United States, Washington should negotiate agreements that serve the national interest. Restrictions on imports, such as tariffs, should be temporary and should be continued only if an industry has a convincing restructuring plan. In other cases, as we argued in Chapter 4, Washington needs to provide training and reemployment measures to help distressed workers and their communities.

America's long-term goal must be the establishment of a new framework for world trading. A future world trading organization, akin to the International Trade Organization proposed and almost established in the late 1940s, would have the authority to work out common rules—including labor and environmental standards—for the production of traded goods. Such a trade organization would thus help reduce destructive competition—based on weak labor rights and environmental degradation—which lowers nations' standards of living. The trade body would also have the power to adjudicate disputes in a timely fashion, thereby providing an alternative to today's lengthy and cumbersome bilateral negotiating process.

The Economic Security Council should consider the following trade and investment proposals:

1. *The Economic Security Council should establish clear-cut goals to help the president and Congress shape trade and investment policies.* We need a more strategic trade policy than the current patchwork of protectionist measures, voluntary export restraints, and antidumping complaints. Setting priorities among U.S. trade objectives would make better use of our bargaining power. For example, America should no longer waste valuable political capital trying to get Japan to open its rice market, which has special noneconomic meaning to Japanese citizens and limited strategic importance for the U.S. economy. The United States needs to balance its deficit by exporting more high-wage, high-value-added goods to Japan, not just more primary products. The council should also develop guidelines for the minimum labor, environmental, and political conditions that must characterize the production of goods traded with the United States.

2. *The Economic Security Council should establish ground rules to evaluate industry requests for trade protection and financial assistance for restructuring.* The following criteria must be in-

cluded: (a) the industry is vital to other industries and to employment; (b) assistance is not too late; (c) intervention is supported by labor and industry leaders; and (d) the restructuring plan includes enforceable commitments from both management and labor to improve the industry's competitiveness.[9]

3. *Washington should extend the Super 301 provision of the 1988 Trade and Competitiveness Act.* Super 301 is a policy tool that allows us to make reciprocity the guiding principle of future trade and investment relations with Europe and Japan. Super 301 allows the U.S. Trade Representative to impose tariffs on goods from trading partners that persistently use unfair trading practices. The threat of Super 301 retaliation has proven to be an effective means of getting Japan to open some of its markets to U.S. producers.

4. *The United States should push forward with a carefully defined set of results-oriented negotiations with Japan.* The basic goal of such negotiations would be to open Japanese markets to U.S. producers. American negotiators should focus on specific sectors that are characterized by structural barriers to trade. To achieve reciprocity, our negotiators would set for a sector a target market share for U.S. and other foreign producers. Key ingredients of any successful trade arrangement are deadlines and mechanisms to monitor compliance.

Some experts have argued that a focus on market-sharing agreements undercuts the liberalization process that the United States has helped to create. Yet in the long run, agreements such as voluntary import expansions, can actually ease the way toward more liberalization. The clear objective of a voluntary import expansion agreement or any other market-sharing agreement is to *increase* trade and foreign competition. As professor Tyson has pointed out: "Paradoxically, in the Japanese context, where many high-technology markets are highly managed, something akin to managed trade is sometimes required to achieve something akin to a market outcome."[10]

5. *The United States should begin negotiations with the European Community to harmonize trade regulations.* Washington should seek to harmonize legal, social, health and safety, and environmental standards between the two trading partners. America should make efforts to establish common rules relating to subsidies, foreign direct investment, and antitrust regulations. Finally, the talks should set up a formal process for handling future trade and investment disputes.

If the proposed North American Free Trade Agreement (NAFTA) is completed, Washington should press for similar negotiations to harmonize regulations between NAFTA and the European Community. (The following chapter contains a more complete discussion of the trade and investment conditions that NAFTA should incorporate.)

6. *The United States should study the feasibility of forming a multilateral trade organization to eventually replace GATT.* Negotiations between the United States and the European Community could be the first step toward a new world trade organization, which, unlike GATT, would consider nontariff restraints on trade. Other countries would join when they were ready to bring their policies and practices in line with those of the United States and Europe. This approach to economic integration would keep alive the U.S. goal of a multilateral trading order while recognizing the reality of regional economic blocs.

Military Security after the Cold War

After World War II the United States designed an international strategy to contain the Soviet Union. The United States built and manned an expensive global network of military bases and forged bilateral and mutual security treaties with its allies. With the collapse of the Soviet Union, the United States now must rethink its security needs and revise its military commitments.

In the 1990s our international policies need to be part of a coherent package that will prevent the emergence of military conflicts that threaten our security. Today a sound security policy based on prevention is best carried out through economic and political channels, not through the deployment of military strength. A recent Brookings Institution study noted, "The future ability of the United States to maintain the conditions of its security will depend as much on its moral authority, diplomatic skills, and economic assets as on its military capabilities."[11] To the extent that the United States maintains military forces in excess of what it prudently requires, it denies itself the resources needed to contribute to world order and to rebuild its domestic economy.

The same Brookings study argues convincingly that current Defense Department projections of military needs and budget requirements are excessive. Based on virtually the same military missions as those foreseen by the Defense Department, the Brookings study calls for savings of $31 to $49 billion by 1997 and $316 billion over ten years (actually $619 billion since the study calculates that the Pentagon underestimates the cost of its own programs by more than $300 billion).[12] This study was written before the collapse of the Soviet Union, and since then larger estimates of the peace dividend have appeared. The task force believes that by 1997 cuts in annual military spending could reach $89 billion. Such reductions would not impair our military security.

A prevention-oriented security strategy must reduce the potential for political chaos and nationalist conflict by focusing first on global economic growth. The United States, for example, can help build order in the old Soviet empire by developing better conceived and funded economic transition plans for the Eastern European countries and the former Soviet republics.

Next, our security policies must also constrain the spread of weapons of mass destruction. Creating with Russia a plan for retraining and employing Soviet scientists, engineers, and technicians once employed in the nuclear weapons industry would be a wise move. The United States also needs an effective nonproliferation policy. This would have to include measures to restrict arms exports and the transfer of military technology. We should, in addition, strengthen United Nations institutions, such as the International Atomic Energy Agency, for monitoring possible nuclear weapons programs.

Finally, America must strengthen the United Nations' collective security system for conflict prevention and international peacekeeping. We should support the creation of a permanent United Nations peacekeeping force to avoid U.S. entanglement in future regional disputes. In addition, we should ask the other leading powers to make available a portion of their military forces for these peacekeeping efforts.

Such prevention-oriented security posture would complement our international agenda for advancing America's national economic, social, and environmental interests. In this chapter we have seen that such an agenda requires us to reassess our strategies for dealing with Japan and Europe. It also requires us to take a fresh look at our relationships with Latin America.

CHAPTER 8

Toward a Community of the Americas

America's Regional Opportunity

FLOWS of goods, capital, immigrants, pollution, and drugs link the United States with its southern neighbors. Our prosperity and welfare are increasingly influenced by events in Latin America. When Latin America's imports nose-dived in the 1980s, U.S. exporters suffered. In the same decade many Latin American countries could no longer make payments on their commercial debts, leaving some of the largest banks in the United States with huge losses. In the Andean region many farmers turned to the cultivation of coca, much of which ended up as crack cocaine on the streets of the United States. And when authorities in Mexico could not find the resources or political support to enforce that nation's environmental regulations, U.S. border communities found their groundwater and atmosphere polluted. Also in recent decades, millions of Latin American citizens fled from poverty and political oppression, making the difficult trip to the United States.

Three historical events have created an opportunity for the United States to establish a mutually beneficial relationship with Latin America. First, with the end of the Cold War, U.S. policies toward Latin America will no longer be tied to old East-West security concerns. The United States has greater freedom in its choice of allies and policies. Second, democratic governments, eager for new policies at home and abroad, have replaced many authoritarian regimes. Third, most Latin American nations are rejecting earlier, inward-oriented economic development strategies and are now seeking to boost exports and attract capital by implementing market-oriented reforms. Latin American reformers are especially interested in gaining better access to the U.S. market, the largest and most prosperous in the hemisphere.

The end of the Cold War, the democratic reforms, and the commitment to international trade and investment give us a unique opportunity to redefine our relations with our neighbors in the Western Hemisphere. We can now build a community of the Americas, a community of democratic and increasingly prosperous nations.

A community of the Americas, unlike the European Community (EC), will not mean the full integration of different national economies. European integration has taken decades to complete. Furthermore, social and economic conditions in European countries are quite similar to each other, while huge disparities separate the nations of the Western Hemisphere. Nor will this community of the Americas mean that different societies will lose their distinctive social and political traditions. Building economic prosperity does not require cultural conformity.

Instead it will involve negotiating a framework for relations based on shared commitments to democracy, economic opportunity, and the protection of environmental and human rights. This framework will promote greater flows of trade and investment. The starting point for discussions of a community of the Americas would be Washington's explicit recognition that democratic prosperity in Latin America is in the interests of the United States and that the economic, social, and environmental problems in the hemisphere can be solved only through cooperative endeavors.

To insure that increasing economic ties benefit average citizens of the United States, the rules that govern trade and investment in this hemisphere must be wisely crafted. This task force believes it is necessary to *link* trade and investment agreements with cooperation and progress on basic social and environmental issues. Linkages provide mechanisms to translate growing commerce into better living standards on both sides of the Rio Grande. Linkages will reinforce shared democratic, economic, and environmental values and strengthen the ties of community.

Common Problems, Mutual Interests

By the 1970s Latin America had become a significant and growing market for U.S. banks and manufacturers. During the 1990s the region will figure even more prominently in our economic prospects. Although U.S. trade with other industrial nations will remain more significant, our exports to Latin America have recently begun to grow again as a share of total U.S. exports.[1] The formation of regional economic blocs in Europe and Asia may reinforce the importance of our trade with Latin America. Social and environmental ties will also focus our attention on Latin America in this decade. It is imperative that we understand the nature of our connections to Latin America—and how they can be improved.

THE ECONOMIC INTEREST
With a population of 715 million and a total gross domestic product of more than $8 trillion, the Western Hemisphere could be vigorously engaged in mutually beneficial trade and investment.[2] But economic links between North and South America and among Latin American countries are still surprisingly modest. Trade within the Western Hemisphere came to less than $300 billion in 1990—about 9 percent of total world trade and only about 35 percent of the trade between members of the European Community. Moreover, U.S.-Canada trade accounted for $178 billion, or 62 percent of that total. Trade between the United States and Latin America is still only $107 billion, or 3 percent of world trade.[3]

Mexico is our fourth-largest trading partner. The United States exports roughly $33 billion of goods to Mexico—significant, but less than 1 percent of the U.S. gross national product (GNP).[4] Given the relatively small size of the Mexican market, the controversy surrounding the proposed North American free trade area may seem exaggerated. The importance of the proposed treaty, however, goes far beyond the size of the Mexican economy.

Economic integration is the process by which two markets are gradually brought together. In cases such as the European common market, economic integration is the result of formal agreements between nations to lower tariffs, investment restrictions, and other barriers to international commerce. Increasingly, however, economic integration occurs informally, the result of broader social or economic forces. Labor markets in North America illustrate this form of integration. Poor conditions in Mexican labor markets cause Mexican workers to seek employment in the United States. On the other hand, conditions in the United States cause some employers to tap into the Mexican labor market by relocating south of the border. As a result, workers and employers throughout North America find themselves in a more integrated job market.

Economic integration has important implications for policymakers both here and in Latin America. Growing trade can be an engine of prosperity: employment, income, and profits may increase as commerce expands. But unifying the markets of countries with greatly different income levels, legal structures, and institutional frameworks also brings risks. In a wealthier nation like the United States, pressure from low-wage countries can undermine wages and labor and environmental regulations. For a less developed country like Mexico, integration attracts foreign investors seeking to exploit the country's lower wages and weaker regulations. This can create powerful obstacles to long-term efforts to raise living standards and preserve environmental resources.

The current trend toward economic integration is partly the result of the financial links forged in the 1970s. In Chapter 2 we described how Latin American nations became large borrowers of recycled petrodollars. At the time, many nations were growing rapidly, manufactured exports were booming, and the prices of commodity exports were rising. Economic prospects seemed rosy, and a number of these countries looked like good credit risks.

Many of the bank loans made to Latin America had variable interest rates. The rates jumped in 1979, squeezing national economies throughout Latin America. Prices of commodity exports slumped, hurting real earnings. The severe global recession of the early 1980s ended the growth of exports, and the boom was over.

When Mexico announced in 1982 that it could not service its debt, the financial crisis began. Brazil, Argentina, and other nations south of the border followed with similar announcements. The rise in interest rates and the decline of export earnings sapped their ability to meet their obligations. According to one estimate, Latin America's debt service alone absorbed 63 percent of the region's 1982 export earnings.[5] Since the region's export earnings were falling rapidly, it could no longer afford the foreign exchange needed to pay for imported capital goods and other items needed to spur development. Chart 8.1 shows the region's bleak trading picture during the 1980s.

In the aftermath of the debt crisis and world recession, both exports and imports plummeted. Not until the end of the

CHART 8.1 Latin America's Merchandise Imports and Exports, 1975-91

Source: International Monetary Fund, *Direction of Trade Statistics*

decade did Latin America's imports and exports surpass the 1981 peak. In addition, falling commodity prices cut heavily into export earnings. Chart 8.2 indicates that declining terms of trade—the price of a nation's exports compared to the price of imports—seriously undercut the balance of payments of Latin American nations even when they managed to boost their exports in the late 1980s.

Chart 8.3 illustrates the extent to which debt still looms over many Latin American countries. Although the growth of debt has leveled off, the total outstanding debt of almost $430 billion remains a major impediment to the region's future development.[6] Large debt-service payments reduce the resources available for current development efforts. For example, partly as a result of its debt problems, Colombia failed to invest in its energy infrastructure. Today the nation is paying the consequences with several hours of daily blackouts.

Thirty-one percent of Latin America's export earnings in 1990 were absorbed by total debt payments to banks and other international lenders.[7] When a nation's debt-service payments amount to more than 20 percent of its export earnings, experts warn that the country has passed a threshold for financial crisis.[8] The ratio of interest payments to exports for the entire

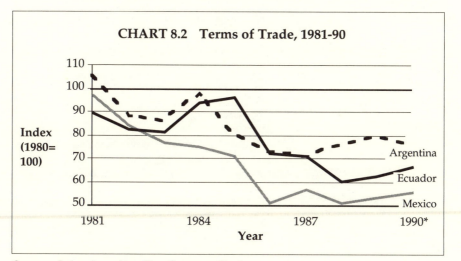

CHART 8.2   Terms of Trade, 1981-90

Index (1980=100)

Year

Argentina
Ecuador
Mexico

Source: Inter-American Development Bank
*Preliminary

213

region was 25 percent in 1990.[9] Chart 8.4 shows this ratio for several countries, indicating that although the debt-service situation has improved recently, many nations remain well above the 20 percent threshold and cannot yet be considered financially secure.

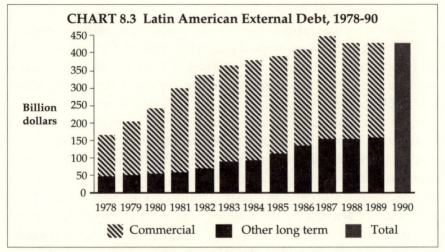

CHART 8.3 Latin American External Debt, 1978-90

Source: Inter-American Development Bank
Note: The breakdown of debt for 1990 is not available.

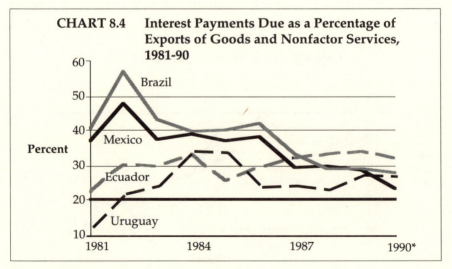

CHART 8.4   Interest Payments Due as a Percentage of Exports of Goods and Nonfactor Services, 1981-90

Source: Inter-American Development Bank
*Preliminary

Another significant resource drain during the 1980s was capital flight. Currency devaluations plus inflation and sagging economies convinced many wealthy Latin Americans to move their assets to the north—precisely when their countries could least afford such an exodus. In many cases the same banks loaning countries vast sums for development purposes were actively promoting flight capital through their private banking departments.[10] One estimate put Latin America's total capital flight between 1973 and 1987 at 43 percent of the external debt built up over the same years.[11] This huge depletion of Latin America's resources further contributed to economic decline and falling living standards.

Finally, as confidence in the economic future declined, business stopped investing. Chart 8.5 shows that during the 1980s the rate of growth of gross domestic investment for Latin America fell to minus 3 percent a year, contrasting markedly with earlier decades' positive growth rates of more than 7 percent.[12]

Given debt-service payments, capital flight, and declining investment, it is no surprise that economic growth in the 1980s failed to keep pace with population increases. During the decade per-capita income fell by an average annual rate of

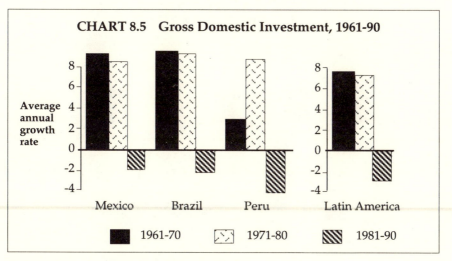

CHART 8.5 Gross Domestic Investment, 1961-90

Source: Inter-American Development Bank

more than 1 percent, leaving many Latin Americans far worse off in 1990 than they were in 1980.[13] Income distribution that was already highly inequitable became more so. Chart 8.6 compares the stark decline of the 1980s with the rising income levels of previous decades. Unemployment and underemployment grew while wage levels fell. Workers' difficulties are demonstrated by Chart 8.7, which maps changes in real wages over the decade for selected countries. Tax revenues declined, and many governments curtailed programs and subsidies that benefited those with the least political clout—workers and the urban and rural poor.

The economic crisis reversed earlier decades of human progress in Latin America. Poverty spread, emigration from rural areas to the shantytown slums surrounding cities quickened, and malnutrition increased: between 1980 and 1988, one out of every ten Latin American children below the age of five was underweight.[14] Another symptom of the problems—and a direct result of governments' failure to make needed public investment—was the outbreak of cholera.

Latin America's reversals had direct and adverse consequences on the United States. The degradation of our

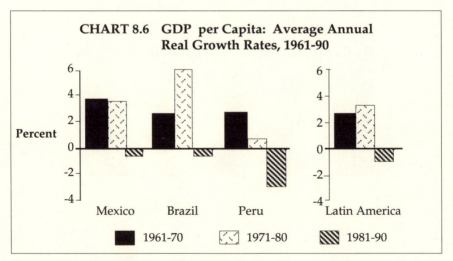

CHART 8.6   GDP per Capita: Average Annual Real Growth Rates, 1961-90

Percent

Mexico   Brazil   Peru   Latin America

■ 1961-70   1971-80   1981-90

Source: Inter-American Development Bank

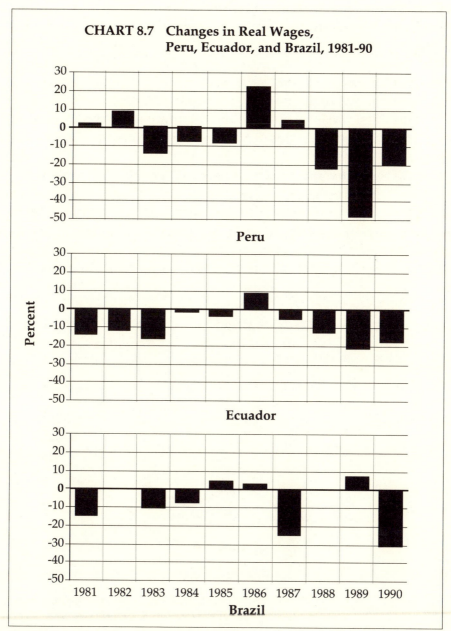

CHART 8.7   Changes in Real Wages,
            Peru, Ecuador, and Brazil, 1981-90

Source: Inter-American Development Bank

hemisphere's environment accelerated and drug trafficking operations flourished. Poverty-stricken and desperate immigrants journeyed to our cities and farmlands in ever greater numbers. The economic decline of the region also crippled what had been a growing market for U.S. goods. The Latin American markets of the 1970s, which had promised good jobs and healthy profits to many U.S. industries, disappeared when the debt crisis forced nations to cut imports in 1982. It took more than seven years for U.S. exports just to regain their 1981 level.

Hampered by onerous debt-service obligations and pressured by international financial institutions, countries were forced not only to dampen their imports, but also to boost their exports. The consequence: U.S. imports from Latin America grew more rapidly than our exports. As a result we ran a trade deficit with the region for an entire decade. (See Chart 8.8.)

THE SOCIAL AND ENVIRONMENTAL DIMENSIONS

Latin America's difficulties affect the United States in multiple ways. The region's problems have played a major role in creat-

CHART 8.8 U.S. Trade with Latin America, 1980-91

Source: International Monetary Fund, *Direction of Trade Statistics*
*Preliminary

218

ing certain social and environmental problems in the United States.

Uncontrolled immigration, especially in times of recession and unemployment, creates social tensions. This can arouse popular opposition against closer ties with Latin America, undermining support for a future community of the Americas.

Fleeing poverty and sometimes political persecution, immigrants have been crossing our southern border in large numbers. Border arrests of undocumented workers peaked at more than 1.7 million in 1986, then declined to a little less than a million in 1989. The numbers began climbing again in 1991—to over 1.1 million—and immigration officials now worry that 1992 border arrests may break the 1986 record.[15] Immigrants from Haiti, Mexico, and other countries are resorting to increasingly desperate measures to reach sanctuary in the United States—from perilous boat journeys to dangerous foot races through U.S. highway traffic. These new American immigrants prefer working long hours in the United States for low wages and few legal rights to no work or political oppression at home. Until the root economic and political causes of immigration are addressed, the United States can expect Latin American immigration to increase.

Growing investment across our southern border by American firms means that U.S. workers must also compete for jobs with workers in Latin America—workers who in many cases have a lower standard of living and little bargaining power. For both of these reasons, it is essential that the trend toward a hemispheric labor market be accompanied by a forceful and sustained effort to institute a common set of rules and enforcement mechanisms.

Mexico and most other Latin American nations have enacted extensive labor laws. In Mexico the constitution guarantees a number of vital rights, including the right to form unions, the right to a minimum wage, the right to an eight-hour day, the right to strike, and a prohibition on child labor. Yet because of lax enforcement there is little correspondence between these rights and the reality of work in Mexico. The close ties between the leadership of the largest union federation and the political party that has governed Mexico for decades have not been used by the union federation as a means to pursue vigorous enforcement of labor laws. At the same time, the government has forcefully suppressed independent unions. Experience has shown that in nations where independent labor unions are not allowed, it is much more difficult to enforce labor laws.[16] Other nations in the Western Hemisphere have the same problem: labor rights on the books are not enforced.[17]

Latin America's environmental destruction affects the United States. Pollution and the effects of environmental degradation do not respect international boundaries. All of the nations of the hemisphere—including the United States—contribute to the ozone depletion and the buildup of greenhouse gases that may devastate the earth's atmosphere in coming decades. Moving toward more sustainable energy forms and forestry practices should thus be a top priority for all Western Hemisphere countries.

Groundwater contamination in Mexico affects the border states of our nation just as U.S. air pollution degrades Canada's atmosphere. Unregulated investment and trade can shift or even increase the cross-border contamination that citizens of both Mexico and the United States suffer. To escape air quality regulations in southern California, many U.S. furniture makers recently moved a few miles across the border.

Another growing concern for U.S. consumers is that unregulated trade will lead to increased residues of pesticides and herbicides in their food. When U.S companies are allowed to export chemicals that are illegal at home to Latin America, "free" trade may mean that imported fruits and vegetables bring those harmful chemicals back to our own supermarkets.

The hard times of the 1980s forced many Latin Americans to return to the countryside, only to despoil it by cutting down virgin forests in their effort to farm the land. Tropical deforestation provides only a few years of economic benefits—the soils are depleted quickly and the settlers must move on. Latin America's environment has also been damaged by environmentally unsound development projects. Many hydroelectric projects, cattle operations, and mining enterprises provided short-term economic gains while destroying natural endowments of forest, water, and wildlife. The indiscriminate clearing of rain forests has destroyed the ways of life of indigenous peoples and resulted in the extinction of plant and animal species with proven economic benefits or potential medical uses.

Another consequence of Latin America's problems in the 1980s has been the growth of the illegal drug trade. When markets for other crops collapsed, farmers in the poorer Andean regions turned to coca cultivation. Entrepreneurs in economies that provided few viable business opportunities established highly profitable drug-trafficking operations. When authorities try to close one such "cartel" or stop production of one drug, another cartel or a new drug soon springs up. Poppy cultivation (to supply heroin to the U.S. market) has recently taken hold in the mountains of Colombia. Until economic growth provides good jobs and income to these farmers, the production of illegal drugs will undoubtedly continue.

For the United States, the surge in drug trafficking and drug use has exacted tremendous economic costs. By the end of the 1980s, drug arrests in America were approaching 750,000 a year. The public expense of arresting, prosecuting, and jailing drug criminals today represents a growing weight on local and state budgets already suffering from declining revenues. According to a recent estimate, at least 100 police officers, U.S. marshals, attorneys, judges, and staff people are needed to secure a verdict for two men arrested for selling crack cocaine.[18]

The U.S. drug war overseas is equally expensive. In 1990 alone, Washington sent more than $141 million to the armies of the Andean countries to fight drugs. Meanwhile, the Pentagon spent another $100 million for antidrug surveillance.[19] Nevertheless, the State Department reports that worldwide production of cocaine and heroin has increased sharply.[20] At the February 1992 drug summit for the Western Hemisphere, Latin American leaders publicly decided to begin pulling their armed forces out of the drug war.[21] While much money was going to unsuccessful military operations against traffickers, they reasoned, the root economic causes were being ignored. By engaging in military and quasi-military efforts to interdict illegal drugs, the U.S. government risks becoming entangled in the internal political affairs of Latin American nations. This raises the danger that we may hedge our support for democratic principles.

Hope for the 1990s

The 1980s brought political and economic change to many Latin American countries. In the 1990s Latin America has the opportunity to consolidate the positive developments recently begun. At the same time there is a risk of the return of stagnation and turmoil. Which way Latin America goes will depend in part on Washington's foresight and leadership.

Democratic governments have assumed power in many nations. In just one corner of the hemisphere, Argentina, Brazil, Chile, and Paraguay held elections. Opposition political parties and trade unions are now allowed to work openly for political and economic reforms.

Yet the movement toward democracy has not touched all nations of the hemisphere. In Haiti and Peru the military still has a determined grip on power. In other nations the army remains a disturbing presence in civilian life.

Mexico, a one-party state for more than six decades, is attempting a number of political reforms, including efforts to crack down on corruption in the government and to allow effective political opposition. According to some journalists and independent observers, progress is occurring, but much work remains to overcome a legacy of undemocratic practices and widespread abuse of human rights.[22]

One significant change has been the closing of the intellectual chasm between the economic thinking of Latin American policymakers and that of their counterparts in Washington. With dwindling trade earnings and an enormous debt overhang, governments have been forced to rethink their economic strategies. Since the beginning of the 1980s, many Latin American leaders have cut back on government ownership and market restrictions, becoming more receptive to direct foreign investment and liberalized trade rules.

Washington has responded favorably to the new economic policies of Latin America. Long-term debt reschedulings under the Brady Plan have helped rebuild confidence in Latin America's future. Under the plan, first announced by U.S. Treasury Secretary Nicholas Brady in the spring of 1989, commercial bank debt for the big debtors has been converted into 30-year bonds (with principal fully guaranteed and interest on the bonds guaranteed for a period of months after any interruption of payments). Mexico, Venezuela, Costa Rica, Bolivia, Uruguay, Argentina, and recently Brazil have negotiated Brady Plan restructurings. The smaller debtors have received somewhat easier terms and some debt reduction.

Despite its ostensible focus on debt reduction, the Brady Plan has resulted in limited debt reduction. Latin America's total external debt at the end of 1991 stood at an estimated $426 billion, the same as the year before. Mexico hoped to relieve its annual debt-service payments by an amount equal to 6 percent of 1989 GNP. Instead, the negotiated relief amounted to less than 2 percent of GNP. Costa Rica was able to achieve debt-service relief of 4.6 percent of GNP—by buying back about 60 percent of its total debt. But since the country had not been fully servicing the debt, its debt-related cash flow problem was not alleviated. Venezuela succeeded in reducing its debt-service payments by about 6 percent of 1989 GNP. Total debt reduction in Uruguay was only about 3 percent of 1989 GNP, while savings in debt-service payments amounted to less than 2 percent of 1989 GNP.[23] As we noted earlier, at the end of 1990, almost one-quarter of Latin America's export earnings were still going to debt-service payments.

Although the Brady Plan has yielded little outright debt reduction, it has boosted the confidence of international investors, partly because the structure of the agreements makes it difficult to renegotiate them. With the old commercial bank debt converted to partially guaranteed securities, new investors in Latin America are less concerned that their money will be caught up in the restructuring maelstrom of the old debts. With the apparent closing of the books on the pre-1990 debt—combined with business-friendly government policies and interest rates offering a far higher real return than in many industrial countries—Latin America is again a favored place for financial investments. Capital inflows, estimated at $40 billion in 1991, together with lower interest rates and the reduction in debt-service payments, are making it possible for debtors to service their debts with relative ease, to increase imports, and even to accumulate foreign currency reserves.[24]

Nevertheless, Latin America's economic recovery is still not secure. Most Latin American economies still lack the productive capacity to satisfy the needs of their growing populations and simultaneously meet their foreign obligations. The debt-linked resource drain of the last decade halted investment and left the continent with a crumbling infrastructure and an outmoded industrial base.

The new liberal regimes are attracting capital from overseas, but financial openness leaves these economies vulnerable to future balance-of-payments problems. The recent capital inflow is financing a surge in imports, satisfying long-suppressed demand, and helping to curb inflation. Imported capital goods can raise the productive capacity of the domestic economy. But if the new money mostly finances imports of consumer goods, then Latin America risks repeating the pattern of the 1970s: mounting deficits, devaluations, capital flight, and debt squeeze.

Some large Latin American economies are experiencing a growing trade imbalance. Mexico's trade deficit grew rapidly in the last two years, hitting $11.2 billion in 1991, with capital goods apparently accounting for most of the increase.[25] Argentina will have a trade deficit this year for the first time in eight years; their imports are heavily tilted toward consumer goods.[26]

If governments try to slow imports by reimposing licensing

requirements, raising tariffs, or devaluing the currency, they risk frightening away the foreign capital they desperately need. Much of the money that has flowed into Latin America in the last two years is "hot money"—short-term investment funds that could leave just as suddenly as they came. By one estimate, of the $40 billion private capital inflow to Latin America in 1991, only $13.9 billion represents foreign direct investment—that is, investment by foreigners in new or existing plant and equipment (this includes investment in privatized state firms).[27]

The rest of the capital inflow is so-called portfolio investment, attracted by high real interest rates and booming stock markets. A 30-day money market instrument in Brazil may yield a 32 percent real annual rate; a 90-day Venezuelan note pays 36 percent. The Argentine stock market yielded returns of 400 percent in 1991. Market capitalization of Latin American stock markets more than doubled from 1990 to 1991, driven primarily by foreign funds.[28] Two-thirds of the capital inflow to Mexico is invested in short-term money market instruments, stocks, and bonds. Much of the money flowing into Argentina is U.S. dollars on deposit with Argentine banks. Sixty percent of the deposit base of Argentine banks is now U.S. dollar accounts, held by foreigners and by Argentinians.[29] Given Argentina's history of instability, those dollars may flee at the first hint of economic trouble. According to the *Wall Street Journal*, 70 percent of the venture capital money invested in Venezuela fled in the weeks following the attempted coup, frightened off by political instability.[30]

While speculative investments surge, total investment in new productive capacity for Latin America remains sluggish. Real long-term investment may pick up as domestic reforms take hold and foreigners gain confidence in Latin America's future. The Mexican government hopes that a North American Free Trade Agreement (NAFTA) will bolster that confidence and bring in more long-term investment. Other countries may seek to join the free trade area for the same reason.

The recent overthrow of the legislative and judicial branches of the Peruvian government provides disturbing evidence that the movement toward democracy in Latin America remains incomplete and that democratic institutions are still fragile. The important political question is whether liberal economic reforms can by themselves insure the prosperity needed to stabilize democratic governments.

Thus far the answer is unclear. In 1989 the Venezuelan government moved to bring its budget into balance by adopting structural reforms approved by both the International Monetary Fund (IMF) and the World Bank. Among other measures, food subsidies were cut, the currency devalued, and bus fares and gas prices raised. Venezuela enjoyed robust economic growth, but the benefits of that growth were not widely shared. Between 1989 and 1991 consumer prices climbed almost twice as fast as did wages.[31] Seeing their living standards tumble, Venezuelans protested in the streets in 1991. More than 300 people were killed in the ensuing riots. This year an even more ominous event rocked Caracas. Five army units attempted to end 34 years of democratic rule in a failed, but bloody, coup.

Unless the governments of Latin America can deliver both growth and equity, the outlook for democracy will remain clouded.

False Choices: Isolation or Laissez-Faire

For the past 12 years, U.S. policies toward Latin America have emphasized the reduction of barriers to international flows of goods and capital. Washington has hailed Latin America's new emphasis on the private sector, and Congress has allowed the executive branch to proceed with negotiations for a North American Free Trade Agreement.

The hope of Washington policymakers is that lowering government barriers to trade and investment will *by itself* yield economies of scale, boost international commerce, and foster growth. But the experience of the United States itself shows this view to be too narrow. Our history and that of our competitors show that markets alone are not sufficient to ensure prosperity. Government has played a key role in building the infrastructure, protecting the environment, promoting social justice, providing economic opportunity, and in helping industries and workers adjust to international competition.

Increased economic ties between the United States and Latin America will bring changes to many U.S. citizens and their communities. Without sound government programs to help manage those changes, many will quickly become detrimental. General Motors may cut costs by moving a parts plant south of the border, but autoworkers in New York may lose their jobs. Mexico runs the risk of increased environmental problems if U.S. companies move production facilities south to escape regulations here. Foreign investment in Mexican agriculture could displace hundreds of thousands of traditional farmers from the countryside, sending more desperately poor immigrants to the United States.

The issue before the United States is not whether we should encourage more trade with our neighbors or put up walls to protect our industry and jobs. Those who put the debate in these stark terms either mislead or misunderstand. Trade can, must, and will occur. The challenge is to insure that growing trade and investment flows promote widespread economic prosperity and human development—in both the United States and Latin America.

Washington has responded to Latin America's economic difficulties with three important measures: the Brady Plan, the proposed North American Free Trade Agreement, and the Enterprise for the Americas Initiative (EAI). Together these policies attempt to address some of the key issues—trade, investment, debt, and environmental degradation. By striving to create some of the conditions essential for stronger commercial ties and economic growth, Washington's current agenda constitutes an advance over earlier thinking.

Nonetheless, the task force believes current policies are too narrow. Washington's policies assume that merely reducing the obvious barriers to trade, such as tariffs, is enough to promote growth and trade. Yet a country's ability to import U.S.-made products also depends on its ability to pay for them.

If the United States forms a regional trading bloc with poor countries that remain poor, then open borders by themselves will have little salutary effect on long-term trade flows, however low tariff rates might be. Another factor influencing the growth of trade is the harmonization of regulations and product standards. The experience of the European Community has demonstrated that the harmonization and the broad distribution of economic gains are necessary components in the expansion of markets and promotion of trade.

The issue is not just how to increase trade, but also how to translate that trade into widespread prosperity for both trading partners. Growing trade and investment flows between countries can bring benefits to small segments of the population but still leave the majority worse off.

THE NORTH AMERICAN FREE TRADE AGREEMENT
The United States, Canada, and Mexico are currently negotiating a treaty that, if approved, will gradually remove obstacles to trade and investment between the three countries.

It is still too early to draw final conclusions about the effects of the 1988 free trade agreement between Canada and the United States. But some of the agreement's weaknesses and strengths are already emerging. Inevitably—and properly— the repercussions of the 1988 agreement form a key part of the debate surrounding the proposed North American Free Trade Agreement (NAFTA).

At present, Canadian wage levels and social services in many instances surpass those in the United States. This has prompted fears among some Canadians as to the trade agreement's effects on employment. Between June 1989 and October 1991, Canada lost 461,000 jobs. Some of these losses are due to recession. Many experts believe, however, that most of the job losses are due to the effects of the treaty.[32] Clearly some Canadian companies have shifted jobs to take fuller advantage of more open borders. Company representatives say that they have shifted production south of the border because of lower taxes, lower real estate costs, lower wages, and proximity to U.S. consumers.[33]

Recent job losses in Canada are a warning to U.S. policymakers. Our nation's competitiveness problems have already taken a toll on employment and income. Hence, the United States can ill afford to suffer further losses of manufacturing jobs. Washington needs to consider mechanisms to avoid or offset such job losses as the three nations of North America move toward freer trade.

NAFTA, however, poses even more complicated issues than the 1988 agreement, which was, after all, between two similar national economies. The question NAFTA presents is how to formulate a trade agreement between two high-income industrial nations and a low-wage developing country. In the United States, debate about the treaty has focused on four crucial issues.

The first is, paradoxically, not trade but investment by U.S. firms. The United States is already largely open to imports from Latin America, including Mexico. Also, Mexico has recently reduced many barriers to exports from the United States. If no new investment occurred in Mexico, a free trade agreement might have little effect on the United States. It is the prospect of U.S. corporations investing in new factories in Mexico at the same time that they are closing them here that is at the heart of the NAFTA debate.

Second, a free trade agreement in North America could result in Mexico's becoming an "export platform" for companies from other countries looking for low wages and secure access to the U.S. market. Foreign companies that in the past might have invested in the United States to gain access to the U.S. market may choose to produce in Mexico instead. Hence U.S firms would be facing new competition without any offsetting gains to U.S workers. Such an outcome would spell significant losses for U.S. industry and workers.

Third, trade agreements without proper regulations could force U.S. workers to compete with Mexican workers, who receive wages amounting to about 10 percent of U.S. wages.[34] Mexico's system of labor relations keeps wages low and enables that country to compete for foreign investment on the basis of low wages. Mexican authorities worry that if they permit wages to rise under a normal process of business-labor negotiations, foreign investors will bypass Mexico for even lower-wage countries.

When workers' rights are suppressed, the normal link between wages and productivity is broken. As several studies have shown, the productivity gap between U.S. companies and their Mexican factories is far smaller than the wage gap.[35] By themselves, then, new investment and greater trade would not necessarily raise Mexican wages.

Mexico's apparent low-wage development strategy raises another critical issue. Under a laissez-faire trade and investment treaty, U.S. businesses would be encouraged to embark on "low-road" competitive strategies, relying on low wages and lax enforcement of environmental and other regulations. This should be of great concern to U.S. citizens and policymakers. As we discussed earlier, the countries that use trade to increase their standards of living—most notably Germany and Japan—compete on quality, productivity, and innovation, *not* on low wages and lax regulation. A narrow trade agreement would create disincentives for American business to make the strategic decisions about investment and training in the United States that are essential for rebuilding our economic strength. Even the threat of moving jobs to Mexico can be used to pressure U.S. workers to accept lower wages, setting the country on a dangerous downward spiral of wage suppression and economic decline.

Mexican barriers to foreign direct investment have been coming down and investment in Mexico, including investment by U.S. firms, is rising. The anticipated NAFTA is an important incentive for investors because it would make it difficult for future Mexican presidents to reverse the current liberalization measures. Similarly, a treaty would make it hard for future U.S. governments to raise new barriers against Mexican imports.

The chief question for the United States is this: what would happen to investment and employment under a laissez-faire treaty? According to one study, such a treaty and the resulting flow in investment from the United States to Mexico could lead to a loss, over ten years, of 550,000 high-wage jobs, concentrated in relatively few industries.[36]

We need an agreement that will encourage prosperity on both sides of the Rio Grande. To guard against Mexico's becoming an export platform, the agreement must include standards for North American content. Second, to discourage wage competition, it must be linked directly to policies that assure Mexican workers fair wages and decent living conditions. Third, the treaty must involve all three governments in programs that protect the environment. Finally, Washington should pursue NAFTA only if it is explicitly linked to domestic programs to retrain and reemploy dislocated workers (see Chapter 4 for a description of such programs). If Washington adopts this long-term perspective, increased trade and investment can benefit Americans. On the other hand, if the United States limits its aspirations solely to a "free," or deregulated, continental market, then the costs to the U.S. economy as a whole will outweigh the benefits.

THE ENTERPRISE FOR THE AMERICAS INITIATIVE
In 1990 the Bush administration announced the Enterprise for the Americas Initiative. To increase trade and investment within the Western Hemisphere, the initiative proposes three policy tracks: reducing Latin American debt, promoting freer markets, and encouraging regional trade agreements. Though the EAI has not received the financial support some experts think it needs to achieve its stated goals, it serves as a framework for U.S. policy. The EAI calls for a reduction in bilateral debt owed to the United States, which results from loans by the U.S. government to governments in Latin America. But as Chart 8.9 shows, this official debt makes up just a small fraction of the region's total debt burden. Even if the EAI succeeds in greatly reducing this part of Latin America's debt, a huge debt over-

hang—composed principally of commercial and multilateral debt—still looms over the hemisphere's economic future.

The EAI encourages nations to focus on narrowly defined economic goals. For example, to qualify for debt reduction under the EAI, countries must develop economic reform plans approved by the World Bank, the IMF, the Inter-American Development Bank, and commercial bank lenders. During the last two decades, the main priorities of these institutions have been macroeconomic and structural reforms designed to increase market efficiency while imposing fiscal austerity. In many cases such reforms remove resources from crucial programs supporting the public welfare. As recent Venezuelan history demonstrates, even long-established democratic governments can see their political support disappear when they implement such policies.

Since Latin American leaders necessarily look to the international lending community for debt relief, the conditions that institutions like the IMF attach to major lending packages strongly influence the course of economic reform. The Enterprise for the Americas Initiative reinforces this influence. If the World Bank and the IMF emphasize just market liberalization

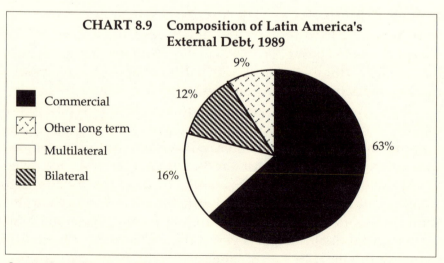

CHART 8.9 Composition of Latin America's External Debt, 1989

Commercial
Other long term
Multilateral
Bilateral

9%
12%
63%
16%

Source: Inter-American Development Bank

and austerity measures, the deeper social and environmental obstacles to development may be forgotten.

One element of the initiative sets an important precedent. Countries that restructure their debt can choose to pay interest (in local currency) into special environmental and social funds. The funds would have strong grass-roots representation and could help countries tackle some difficult environmental and social problems. Their scope is limited, though. One authority recently estimated that they would provide only about $50 million annually for 20 years.[37]

LESSONS FOR THE 1990s: THE EUROPEAN COMMUNITY

As leaders in the Western Hemisphere struggle to find the right policies to stimulate their economies, Europe's long experience with economic integration provides some interesting lessons.

One lesson from the European Community is that integration is a long process: creating the social and economic foundations for the EC has taken almost 40 years. The process of European integration began in 1958 when six countries signed the Treaty of Rome. It took another decade for the original members to eliminate trade barriers for goods. Throughout the 1960s and 1970s, restrictions on investment, migration, and services still blocked the creation of an integrated internal market. In the 1980s the push toward integration accelerated. The Single European Act of 1986 set 1992 as the date for completing the single market, and the 1989 Charter of Fundamental Social Rights sought to address problems caused by the unequal development levels of member countries.[38]

The gradualness of European integration is especially noteworthy when the socioeconomic differences between poorer and wealthier countries in Europe are compared with the gaps between Latin America and the United States. Some supporters of the proposed North American Free Trade Agreement believe that the entry of Spain, a relatively poor European country, into the European Community illustrates the feasibility of including Mexico in a greater NAFTA. But while Spain's per-capita income level in 1988 was about 60 percent of the EC average,

Mexico's is less than 10 percent of the U.S. average. Indicators of Spanish healthcare and education are much closer to those found throughout Europe than are Mexico's to comparable U.S. figures.[39] Boosting Spain's development to the general European level clearly will require less than lifting Mexico to the level of the United States and Canada.

The members of the European Community have recognized that they cannot reduce barriers to trade without also harmonizing rules of commerce and setting common standards for the production of traded goods. Where the United States has acted as though trade by itself will be sufficient to improve conditions in our poorer southern neighbors, Europe has favored a broader strategy that includes trade, regulatory harmonization, development assistance in the poorer countries, and adjustment help throughout the community. The EC has earmarked over $68 billion for adjustment assistance and regional development over the next four years.[40]

The European Community has now taken a further step by adopting a social charter. The charter, and its accompanying action plan, emerged as a response to fears of "social dumping." Labor leaders and policymakers argued that large differences in labor costs create incentives for business to move to poorer countries where wage levels, labor standards, and workplace safety regulations are lower. If such a capital movement becomes widespread, it could produce pressure to lower wage and labor standards in the more developed countries. In effect, social dumping would erode the prosperity and cooperation that form the EC foundation. Through its social charter, the European Community is working to prevent this by establishing fundamental labor rights for all member countries.[41]

Currently the charter is not a binding mechanism for securing those rights, and the actual implementation of the charter remains an unresolved issue. Nevertheless, the European Community states have recognized the necessity of linking trade and investment accords with social progress.

The European Community has also used a combination of mutual recognition, harmonization, and multilateral standards to accommodate the myriad national laws and regulations within the community. "Mutual recognition" is used where national standards are roughly comparable. "Harmonization" is used to bring them closer when large gaps exist. EC standards are adopted when all the members agree on what minimum communitywide standards should be.

The European Commission, composed of appointed officials, is mainly responsible for proposing EC legislation. The commission may also take member countries to the European Court of Justice over matters concerning community laws. The European Council of Ministers, comprised of leaders of national governments, is responsible for debating and adopting commission proposals, and may request studies from the commission. Finally, the European Parliament, whose members are directly elected, provides opinions on commission proposals before council decisions are made.[42]

Multilateral institutions such as these insure that the economic integration process reflects the broad and long-term interests of the EC. In North America such multilateral bodies do not yet exist because no one is proposing full integration or political union. But even the partial integration that will follow from the creation of a free trade area requires the adoption of minimum common standards over time. Although the need for a social charter would seem greater in North America—where the disparities in living standards are far greater than in Europe—government negotiators have thus far failed to consider the idea. The United States and its free trade partners should look at the possibilities of mutual recognition, harmonization, and perhaps multilateral standards and enforcement mechanisms.

Even though the European experience of integration is not identical to the process we envision in the Western Hemisphere, we would be foolish to ignore its virtues. Spain, Portugal, and Greece were not allowed to join Europe's common market until they accepted the basic political and social standards prevailing in northern Europe and began moving toward them. This did not mean that overnight Portugal was expected to have Germany's occupational safety and health laws; rather, Portugal committed itself to a process of harmonizing its regulations with those of its northern neighbors. Northern European countries took this position to protect their own economies and standards of living. The United States and Canada should ask the same of Mexico, Chile, and any other Latin American country that desires closer economic ties.

Trade, Development, and Environment: Necessary Linkages

To forge a community of the Americas, U.S. policies should reflect both our interests and our values. This means trade and investment agreements must link market access with progress on social and environmental issues.

Linkage is necessary for a number of reasons. Requiring that our trading partners observe common standards of human and labor rights reduces the likelihood that low-wage competition will erode American standards of living. A commitment by our southern neighbors to democracy will diminish the influx of political refugees. Having our neighbors adhere to collective environmental rules means that Americans will be better able to enjoy the natural resources we share with Mexico and other Latin American nations.

As Chapter 4 argued, Washington has a responsibility to encourage U.S. business to compete on the basis of high-quality, high-wage domestic production. Companies that operate in Mexico with free access to the U.S. market but without any environmental safeguards and minimal regard to worker safety, child labor laws, or freely negotiated wage scales may enjoy a cost advantage over companies in Canada or the United States. By linking the privilege of increased market access to social and environmental progress, the United States can help insure that this destructive form of competition does not intensify.

A policy agenda for a community of the Americas should move on three fronts: trade agreements, parallel talks with individual nations, and multilateral forums. Trade agreements are the natural forum for dealing with issues related to the conditions of production. This task force recommends that social and environmental safeguards be built into the treaties themselves. Social and environmental issues also need to be given a higher priority in our bilateral and multilateral forums, such as those that deal with debt and development assistance. We also propose that the United States initiate a dialogue with the nations of the Western Hemisphere on common political and environmental rights (to which everybody would be entitled) and standards (which would vary with a nation's level of development). Once such a social and environmental charter of the Americas had been agreed to, it would shape trade and investment treaties within the hemisphere.

TRADE AGREEMENTS THAT ADVANCE THE PUBLIC INTEREST

Properly conceived, NAFTA and future trade and investment treaties with other Latin American nations can lead toward a more prosperous and equitable hemispheric community. Unfortunately, current proposals lack any mechanisms to link the benefits of growing commerce to social, economic, and environmental progress.

One approach for addressing broader social and environmental issues is through parallel talks. Trade officials negotiate a trade treaty; in separate talks, environmental officials haggle over an environmental treaty. This is the method Canada, the United States, and Mexico are currently employing to address labor and environmental issues. Advocates of this narrow strategy are relying on the flawed laissez-faire assumptions discussed above. They believe that tighter linkages are not needed because trade by itself will spur growth and rising living standards. Once better living standards are secured, they further assume, each country will have more interest in protecting the environment and more resources to devote to environmental protection.

Whether this strategy will insure social and environmental progress in the Western Hemisphere is doubtful. It is true, at least in the United States and in Western Europe, that growth has been associated with rising living and environmental standards. But these are countries with long traditions of democratic institutions and guaranteed rights. Countries in Latin America, which do not have secure democratic traditions, have not been subject to the same pressures and processes of negotiation as the United States and the nations of Western Europe. Particularly relevant are the rights of freedom of association and collective bargaining. Without these, it is hard to see how labor can bargain for a share of the benefits of growth.

Furthermore, with parallel talks the United States loses much of its leverage over Mexico's compliance. Once a nation has achieved an agreement guaranteeing it access to the American market, its incentive to consider positive reforms diminishes. U.S. citizens cannot be asked to pay the consequences of an incomplete treaty. Already, the jobs lost to Mexico, the destruction of the border environment, and the continuing pressure from new immigrants have deeply affected the lives of many U.S. communities. Building social, labor, and environmental conditions *into* NAFTA is thus an imperative for renewing our domestic prosperity. Parallel and nonbinding discussions are not enough. The enforcement of labor and environmental standards depends upon their inclusion in the original trade agreement.

1. *A North American free trade agreement should provide for the upward harmonization of labor, environmental, and product standards within an explicit and reasonable timetable.* The U.S.-Canada agreement calls for the two countries to work toward equivalence of regulations in, for example, food safety. The text does not call for harmonizing standards toward levels most protective of the public health and the environment. This omission, especially if carried over to a North American agreement, could weaken the efforts of state or national governments to regulate pesticides, food additives, and fertilizers.

The need for upward harmonization is also apparent in labor issues. Mexico has a minimum wage far below that of the United States and Canada. A commitment by the Mexican government to move, over time, its minimum wage closer to those of the United States and Canada should be incorporated into the treaty. So should a commitment to freedom of association, prohibitions on child labor and forced labor, and upward harmonization of workplace safety rules and environmental standards. We do not expect Mexico's standards to approximate those of the United States in the near future, but we consider a commitment by all governments to upward harmonization as crucial for U.S. workers and consumers. This commitment is also necessary, we believe, to insure that most Mexicans can share in the benefits of growth. The agreement should stipulate a time frame for accomplishing much of the harmonization and provide that failure to harmonize in an upward direction would lead to a suspension of privileges under the treaty. The treaty should also recognize that the nations may stipulate common, harmonized standards in another forum, such as a social charter, which would then be incorporated into the treaty.

2. *A North American trade agreement must stipulate that existing labor and environmental laws and regulations are not barriers to trade and thus cannot be superseded by the trade agreement.* Harmonizing laws and regulations will take time, perhaps decades. While this process is under way, it is imperative that the trade agreement not be used to undercut existing laws and regulations.

3. *The North America Free Trade Agreement should include a process for settling disputes about compliance with the treaty.* The treaty could stipulate that if consultation between the nations did not resolve disputes, the issues would be referred to tri-national panels for binding arbitration. The panels would be empowered to hear complaints about firms that seek to produce for the vast North American market without adhering to the laws and regulations of the United States, Canada, or Mexico. A company that exports under the NAFTA umbrella and is found by the arbitration board to be violating environmental laws or basic labor protection laws (for example, the

right to organize, rules against child labor, and the minimum wage) of the country in which it is operating would be deemed in violation of the agreement. The United States, Canada, and Mexico would agree on probationary periods for companies to comply with local laws and on fines to be imposed by the national governments if there was no compliance within the set period.

These panels would thus provide an avenue for citizens of the three countries to secure enforcement of labor and environmental regulations. If the panel concluded that products were made under substandard conditions, it could, after the probationary period, withdraw from the products in question the privileges accorded by the trade treaty. To cross North American borders, in other words, a tariff would have to be paid on such products.

The agreement establishing these dispute-settlement bodies should explicitly recognize that the violation of social and environmental standards constitutes an unfair trade practice and is thus a barrier to trade. An important precedent for the regulation of untraditional barriers to trade has already been set by the United States. Since 1984 United States trade law has required that developing nations seeking preferential market access must meet internationally recognized workers' rights.

4. *The dispute-resolution panels must be open to the public and the media and to the participation of environmental, social, and labor experts. Public scrutiny is necessary to protect public welfare.* Similarly, because trade can involve broad interests beyond those of the immediate parties to disputes, and because the immediate parties may not have the resources to bring in expert testimony, the panels need to have a process for incorporating the participation of experts, nongovernmental organizations, and other concerned parties.

TOWARD A PERMANENT SOLUTION OF THE DEBT CRISIS
The debt restructurings that have occurred to date have failed

to reduce the debt burden of most debtors to levels their economies can support *without* substantial capital inflows—inflows that may or may not continue the rest of this decade.

The Brady Plan deals have guaranteed that 100 percent of the principal and much of the interest will be paid to the holders of the debts. However inadequate—from the debtors' point of view—these deals may prove to be in the long run, the banks and other creditors are unlikely to reopen negotiations at the present time. Thus, near-term efforts to ease the debt burden must focus on official loans and on commercial debt not already restructured.

1. *The United States should organize a Latin American debt conference, bringing together all official lenders, bilateral and multilateral, to reach agreement on a comprehensive, long-term debt reduction for the region.* Official debt restructurings have been done debtor by debtor and lender by lender. In some cases the scale of the deals is so small that only payments due over the next year or two are covered. That means debt restructuring has to be repeated again and again, thus perpetuating the uncertainty about the debtor's future payment situation. The multilateral agencies, which hold the largest portion of official claims and which never reschedule (in principle, at least), have dealt with mounting payment arrears on an ad hoc basis.

Debt conference participants would agree on what is a manageable burden for each debtor through the year 2000. Based on these assessments, they would allocate debt reductions between the creditors, including the multilateral agencies. The agreement would encompass a menu of options that creditors could choose from to make their contributions. The menu, for example, might allow debtors to extinguish their debt by paying in local currency to environmental, health, education, and infrastructure projects in their countries, such as the environmental or development funds proposed by the Enterprise for the Americas Initiative. The emphasis should be on debt conversion and reduction, rather than on the creation of more debt.

241

2. *The U.S. government should support deeper debt reduction in future Brady Plan agreements.* A few more Latin American debtors, including Peru and Jamaica, will likely seek Brady Plan deals in the next year or two. World Bank and other official support for guaranteeing the remaining debt should be conditioned on the commercial banks' agreeing to debt reduction sufficient to assure the debtor's ability to repay through the end of this decade.

3. *The U.S. government should encourage appropriate debt-for-nature and debt-for-development swaps by both private- and public-sector holders of debt.* Private-sector involvement in debt-for-nature and debt-for-development swaps is heavily influenced by the tax treatment those swaps receive. The Treasury Department should rule unambiguously that commercial bank donations for such swaps are charitable, thus providing additional incentives for debt reduction, environmental conservation, and development. The federal government can also take a more direct role. As federal institutions, such as the Resolution Trust Corporation, acquire the assets of troubled financial institutions, they become the owners of the debt. Although the federal government may not be a large owner of debt, its donations of the debt it holds could benefit debtor nations—and spur the expansion of debt-for-nature swaps.

REFOCUSING AID ON THE BARRIERS TO LONG-RUN PROSPERITY

Aid programs provide important resources and direction to Latin American development. With commercial lending drying up in the aftermath of the debt crisis, such assistance is even more critical to the success of regional adjustment programs. Both the United States and the multilateral financial institutions have a responsibility to make certain their aid programs target the fundamental obstacles to economic growth and competitiveness. Otherwise, scarce public resources are being ill-spent.

1. *The United States should reassess its foreign aid priorities.* Washington should first increase America's level of overseas development assistance. Second, it should raise the portion of development assistance that goes to the social sector (nutrition, health, and education) to a target rate of 25 percent. Third, it needs to increase the proportion of U.S. social-sector aid allocated to priority areas (primary healthcare, basic education, family planning, and rural water supply) to 50 percent. Multiplied together, these three ratios give what the United Nations Development Program calls the "aid human expenditure ratio," an important indicator of industrial nations' commitment to human development in the Third World.[43] Of the 12 industrial countries examined by the United Nations Development Program, America's aid human expenditure ratio is by far the lowest (0.012 percent of GNP, compared to the 0.026 percent average for the 12 countries).[44]

It is important to note that what is being proposed here is not simply *new* spending, but a *reordering* of funding priorities. For too long, priorities in U.S. foreign aid were dictated by the political concerns of the Cold War. That meant funding military needs as opposed to human ones. With the end of the Soviet Union, those old priorities have lost whatever justification they may once have had. We are free now to shift billions of dollars from military assistance to development assistance—and we should do so.

Support for public investments in infrastructure and needed social services will increase the likelihood that more Latin Americans develop into productive citizens. By restructuring our aid budget, we can better promote long-term growth in the Americas—and throughout the Third World.

2. *Similarly, the United States should encourage the multilateral development banks to give greater weight to the development of democratic institutions and the improvement of social and environmental conditions.* The IMF, the World Bank, and the Inter-American Development Bank are sensitive to the signals they

receive from the United States.[45] Since debt-burdened nations must rely on development banks for resources, those financial institutions can strongly influence Latin America's economic strategy. It is imperative that these institutions send the right message. The United States should formally urge them to consider more than just macroeconomic and investment conditions in their adjustment programs. Washington should insist that equal importance be given to the environment, healthcare, education, and human rights. By stimulating immediate growth while laying the foundation for long-term prosperity in the Third World, the world's financial institutions can help move the world economy toward stronger and more balanced growth.

U.S. IMMIGRATION POLICY

The United States has long been a magnet for Latin American immigrants fleeing poverty and political oppression. In the long run, our economic strategies will work to ease the pressure to immigrate. In the meantime, immigration flows are likely to continue and may even increase if market integration displaces large populations from their traditional occupations.

Recent immigration legislation has taken important steps toward bringing portions of the immigrant community into the political and economic mainstream. The emphasis of these laws on family-based immigration should remain the cornerstone of U.S. immigration policy. But a large population of "undocumented aliens" still resides and works in the United States—without basic civil, human, or workers' rights. The lack of fundamental rights for these individuals violates the democratic principles of the United States and undermines labor rights for all workers.

A liberal, fair, and equitable immigration policy serves U.S. interests. Congress should therefore consider reforming immigration laws by:

- Making asylum and safe haven laws more sensitive to political and social conditions in countries of Latin America (and elsewhere). Our refugee policy should reflect greater concern for human rights abuses in sender countries.

- Repealing legislation that imposes sanctions on employers for hiring undocumented workers. This law was intended to help reduce illegal immigration and improve wages and working conditions of U.S. workers. Unfortunately, it has had minimal impact on illegal immigration and seems to have increased discrimination against minority workers.

- Providing some form of legalization to undocumented workers. Their vulnerability to abuse and exploitation does not serve the democratic interests of America.

AN AMERICAS SUMMIT: A STATEMENT OF SHARED SOCIAL AND ENVIRONMENTAL STANDARDS

Free trade areas offer one mechanism for regulating trade and investment flows. Yet their influence is necessarily limited. The United States will continue to trade with other countries in the hemisphere, and conditions in those countries will influence decisions about production and investment in North America. Efforts to maintain and/or improve social, labor, and environmental standards within a North American free trade area necessarily must be complemented by other hemisphere-wide efforts to raise standards.

If Mexico, in an effort to improve its citizens' quality of life, increases wage levels and labor and environmental standards, then it inevitably creates new costs for business. A regional charter could reduce the incentive of companies to abandon Mexico in favor of nations with weaker labor and environmental standards. Instead, business would be encouraged to stay in Mexico and to improve competitiveness through technological change and innovative management.

Economic and social conditions within Latin America are diverse; different countries find themselves at widely varying levels of development. Yet despite these differences, many of our hemispheric neighbors recognize the need to work together to improve the lives of people throughout the Americas. Working with its neighbors, the United States can help formulate a charter of basic social rights and environmental standards. The charter would serve as a statement of principles that would be incorporated into existing and future trade agreements within the hemisphere.

The United States should ask the Organization of American States to begin a process, with the input from governments and nongovernmental organizations throughout the hemisphere, for drafting a social and environmental charter for the Americas. The charter would establish fundamental human and workers' rights and basic social and environmental standards. The International Labor Organization has already proposed a number of basic rights that could serve as a basis for beginning the dialogue: the freedom of association, the right to bargain collectively, the abolition of forced labor, equal remuneration for men and women, and freedom from discrimination in employment.[46] The Organization of American States provides a natural forum for a hemispheric dialogue on rights and standards. After working groups have agreed on the contents of this social and environmental charter, the heads of the governments can meet at a summit of the Americas to commit their governments to the charter.

The charter would also stipulate that trade and investment agreements among the signatories would contain mechanisms for enforcing the provisions of the charter. The dispute-settlement panels that we propose for the North American Free Trade Agreement offer one model of how this could be done.

The establishment of a social charter for the Americas should be part of a broader global strategy by the United States to encourage our trading partners to respect minimum labor and human rights. Recently the United States began supporting more vigorously the efforts of the International Labor Organization to build consensus among governments, employers, and workers. With that consensus, the International Labor Organization tries to persuade other governments and business to "come up to internationally agreed upon labor standards and provide incentives to improve upon the standards of living and conditions of work of [their] citizens."[47] This task force believes that in the long run, human and labor rights will be best protected through a global process, involving perhaps a post-GATT multilateral trade organization. In the meantime, a social and environmental charter of the Americas should be seen as a way to gain regional support for a global process.

Growth, Prosperity, and Community

The rules that govern international trade and finance affect the ability of the global economy to grow—and global growth has a direct influence on U.S. domestic prosperity. Unless we take an active role in shaping the emerging international order, our economic goals will be difficult to achieve.

This is particularly true in the Western Hemisphere. Because of its sheer size and wealth, U.S. policy heavily influences the evolution of economic, political, and environmental relations in the hemisphere. Retreating from the leadership role conferred by our position in the region will not advance our national interests.

The important question is not whether we play an active role, but the kind of active role we will play. Only economic programs combining equity with economic liberalization can secure democracy and improve living standards for the broad spectrum of Latin Americans. Only policies that mix market-based economics with social and political reforms will build a stable and prosperous community of the Americas. The West worries about social and political upheaval in the former Soviet Union and stands prepared to spend billions of dollars to ease the pain of that region's economic and political reform. We should recognize that the same pain haunts the efforts of Latin American nations to make the transition to democracy and market economics.

The United States, in its own interest, should institute

policies that steer the process of hemispheric integration toward growth, prosperity, and community.

That is what we have proposed. In our program for a community of the Americas, we offer a strategy of continental development that attacks the deep roots of stagnation and poverty, providing constructive measures to improve economic, social, and environmental conditions throughout Latin America.

Our reforms will require new resources and farsighted leadership. But the rewards will be long lasting: growing U.S. export markets, rising standards of living throughout the Americas, declining levels of illegal immigration and drug trafficking, a sustainable relationship with our environment, and reinforcement of the democratic institutions that safeguard the political and human rights we have so long espoused.

PART III

Leadership

CHAPTER 9

The Macroeconomics of Investment-Led Growth

A Damaging Dynamic: Slow Growth and Huge Deficits

FOR the past two decades, Washington's policymakers have had difficulty managing the economy to achieve the traditional goals of healthy growth with full employment and stable prices. In the 1970s policymakers oscillated between anti-inflation policies to slow the economy and economic stimulation to reduce unemployment. After aggressive anti-inflation policies caused a deep recession in 1981-82, the Reagan administration pursued vigorous economic growth by running large deficits and expanding credit. For six years the economy grew, but so did the nation's debts and its structural problems: low investment, stagnant productivity, an inadequate education system, and widespread social problems. By the late 1980s the accumulation of economic and social problems had sapped the nation's ability to grow and prosper in the increasingly competitive global economy. Since 1989 growth has virtually halted. Slow growth meant falling tax revenues and rising expenditures on welfare and unemployment. In short, slow growth widened the federal budget deficit.

To manage the economy now requires more than modulating the business cycle to control inflation and reduce unemployment. Instead, policymakers have to extract the nation from the damaging dynamic of slow growth and huge federal budget deficits.

Washington's attempts to restart growth and reduce the deficit have been unsuccessful. In October 1990 Congress and the president agreed on a package of tax increases and spending and investment cuts that promised to slash the deficit. Because of the structural weaknesses that have impaired investment rates and competitiveness, these short-term measures for deficit reduction backfired.

The Commission believes that the deficit needs to be reduced. We also believe that federal budget policies must address the constraints on the nation's ability to grow. Paradoxically, these positions complement each other. Slashing key programs today can actually raise tomorrow's deficit. On the other hand, investing in the nation's ability to produce wealth can create the growth needed to help bring the federal budget back to a manageable balance.

The critical question is whether government spending and taxation address our fundamental problems, particularly the need for investment. If, during the 1990s, Washington spends wisely on public infrastructure and human resources while encouraging private investment, the economy will grow and the deficit will diminish. But if the nation does not invest, it will remain mired in slow growth, while the federal Treasury posts huge deficits.

The Policy Impasse

The nation's leaders have struggled to reach an agreement on new fiscal policies. One group in Washington believes the deficit is so large that they support only those measures that will reduce the deficit immediately. They oppose new spending and favor cuts in existing programs. They also support proposals, such as the balanced budget amendment to the Constitution, that create mechanisms for automatic, across-the-board spending cuts. They do not believe, as do some Keynesian economists, that the budget deficit can be safely increased during this time of slow growth. Furthermore, they point out that if deficits are stimulative, the present deficit—

expected to be $352 billion in 1992, up from $269 billion in 1991—is already providing plenty of stimulus.[1]

A second group of policymakers opposes immediate reductions in spending. They know the pain that budget cuts will bring to their constituents and they worry that large spending cuts now will jeopardize the anemic recovery. Rejecting the idea that fiscal policy is already extremely stimulative, they point out that much current spending is not generating demand for domestic industries. The $67 billion spent on the savings and loan bailout simply replaces savings, so that it creates no new demand for goods and services. Much of the $100 billion the United States spends defending European countries stimulates their economies, not ours.[2]

A third group, less concerned with spending, is demanding tax cuts. Some of the tax cutters favor the middle class, whose standard of living has suffered, while other legislators want across-the-board cuts in the capital gains tax, claiming that this will spur investment.

Given these splits, Washington policymakers have been unable to agree on a new fiscal policy. Furthermore, none of these three groups has a strategy for dealing with both slow growth and the federal deficit.

The Commission believes the nation can end the impasse by simultaneously addressing weak growth and huge deficits. Our approach recognizes the pitfalls and shortcomings of economic policy during the last two decades. Demand-side fiscal stimulation is by itself incapable of sustaining growth. In the 1970s and 1980s demand-side policies failed because they did not address structural, supply-side issues—the energy crisis, the decline in productivity growth, and America's loss of international competitiveness. Fiscal stimulation spurred growth, but because it failed to promote the new investment and innovation American industry needed, growth could not be sustained.

The supply-side economists criticized the Keynesians for this shortcoming and promised to revitalize our industries by providing incentives like lower taxes and deregulation to encourage business investment. The supply-siders claimed that their policies would give such a strong boost to investment that the economy would grow rapidly, reach full employment, and generate the tax revenue needed to reduce the deficit. Less government and freer markets were supposed to reinvigorate the nation, making America's companies more productive and strengthening the financial sector. Although called "supply-side economics," this approach ignored the supply-side factors—public investment, education, training, and technology—for which government has traditionally assumed responsibility.

Critics of the supply-side strategy objected that the massive tax cuts would worsen the already-large federal deficit. The supply-siders countered that their tax cuts would actually generate more revenues and smaller deficits. This turned out not to be true. The supply-side strategy produced the same tepid growth that the economy experienced in the 1970s. The major difference between the decades was the unprecedented increases in the federal deficits—deficits that have made it difficult to finance the investments the nation needs.

Investment-Led Growth

To escape from the quagmire of large deficits and slow growth, the nation needs a new economic strategy. Our strategy—investment-led growth—addresses the structural constraints on growth as well as the cyclical problem of increasing demand. New public and private investments will boost productivity and enhance our ability to compete internationally. New spending will also provide an immediate stimulus, fueling a strong recovery.

Our strategy overcomes the major shortcomings of Keynesian and supply-side approaches. The Commission recognizes that *what* the federal government spends its money on is just as important as *how much* it spends. Macroeconomic policies should be complemented by microeconomic measures to improve productivity and competitiveness. The United States needs policies that improve its ability to produce over the long run, not just to manage demand over the business cycle. Because rebuilding competitiveness will take time, perhaps a decade or longer, policymakers need to have long-term agendas. In addition, unlike either the supply-siders of the 1980s or the demand-siders of the 1960s, the Commission has taken into account the constraints on growth imposed by diminished competitiveness and by the problems of the global economic system.

The agenda outlined in Chapter 4 addresses the nation's industrial competitiveness problem. Foreign producers have captured large and seemingly permanent shares of our domestic market. That means a sizable portion of consumer demand "leaks" abroad. The lesson for policymakers becomes clear if we compare the effects of two famous tax cuts. The Kennedy administration's tax cuts, which occurred at a time when American industry was still preeminent, promoted strong domestic growth. In contrast, the tax cuts and budget deficits of the 1980s, when our industry was struggling, generated modest growth and unprecedented trade deficits. As we restore U.S. competitiveness, American workers and companies will receive more benefits from stimulative fiscal policies.

An agenda for investment-led growth will not only help America rebuild competitiveness; it will also attack some of the causes of inflation. Without a low and stable rate of inflation, it is difficult to sustain growth. Traditionally U.S. macroeconomic policy has combated inflation by raising interest rates—on occasion raising them so high that a recession followed. A better option, one utilized by other countries, is to implement forward-looking policies to raise productivity.

Most economists believe that achieving high rates of economic growth without inflation is difficult *unless* productivity also improves at a healthy rate. Since U.S. productivity has lagged in recent decades, some experts counsel that we must accustom ourselves to slow economic growth: our low productivity will not allow anything better. The Commission's policies, by promoting the public and private investment needed to improve industrial competitiveness, will encourage better productivity performance.

In open economies that are lagging competitively—for example, Great Britain's economy in the 1970s—a falling currency generates inflationary pressure, by raising the prices of imports, of goods produced with imports, and of goods competing with imports. Bolstering U.S. competitiveness means that Washington will be less likely to turn to dollar devaluation as a means for reducing the trade imbalance.

At the time of this report, the possibility of an inflationary increase in the price of crude oil or other imported commodities seems remote.[3] Before this situation changes, America should invest in alternative energy sources and conservation measures that will help insulate the economy from future increases in oil prices.

The United States can also learn from the strategies pursued by some of its industrial competitors. In Germany, Sweden, and other European countries, business, labor, and government sit down together to discuss the prospects for real economic growth and to forge wage settlements that reflect changes in productivity and thus do not contribute to inflation.[4] In the United States we have been reluctant to negotiate such accords. During the 1970s both labor and business were hoping to get bigger slices of the economic pie, but the pie was not growing rapidly enough to give everybody what they wanted. Predictably, wage and price increases resulted only in inflation, and not in higher *real* wages or profits. If the federal government took the lead in a dialogue, labor and business would be better able to negotiate wage and price changes consistent with productivity gains.

The Commission's measures to promote public and private investment will increase the capacity of the private sector, thus reducing the likelihood that demand will outpace supply and overheat the economy. By ameliorating the supply-side sources of inflationary pressure, the country can reduce the need for the Federal Reserve to raise interest rates when economic growth increases. Allowing the Federal Reserve to keep interest rates down will make it easier to sustain high rates of growth.

OVERCOMING THE STRUCTURAL CONSTRAINTS ON GROWTH
Chapters 3 and 4 present the major investment and competitiveness recommendations. Here we review the implications for fiscal policy.

1. *Increasing Public Infrastructure Investment*
Substantial investment in infrastructure networks—transportation, water and wastewater, and telecommunications—is one cornerstone of the new pro-growth economic agenda. State and local governments should be partners in this investment program.

Public infrastructure has been so neglected that simply meeting existing infrastructure needs could consume an additional $101 billion per year. With the nation confronting a large budget deficit and many other unmet needs, we cannot recommend an increase of this magnitude. On the other hand, the more easily financed increases of $10 billion to $20 billion per year would not stem the decline of infrastructure and would do little to promote growth. The Commission advocates a middle course: the federal government should raise infrastructure investment by $48 billion next year, by $65 billion in 1994, and then maintain that level of commitment for eight years. Recently a group of 100 economists reached a similar conclusion in their statement calling for a $50 billion increase in public investment.[5]

2. *Public Investment in People and Technology*
The nation needs to invest more in human resources. To implement the recommendations made in the chapters on industrial competitiveness and urban poverty, the Commission proposes a total increase of approximately $22 billion in annual spending in 1993, rising to $30 billion for the next four years.

To attack the causes of inner-city poverty and improve the

quality of the work force, the United States needs a new national public employment program. The program, costing approximately $3 billion per year, should be structured to provide important public services while not displacing current public employees. It should provide temporary employment and training, so that participants get the experience they need to find private-sector jobs.

In Chapter 4 we proposed a strategic initiative for technological preeminence: a multiyear plan to increase research and development (R&D) in critical technologies. This should cost $3 billion in the first year and then rise to $5 billion per year.

Although the magnitude of the new public investment program will depend on the level of economic growth and on political compromises for reducing the deficit, the Commission believes the nation can and should commit itself to this agenda, a ten-year, $1 trillion public investment program.

3. *Stimulating New Private Investment*
Better public investment will improve the climate for private investment. Additional tax incentives will also encourage private investment. A 10 percent net investment tax credit, if it generates an additional $100 billion to $120 billion in net investment, will have a direct cost of $10 billion to $12 billion. We also propose an increase in the R&D tax credits which will cost $1 billion per year. The proposed sliding-scale capital gains tax should be revenue neutral.

4. *Industrial Competitiveness Policies*
Policies to improve America's international competitiveness cannot wait until the economy is growing again. In Chapter 4 we proposed a national quality-in-manufacturing initiative, including new support for employee ownership and participation; an industrial conversion program, including industrial innovation grants to the states; new work force training and retraining systems; and effective export promotion policies. These initiatives will cost the federal government approximately $12 billion in fiscal year 1993.

5. *Eased Access to Credit*
The Federal Reserve Board's interest rate cuts are an indispensable part of a strategy for a strong recovery. But so far monetary policy has not had a strong effect because of the weakness of the financial sector. The Commission's recommendation that the Federal Reserve inject needed capital into the commercial banks would increase the banks' ability to lend. This injection of capital can be financed from internal resources of the Federal Reserve and will have no effect on the deficit.

6. *Promoting Growth Abroad*
Chapters 7 and 8 call for measures by international public-sector agencies to promote growth overseas. Although the United States may need to make modest contributions, the bulk of the resources should come from Japan and Germany as part of a package to give them a larger voice in international institutions. In addition, the United States will need to refocus its international assistance from military priorities to economic and environmental ones.

Latin America deserves special mention. An additional $5 billion in U.S. resources, leveraged by international lending institutions, would greatly help growth in Latin America. This, in turn, will diminish the economic pressures that push immigrants across our borders, as well as expand the demand for U.S. exports.

BOOSTING DEMAND FOR A STRONG RECOVERY
The current recovery has been sluggish at best. Past recoveries began with growth at 5 to 6 percent, but the outlook now is for 2 to 3 percent growth next year. We propose two measures to stimulate economic growth directly:

1. *Emergency Revenue Sharing with States*
State and local governments have been forced to raise taxes and cut spending, producing a deflationary impact on the economy. Eighty-five percent of Americans live in states with serious fiscal problems. According to recent estimates, state and local

tax increases, combined with spending cuts, took $50 billion out of the economy in 1991.[6] In 1992 the outlook is for another round of tax increases and budget cuts at the state and local levels. Emergency revenue sharing with the states of $10 billion would help counteract the fiscal drag of state and local budgets. The money should be earmarked primarily for investment in public infrastructure.

2. *A Temporary Tax Cut*

We propose a one-year cut in Social Security payroll taxes. This action will provide taxpayers with some relief and will reduce business's labor costs. As economists Robert Solow from MIT and Francis Bator from Harvard have pointed out, lower Social Security withholding rates would generate an immediate increase in take-home pay and consumer spending.[7] The reason for emphasizing consumer spending in the short run is that we can make it happen more quickly and thus effectively boost the economy. A permanent tax cut would, of course, provide more stimulus, but our primary long-term goal should be growth through public and private investment, while still reducing the deficit.

A Budget for New Priorities

Although the Cold War has ended, America's fiscal priorities have not significantly changed. The United States is still allocating $150 billion per year to defend the affluent nations of Europe from the former Soviet Union. Despite the emerging consensus on the need for public investments in infrastructure and human resources, budget policies have yet to shift substantial resources into the domestic investments that will secure America's future prosperity.

Washington's ability to formulate constructive budget policies is hampered by the way the federal government keeps its books. Unlike corporations, most states, and many European governments, the federal budget lumps together all of its expenditures, regardless of their economic effect. A better

approach would be a capital budget that distinguishes investments in better roads or education from interest payments on
the national debt or entitlements such as Medicare. A capital
budget will segregate the public investment outlays that lead
to higher productivity and greater production of wealth. Other
expenditures may be equally important to society but have
little effect on the nation's ability to produce goods and services. The Commission believes that a capital budget will help
policymakers and the public understand this crucial distinction and thus will lead to better policy decisions.

FINANCING OUR PROGRAM

Since investment programs eventually lead to higher income
and increased tax revenues, they can be financed, at least in
part, by borrowing. In Chapter 3 we proposed that Washington
create a Public Investment Trust fund. Properly structured, the
trust's revenues would cover all financing costs, thus not increasing current operating expenses. Revenue to pay the interest and principal on the debt issued by the Trust would come
from a dedicated tax and from existing sources of money such
as the highway and airport trust fund. (The highway fund has
a current surplus of $17 billion, which earns approximately $1
billion per year in interest.)

The major source of money for the Trust would be the peace
dividend. Some have suggested that the peace dividend be
used to reduce the budget deficit or to grant permanent tax
cuts. While both goals are desirable, the Commission believes
that the nation's highest priority should be revitalizing the
American economy. Therefore the peace dividend should primarily be used to invest for long-term growth.

According to a recent Brookings study and to other experts
in the field, the defense budget can be dramatically reduced.
Estimates of the peace dividend range from $75 billion to $150
billion per year. We believe that a peace dividend of $29 billion
next year, climbing to $97 billion in 1997—$89 billion more than
Washington anticipates for 1997—is justifiable.[8] While some of
these funds may need to go to other obligations, a substantial

portion should be committed to rehabilitating and modernizing the public infrastructure and supporting the other elements
of our economic strategy.

New investment will lead to growth, which in turn will
increase tax revenue. But America cannot simply grow its way
out of the deficit. The federal government needs to trim its
spending and expand its revenues. Because investment spending must be the nation's priority, spending cuts should fall on
consumption, such as entitlements. Cost control measures for
healthcare will sharply reduce the growth of federal spending
for medical care entitlements. In addition, further cuts will
have to be made in entitlements, and Washington needs to
increase the taxation of Social Security benefits received by
those with high incomes. These two measures should produce
savings of at least $8 billion in 1993.

The United States should raise the top income tax rate to 38
percent for taxpayers making over $200,000 per year. This
would yield approximately $4 billion in 1993 and more there-
after. And the government must do a better job of collecting
taxes. A dollar spent on enforcement may yield four or five
dollars in new revenue.[9]

It will be politically difficult to pay for new spending while
reducing the budget deficit over the long term. We could
propose specific tax increases and spending cuts. But if the
president or congressional leaders were to show any interest in
these proposals, numerous organized groups would quickly
set about to block action on them. To avoid gridlock in Washington, it would be better for the president and Congress to
convene a National Budget Commission with a mandate to
identify the tax increases and spending cuts needed to secure
long-term deficit reduction while still financing the new economic agenda. The president and Congress would identify a
target for the commission, approximately $70 billion to $75
billion in deficit reduction by fiscal year 1997.

In Table 9.1 the Commission presents a summary of the
estimated costs of its initiatives and ways to pay for them,
including the savings the National Budget Commission would

TABLE 9.1 New Initiatives (excluding Healthcare)
(in billions of dollars)

	1993	1994	Year 1995	1996	1997
Additional pubic investment:					
Infrastructure investment	$ 48	$ 65	$ 65	$ 65	$ 65
Education and training	22	30	30	30	30
Strategic technology (R&D)	3	5	5	5	5
Total public investment	73	100	100	100	100
Additional other spending:					
Public employment program	3	3	3	3	3
Net investment tax credit	12	15	17	19	22
R&D tax credit	1	1	1	1	1
Competitiveness, adjustment	12	10	7	7	7
Emergency revenue sharing	10	—	—	—	—
Global growth	3	3	4	4	4
Latin American initiative	5	5	5	5	5
Social Security tax cut	23	—	—	—	—
Total other spending	$ 69	$ 37	$ 37	$ 39	$ 42
Sources of additional funds:					
Additional peace dividend savings	$ 29	$ 41	$ 55	$ 70	$ 89
Existing trust surpluses	4	3	2	1	1
Income tax rate of 38 percent over $200,000 income	4	7	7	7	7
Reduced entitlements	4	5	5	6	7
Increased taxation of social security benefits	4	10	10	10	11
Space station, tax enforcement, and misc. savings	18	25	28	28	29
National Budget Commission	10	26	41	57	73
Total funds	$ 73	$117	$148	$179	$217
Net cost of new initiatives	$ 69	$ 20	$ –11	$ –40	$ –75

263

identify. This is not, of course, a complete budget, since it presents only the *changes* we recommend, not current spending.

The commission format is a useful device to help form a consensus on the difficult choices, just as the Greenspan Commission created a consensus on reforming Social Security. The establishment of the commission would not prevent Congress and the president from enacting the new economic program and those deficit reduction measures that already command sufficient support.

The mandate of the National Budget Commission would also specify that any new revenue increases, as a package, had to make the tax burden more progressive. As the commission considered new taxes, such as the carbon tax proposed by European representatives at the Earth Summit in Rio, it would also consider ways to address the regressive impact of such taxes.

THE HEALTHCARE DIVIDEND

Table 9.2 provides a rough estimate of the costs of our proposed healthcare reforms and how to finance them. Tentatively we estimate that administrative savings could amount to $21 billion in the first year. (This estimate reflects savings from electronic processing and standardizing prices and benefits packages.) Other experts have argued that greater administrative savings are available; the General Accounting Office has estimated that moving to a publicly financed system could yield $34 billion in savings on insurance overhead and $33 billion in hospital and physician administrative costs.[10] Our estimated savings also include cost reductions from trimming the growth of Medicaid and Medicare. We stress that these are only approximations; the actual costs and savings will depend on how many states choose the more expensive play-or-pay option or a less expensive tax-financed option. These measures will not cover all the costs of the new system, so we also propose a new 0.5 percent payroll tax.

TABLE 9.2 Healthcare Initiative
(in billions of dollars)

	Year				
	1993	1994	1995	1996	1997
Additional Spending					
Healthcare coverage for employees in national plan*	$25	$26	$27	$29	$30
Universal access for those without jobs	40	42	44	46	49
Total spending	$65	$68	$71	$75	$79
Sources of additional funds					
Contributions for employees in national plan*	$25	$26	$ 27	$ 29	$ 30
Payroll tax of 0.5 percent**	15	16	17	18	19
Repeal the Medicare taxable maximum	3	6	6	7	7
Administrative savings	21	24	32	37	44
Total sources	$64	$72	$ 82	$ 91	$100
Net cost of healthcare reforms	$ 1	$ –4	$–11	$–16	$–21

*In states with a play-or-pay financing system, for employees whose employers opt to pay into the national plan, rather than provide private insurance.

**In states with a play-or-pay financing system, this will apply to all employers. States with a publicly financed system might have only one additional revenue stream.

REDUCING THE DEFICIT

Table 9.3 summarizes the information in Tables 9.1 and 9.2, showing how the Commission's initiatives will effect the federal deficit. Our calculations begin with the estimates of the deficit from the Congressional Budget Office (CBO). Because government spending and revenue depend on the health of the economy, estimates such as these rest on assumptions about the rate of economic growth. The CBO's estimates assume that the economy will grow by 1.6 percent in 1992, 3.6 percent in 1993, and 2.6 percent in 1994 through 1997. To the extent that growth is lower than expected, the deficits will be even larger.[11] For example, the CBO calculated that a 1 percent reduction in growth will translate into a $133 billion increase in the deficit by 1997.[12]

Implementing this agenda will require additional borrowing over the next two fiscal years. By 1997 these policies will have led to a $97 billion reduction in the deficit. These estimates do not take into account the positive feedbacks stemming from increased growth. Preliminary calculations indicate that the program would increase the rate of growth.[13] Over time such increased growth would have decisive effects on the deficit.

TABLE 9.3 Effects of Initiatives on the Deficit
(in billions of dollars)

| | Year | | | | |
	1993	1994	1995	1996	1997
CBO baseline total deficit*	$327	$260	$194	$178	$226
Additional public investment	73	100	100	100	100
Additional other spending (exc. health)	69	37	37	39	42
Additional funds (exc. health)	73	117	148	180	218
Net cost of healthcare reforms	1	−4	−10	−16	−21
Deficit	397	276	173	121	129
Change from baseline deficit	70	16	−21	−57	−97

*Includes on-budget and off-budget expenses and revenues.

Strong Growth and Diminishing Deficits

The proposals outlined above—private investment incentives, infrastructure and human resource investments, and industrial competitiveness policies—reflect our conviction that spending priorities must match national goals for investment and wealth creation. The new budget will help America address both the supply-side and demand-side constraints on growth. By raising investment, the nation can improve its competitiveness, reducing a supply-side barrier to growth. At the same time, the large increase in investment will boost demand and ensure a strong recovery.

Growing sales and incomes will generate increased tax revenues—without higher tax rates—making it easier to finance needed services and to cut the budget deficit. Although growth makes reducing the deficit easier, growth by itself will not provide the deficit reduction the nation needs. When policymakers recognize the importance of investment spending, it is more likely that the budget axe will fall on consumption expenditures. By promoting growth and helping the nation make rational decisions about spending, these policies can help America achieve a beneficial dynamic of strong growth and diminishing federal deficits.

CHAPTER 10

Choosing Our Future

A Social Vision, a Pragmatic Program

"PROGRESS," wrote the British playwright and critic George Bernard Shaw, "is impossible without change; and those who cannot change their minds cannot change anything."[1]

This report provides an agenda for progress. By acting on its recommendations, we will create a more participatory system—a strong economy capable of raising the standard of living of all Americans. Achieving this will require changing the way we Americans think about our present policies and institutions. But unless our policymakers are prepared to consider today's problems in new ways, progress will elude us.

For the past 12 years, American economic policy has relied upon a simple, powerful idea: the motivating force of economic progress is self-interest. Since markets allow people to realize their self-interest, policymakers reasoned, deferring to markets is the surest way to achieve general prosperity. As a result Washington's policies undervalued government's responsibility to provide the goods and services that markets do not provide, with the exception of military security. The litany is by now familiar: the public needs a modern, efficient transportation system, a clean environment, and effective schools for all Americans. These are more than just public needs. They are also necessary for companies to compete successfully at the global level. Thus the private sector needs government to do its job.

Not only did policymakers in the 1980s misunderstand the

relationship between the public and private sectors, but their strict reliance on markets led to a business climate that devalued both cooperation and long-term planning. Many companies treated their suppliers as adversaries. Too many top managers became preoccupied with short-run strategies, not the long-term growth of their corporations.

The breakdown of cooperation in labor-management relations has been costly. Productivity suffers when the workplace is beset with mistrust and rancor. But companies that plan for the long run can introduce new technologies that enable them to maintain their competitiveness. The new technologies require employees who can solve problems, work as part of a team, and learn new tasks and skills with ease. Building for the long run leads successful companies to more cooperative relations with suppliers and workers.

The lesson the Commission has drawn from this examination is that individual effort and its reward are necessary to a successful economy, but they are not enough. Private enterprise works best when it takes place within a web of mutual commitments, a common focus on teamwork, and an ethic of stewardship for our shared future. These values are not foreign to our nation—indeed, they have guided us for much of the past two centuries.

The program the Commission has presented tries to move the nation beyond the one-sided approaches of the 1980s and earlier decades.[2] Throughout its history America has sought a balance between the values of the marketplace and those of community, between competition and cooperation, individualism and solidarity. In the 1980s the nation lost that balance. Washington emphasized individual enrichment while it ignored social welfare. The federal government acted as if a commitment to family and to community could be sustained without economic and governmental support.

This must change. Our job now is to actively foster the institutions that will restore balance to our society and economy. America needs entrepreneurship, *and* it needs cooperation. Americans want competitive industries, *and* they want excellent public institutions. Government, business, and labor must work together. This is a visionary program, yet it is also pragmatic. It is based on a careful diagnosis of our problems. The Commission has avoided the easy responses of preconceived ideologies.

The program presented here is financially responsible. In the previous chapter we pointed out that most of the money needed is already in the budget. The challenge, put simply, is to change the nation's fiscal priorities from military security to economic security. This program is within America's means. Indeed, it is a bargain compared to the cost of continued economic decline.

The Commission's program is comprehensive, and its elements form an integrated program. Take, for example, school-to-work programs. They help industry find skilled, experienced workers and they help youths, especially in the inner city, forge links to the world of work. High-speed rail lines are another good example. They dramatically reduce highway and air-corridor congestion, cut atmospheric pollution, and make transportation cheaper. With them, American businesses will reach larger markets more quickly and thus will have additional incentives to modernize. The Commission's proposed initiatives for Latin America will benefit the United States in several ways: higher employment in our exporting industries, and less drug trafficking and environmental destruction. Reforming our healthcare system will buttress our antipoverty program while providing security to families and helping the private sector compete.

Greater employee participation will enhance the quality of U.S. products and reinstill Americans' pride in their work. Corporations that move to long-term strategies will produce higher-quality products relying on skilled, high-wage workers. By putting American wages back on an upward trajectory, the nation will expand the purchasing power of families and enlarge the domestic market.

Making American industry more competitive will allow the

economy to grow faster with little or no inflation. More rapid growth, in turn, will boost revenues without raising tax rates.

We have seen time and time again how the economic challenges we face are interwoven. Narrow, ad hoc programs do not work. Their failure only feeds the growing public cynicism toward government.

Our program is also pragmatic in a political sense. The Commission is confident that its recommendations will attract broad public support. Indeed, many of the specifics—including public investments in people and infrastructure, a technology policy, and comprehensive healthcare reform—are already recognized as urgent necessities.

Maintaining American Values

The Commission's agenda will strengthen the nation's economy, but that is not its underlying purpose. Economic strength is a means to an end.

Our objective is not simply a rise in America's general prosperity, although this is important. The Commission's goal is to sustain a just and caring society—to maintain values that general prosperity makes possible.

First among these traditional American values is a commitment to the process of democracy—of vesting final authority in the people themselves. This commitment means that market forces by themselves should not determine the direction of our society.

Traditionally open to diversity, the United States, more than any other country, is composed of people from around the globe. Out of many ethnic, racial, and religious differences we have created a single nation through participation—by giving people a chance, a voice, and the right to share in the decisions that shape their lives.

The spirit of cooperation and a concomitant belief in compromise have shaped many of our institutions. When most Americans saw that their fortunes were inextricably linked to the national good, such cooperation was easy. After America gained its independence, large states cooperated with small states to create a form of government that would protect the rights of both. The United States was one of the first industrial nations to build an educational system open to all, so that everyone could have the skills and knowledge needed to become productive citizens.

During World War II, Americans from all walks of life joined efforts to build an economic engine capable of supplying the Allied forces. Throughout most of the postwar period, labor and business came together to form contracts that shared the fruits of rising productivity.

Americans have always placed a strong value on the future. The nation saved to invest in future growth. Business built the world's most modern plants and research labs. Government constructed and maintained efficient infrastructure, improved the educational system, and supported key research and development. Working women and men endeavored to bequeath a proud and prosperous nation to their children. This, after all, was perhaps the most comforting consequence of America's strength—the knowledge that our children would enjoy the same opportunities and rising living standards that we experienced.

In recent years maintaining these values has become increasingly difficult. The economic policies of the past decade have weakened the abilities of breadwinners to support their families and made it more difficult to participate actively in our society. More and more Americans have had to rely on welfare and other government handouts, even as the size of these handouts has diminished and the eligibility restrictions have tightened. Confronted by a stagnant economy, more Americans have come to blame foreigners and immigrants for the nation's economic problems. The nation must reject this search for scapegoats. Neither Japanese corporations nor Mexican immigrants are responsible for Washington's neglect of infrastructure, its misguided financial deregulation, or its failure to control the costs of medical care.

Economic insecurity has not been the only reason the nation has found it difficult to live up to its ideals. Our leaders need to set goals that can mobilize the nation to work for the common good. For most of the past 40 years Washington did offer a clear sense of direction: the national good consisted of containing the Soviet threat, while constructing an economic system that maintained prosperity at home and promoted the economic rebuilding of Japan and Western Europe. We succeeded on all fronts. Today, as a result, the nation no longer has such unifying goals. Without a sense of national direction, too many of our leaders—in both the private sector and the public—seem to have put their personal interests above those of their organizations, communities, and the nation as a whole.

Poor economic policies do more than slow growth and raise unemployment. They splinter society into economic enclaves of poor and rich where little is shared. Increasing inequality harms the American sense of community. The collective beliefs that made us a single nation slip away, replaced by a growing factionalism. Too many people and groups grab for themselves, threatening what we once treasured most in our country—the values that made us a model to the rest of the world. It is time to reverse the policies that threaten those values.

Listening to the People

The American people know that the nation is headed in the wrong direction. They understand that inaction is costly. They want change.

Indeed, many are already implementing some of the ideas put forth in this report. Many companies are becoming more competitive. Workers and managers are adopting employee participation and ownership programs. Institutional investors are flexing their muscles and organizing themselves to reform the way American corporations are governed. Prodded by dissatisfied parents, communities are reforming their school systems. Individual states are working to improve their healthcare systems and refurbish their infrastructures.

But these efforts can only go so far without federal support. State and local governments lack the financial resources required to do the job. Smaller businesses often lack both the money and expertise needed to take advantage of the opportunities more cooperative labor management systems offer. Only the federal government can provide the resources and coordination that the states, communities, businesses, labor, and the poor need.

Throughout our history Americans have used the government as an agent of economic and social change. Public schools have helped millions of Americans develop valuable skills. America's network of interstate highways has allowed companies to reach new, larger markets more quickly. Social Security has made it possible for the elderly to live in dignity. Federal support for critical technologies has contributed to the development of the computer industry. Federal mortgage programs have helped middle-income families afford their own houses. Federal and state regulations have made many American workplaces safer and the environment cleaner.

The issue is not big government versus small government. No one favors large, unresponsive bureaucracies. The issue instead is whether the federal government will make it possible for Americans to better their economy and their society.

In the past the president has articulated a vision of the nation's future, rallied public support for his ideas, and worked with Congress to carry out the needed changes. But at present Washington seems unwilling to act. Paralysis has become the normal state of governmental affairs. The president has one agenda; congressional leaders have their own, different agendas. The vacuum of leadership has been filled by a powerfully financed army of special-interest lobbyists who have little concern for the broad national interest.

Voters are angry. But the electorate wants more than to punish the old guard and replace them with new faces. Voters are ready to act, to move. Beneath the anger is a yearning for leadership and a willingness to work together to restore America's economic strength and to push the nation to the next stage in its history. Americans see the need for individual responsibility and are poised to assume it. They understand the role of private initiative and are ready to take it. But they need positive, effective government—and we mean government, not bureaucracy—to coordinate and support their efforts.

Without leadership from Washington, the ideas we have proposed will remain only ideas, and the efforts of ordinary Americans to better their lives will encounter only frustration. The key political issue now is how to break out of the gridlock in Washington.

Breaking Out of the Gridlock

Some observers have said that the way to break out of the gridlock is to make procedural political reforms. Pointing to the clout of special-interest groups, they urge a variety of reforms, including changes in the campaign finance and lobbying laws, to reduce the influence of moneyed factions.

These reforms may indeed make politicians less responsive to special interests and more capable of addressing the general interests. But this is not sufficient. Not only must we reduce the influence of the best financed groups; we also need to carry out the *positive* task of persuading political leaders to commit themselves to change.

America's political problems cannot be blamed entirely on the stranglehold of special interests. Many citizens regularly vote to reelect their state and federal representatives. In the final analysis sovereignty rests with the American people. The emergence of the more participatory economic system we have advanced requires more political participation from the American people.

It is up to all of us to demand a demonstrated commitment to change from those who would be our leaders. Such a commitment could take the form of supporting the proposals the Commission has presented. The next president and the next Congress should commit themselves to carrying out the major recommendations of this report. Americans should insist that

Washington increase public investment, provide incentives for private investment, reform the medical care system, invest in human development, create an Economic Security Council, and construct a new international policy. Political leaders who are attentive to these needs will soon find themselves the objects of praise rather than the butts of criticism.

The American people are ready to face the challenges of a changing world. The Commission offers this report as an act of confidence in the nation's ability to shape its future. The members trust that the report will contribute to the creative ferment the nation needs.

GLOSSARY OF TERMS

all-payer fee schedule A uniform set of prices for medical services to prevent medical providers from shifting costs from one type of payer to another.

automatic stabilizers Mechanisms that stimulate the economy during times of recession and dampen it during periods of rapid growth. Spending for unemployment insurance, for example, tends to increase during recessions and diminish during recoveries. Automatic stabilizers serve to smooth out the peaks and the troughs in the business cycle.

beggar-thy-neighbor policy A policy designed to enrich one nation at the expense of its trading partners. At times of worldwide unemployment, a country can increase its own levels of employment and output by bettering its trade balance, which results in falling employment and a worsening trade balance in other countries. To accomplish this a country might impose protective tariffs or maintain an artificially low exchange rate, so that its exports are inexpensive abroad while imports are expensive at home. (See also **trade balance**.)

bilateral negotiations Negotiations conducted between two nations.

Brady Plan The plan outlined by U.S. Treasury Secretary Nicholas Brady in 1989 to negotiate long-term debt rescheduling—and some debt reduction—with Third World countries.

Bretton Woods agreement The 1944 accord among the Western powers that established the postwar international economic order of liberalized trade and fixed exchange rates. The agreement aimed at promoting both trade and employment. Major components of the Bretton Woods agreement include the International Monetary Fund and the World Bank.

budget deficit The amount by which a government's revenue falls short of its expenditures, which it finances by borrowing.

capital adequacy ratios The amount of capital required by regulation to support bank assets, expressed as the percentage of capital compared to assets. (Banks' assets are their loans.) Recent regulatory changes have required banks to increase their capital (which includes equity, subordinated debt, and loan loss reserves) as a percentage of assets. In part because they have been increasing their capital adequacy ratios, banks have experienced a shortage of loanable funds, creating the so-called credit crunch. (See also **credit crunch**.)

capital flight The transfer by individuals or corporations of investment funds from one nation or region to another to escape domestic taxation, inflation, political instability, devaluation, or some other unfavorable political or economic circumstance. Many Latin American countries have suffered from capital flight spurred by weak economies and unstable governments.

capital flow The movement of investment and loanable funds between nations. This flow includes private and government loans and investment in stocks of companies abroad.

capitation A system of payment for healthcare services in which a medical provider is given a fixed amount per patient per year regardless of the services utilized by any individual patient.

Comer model The school development program designed by Dr. James P. Comer that brings together families, educators, and social service providers in troubled schools. The program seeks to bridge the gap between children's homes and their schools and to improve academic and behavioral performance by involving parents or guardians in students' school activities.

community rating A method that insurance companies use to set their rates. Premiums are based on the health status of the entire group, thus spreading the expenses of healthcare over the community as a whole.

consumption Using products to satisfy immediate needs. Consumption is typically opposed to investment. (See also **investment.**)

credit crunch A period in which credit is not available due to reduced lending by banks and insurance companies.

current account (surplus or deficit) An account of the difference between the money value of the total export and import of goods and services of one nation. The current account balance is determined not only by the exchange of merchandise between a nation and its trading partners but by trade in services such as insurance and banking; expenditures by travelers; profits earned abroad; interest; and one-way transactions such as foreign aid or individual gifts. (See also **trade balance.**)

debt service Payments of the interest on a debt plus any repayments of the debt itself that are due.

demand Willingness and ability to buy.

demand management Government's use of fiscal and monetary policies to regulate the overall level of demand.

dollar devaluation The decrease in the value of the dollar relative to the currencies of other nations. For example, since 1985 the United States has allowed the value of the dollar to fall versus the yen. Since the Japanese can receive more dollars for their yen, American goods become less expensive. The government uses dollar devaluation policies to promote exports and discourage imports.

dumping The practice of selling products below cost to increase market share. Under international trade agreements, dumping is considered an unfair advantage, and injured industries may seek import restrictions against producers that dump.

economic integration Integration means to bring parts together into a whole. There are varying degrees of economic integration. The loosest form of integration is a free trade area, in which member countries eliminate barriers to trade between themselves, while allowing each country to maintain its tariffs and quantitative restrictions against other countries. The European Community began with such a loose form of integration and is now moving toward tighter integration, which will include common trade and monetary policies. Integration sometimes begins without formal treaties. For example, the Mexican and American economies are now becoming more integrated.

Enterprise for the Americas Initiative (EAI) A Bush administration proposal to increase trade and investment within the Western Hemisphere, reduce Latin American debt, promote freer markets and business initiative, and encourage regional free trade agreements.

entitlements Government transfers of particular services or benefits to individuals according to law. In the United States, entitlements can be actual payments such as Social Security checks and unemployment insurance payments. Other entitlements include in-kind benefits such as food stamps.

exchange rate The number of units of one currency that can buy a unit of another currency. For example, a yen-dollar exchange rate of 123 means that 123 yen will buy one dollar.

experience rating A method that insurance companies use to set their rates. Premiums are determined by the health status of the individuals in the plan.

export-driven development A national strategy successfully used by Japan—and now by some Third World nations—that finances industrialization by orienting production toward foreign markets. South Korea is a leading practitioner of export-driven development. It has invested much of its capital in steelmaking, automaking, and other production designed for export to the advanced nations.

Federal Reserve The central monetary authority of the United States, established by the Federal Reserve Act of 1913. The Federal Reserve determines monetary policy through the regulation of the money supply and interest rates.

fee-for-service A system of payment for healthcare services in which the patient is reimbursed for specific services. The provider bills for each service given to the patient.

fiscal policy The overall program for directing spending and taxation to achieve economic goals. For example, during a business decline and high unemployment, the government may attempt to spur growth by increasing spending, cutting taxes, or both. Conversely, in times of overexpansion, the government may try to counter inflation by decreasing spending, raising taxes, or both.

fixed exchange rates Set rates agreed upon by nations to fix the value of their currencies. From the 1950s until 1971, most advanced countries fixed the value of their currencies relative to the dollar.

floating exchange rates Under this system the value of each currency is determined by supply and demand on the international market. For example, if demand for dollars increases, the price of the dollar will rise.

free trade Trade between nations unrestricted by tariffs, subsidies, quotas, or other barriers. The agreement between Canada and the United States is an example of a free trade treaty.

G-7 Nations The seven advanced nations: Canada, France, Germany, Italy, Japan, the United Kingdom, and the United States.

General Agreement on Trade and Tariffs (GATT) An international agreement devoted to reducing and eventually eliminating national barriers to trade. Adopted by 22 nations in 1947, the GATT now sponsors negotiations among almost 100 nations to reduce tariffs and quotas.

globalization and interdependence The increasing interaction of nations' economies. Goods and services are now bought and sold on a worldwide basis. When markets become globalized, the economic policies of individual nations affect other countries. For instance, because so many nations now depend on American consumers to buy their products, a recession in the United States can trigger a worldwide recession.

gold standard An international monetary system in which nations agree to redeem their currencies for definite quantities of gold.

gross domestic product (GDP) The value of goods and services produced domestically for final use. This includes goods and services consumed by households and government, as well as exports, but does not include materials used up in production.

gross national product (GNP) GNP differs from GDP primarily by including the repatriated income from a nation's business, property, and investment holdings in foreign countries, minus the repatriated income received by foreign companies operating within U.S. borders.

Head Start A federally funded preschool program combining education, counseling, and healthcare for poor and disadvantaged children.

high definition television (HDTV) Advanced television and computer screens that provide very sharp picture quality and have wide-ranging applications in high-tech industries such as medical imaging and computer graphics.

industrial policy Structural or microeconomic policies that aim at strengthening industries. Industrial policies include measures such as subsidizing research, encouraging exports or restricting imports in key sectors, and government procurement policies.

intellectual property rights A corporation's or individual's claim on technology, trademarks, and other patented ideas. For instance, a new semiconductor-making process represents an intellectual property right. In recent years, controversy has arisen over the alleged theft of intellectual property rights of U.S. corporations by foreign manufacturers—particularly East Asian producers—which duplicate everything from designer jeans to software without paying licensing fees or other compensation to the original trademark or patent holder.

International Monetary Fund (IMF) Established at Bretton Woods, the IMF lends funds to member nations to cover balance-of-payments deficits. Affiliated with the United Nations, the IMF promotes exchange rate stability and encourages nations to cooperate on monetary policy.

investment To invest is to acquire an asset that can be used to produce or maintain wealth. Investments increase the nation's stock of productive capital. This stock includes, among other things, factories, publicly owned transportation networks, and the skills of the work force.

just-in-time inventory (JIT) A system that allows companies to order smaller amounts of products from their suppliers. JIT eliminates the need for large inventories.

keiretsu A corporate system that consists of a closely knit family of companies. Keiretsu are composed of firms that have long-standing business relations among their members. These firms are connected through cross shareholdings, time-honored buyer-supplier arrangements, shared directors, and the interchange of personnel. Furthermore, keiretsu enjoy privileged relationships with government agencies, enabling member firms to secure crucial procurement contracts.

leakage Channels by which income is diverted from respending by domestic households, for example the loss of dollars (which might otherwise stimulate the domestic recovery) through the purchase of imports.

"locomotive" theory of global growth A description of the U.S. economy's postwar role as the engine that drove the global recovery. U.S. market demand fueled domestic economic expansion and allowed Europe and Japan to reconstruct their devastated industries.

macroeconomic policies Policies directed at influencing aggregate national economic phenomena such as inflation, unemployment, and growth. Macroeconomic policies are carried out through controlling interest rates, intervening in financial markets, and government spending and taxing. The government's decision to raise spending during recession is an example of a change in macroeconomic policy. (See also **fiscal policy** and **monetary policy**.)

managed care A delivery system for medical care that controls utilization. Managed care systems often require review of practitioners' decisions and may limit patients' choice of providers and services.

managed trade A policy of negotiating the levels of imports and exports of particular products. The Multi-Fiber Agreement is an example of managed trade. Signatories agreed to rules governing the import and export of apparel according to the needs of various nations.

Marshall Plan The postwar program established in 1947 by the United States to fund European reconstruction. Proposed by Secretary of State George C. Marshall, the plan gave European nations $5 billion in loans and gifts (the beneficiary nations were required to match the funds) for reconstruction of industry and infrastructure.

Medicaid The federal-state health insurance program for low-income Americans. Created in 1965, the program is run by the states subject to federal guidelines. At both the state and the federal levels Medicaid is funded out of general revenues.

Medicare The federal health insurance program for the elderly and the disabled. This program is administered directly by the federal government. Medicare has its own trust fund, which is financed from payroll taxes, premiums, and general revenues.

monetary policy A nation's overall program for regulating money and credit to achieve desired goals. In most countries, the central bank implements monetary policy. In the United States, the formulation and implementation of monetary policy is the responsibility of the Board of Governors of the Federal Reserve System, working through the 12 Federal Reserve banks. The "Fed" expands the money supply by buying government securities and restricts the money supply by selling government securities.

multilateral negotiations Negotiations conducted by more than two nations. The GATT talks are multilateral negotiations.

neomercantilism A term used to describe the policies and practices of nations that seek to increase their wealth by accumulating large export surpluses by promoting exports and restricting imports.

newly industrialized countries (NIC) The "Four Tigers" (Singapore, South Korea, Hong Kong, and Taiwan), Malaysia, Brazil, Mexico, and other Third World nations that have rapidly developed industrial economies over the past 25 years and are now producing advanced manufacturing goods.

North American Free Trade Agreement (NAFTA) The proposed free trade agreement between the United States, Canada, and Mexico to eliminate almost all trade and investment barriers.

Special Supplemental Food Program for Women, Infants, and Children (WIC) A program that provides poor mothers with vouchers to buy milk and food for their infants.

outsourcing A manufacturing strategy to reduce costs by subcontracting out either domestically or abroad for materials or finished products. This strategy is often employed by domestic manufacturers who purchase product components from foreign, low-cost producers.

play-or-pay Requiring employers either to provide health insurance for their employees ("play") or to pay a payroll tax that will provide the employees with publicly financed coverage.

productivity A measure of how much of a commodity can be produced with a given amount of input. The most commonly used definition of productivity is output per labor hour. Over long periods of time, increases in living standards have corresponded to increased productivity.

protectionism The use of trade barriers to protect domestic manufacturers from foreign competition. Some view protectionism as a policy of protecting uncompetitive and inefficient industries at the expense of both consumers and foreign producers. Others view certain forms of protectionism as necessary to protect domestic producers from unfair competition, for instance from foreign manufacturers who pay exploitive wages or who sell their products below cost in other countries' markets.

real wages A measure of what the money received as wages will buy. If prices rise (inflation), a given wage will buy less, so the real wage falls; as prices fall, a given wage will buy more, thus the real wage is higher.

recession During a recession the economy slows down as demand falls and investment and purchasing power decline. As demand falls, unemployment rises, which in turn creates even less demand. The government sometimes uses fiscal and monetary policies to induce recession and slow inflation.

rescheduling and writing off debt A bank that reschedules debt delays the due date for the principal. When a bank writes off debt, it takes a loss against its reserves. Until recently, most banks dealt with the Third World debt crisis by rescheduling loans. Realizing that most nations are unable to pay back their enormous debt, many banks have increased their loan loss reserves in anticipation of default or of writing off the debt. (See also **Brady Plan**.)

reserve currency A national currency, such as the dollar or the pound sterling, or an international currency, such as the IMF's Special Drawing Rights, that is held in reserve to meet international obligations. Throughout the postwar era the U.S. dollar has been the leading reserve currency, and every major trading nation (except Switzerland) maintains a substantial portion of its reserves in dollars.

savings Income that is not used for consumption. The financial system may channel savings into productive investments.

Special Drawing Rights (SDRs) The IMF created SDRs as an international reserve currency based on the value of a "basket" of national currencies. The agency allocates SDRs to member nations, which may sell them to other members to fund balance-of-payments deficits.

supply Willingness and ability to sell.

supply-side economics Also known as Reaganomics, supply-side economics holds that government should promote economic prosperity by focusing on the suppliers of goods and services—businesses and their owners—rather than by influencing demand. Supply-side economists advocate financial incentives such as tax cuts to increase the supply of savings and deregulation to encourage business to increase production.

targeting A national strategy of identifying a specific market to penetrate and dominate. The Japanese successfully targeted the U.S. electronics market and have achieved a significant share of the American auto market. The South Koreans have built a steel plant specifically designed to produce steel for the U.S. market. (See also **industrial policy**.)

third-party payers A system in which someone other than the recipient of care pays the care provider. Private insurers and the Medicaid program are third-party payers.

trade balance (surplus and deficit) The difference between the money value of a nation's merchandise exports and the money value of its merchandise imports. When a nation exports more than it imports, it maintains a trade surplus; when imports exceed exports, a nation runs a trade deficit.

trade barriers (tariffs, quotas, etc.) Mechanisms that restrict imports. Tariffs are a surcharge levied on goods entering a nation, while quotas limit the amount of goods that may be imported. Trade barriers can be applied to a particular country (or countries) or particular kinds of products.

unfair trade practices Market strategies that seek an advantage over foreign producers by selling below cost, paying exploitive wages to workers, exceeding markets quotas, or engaging in other practices that injure competitors.

U.S. Trade Representative (USTR) The individual, appointed by the president, who is responsible for negotiating the nation's international trade agreements. Congress created the office of the U.S. Trade Representative in 1962.

World Bank Established by the Bretton Woods agreement, the World Bank channels multilateral aid to developing countries by lending funds for economic development at below-market rates.

NOTES

1. THE NEED FOR A NEW COURSE

1. Jeff Faux and Todd Schafer, "Increasing Public Investment: New Budget Priorities for Economic Growth in the Post-Cold War World," Economic Policy Institute, 1991, p. 5.

2. Ibid., p. 7.

3. Ibid., pp. 6-7.

4. Steven Greenhouse, "Lift Taxes, Economists Vote Yes: Eventual Rise Seen to Meet U.S. Needs," *New York Times*, January 27, 1992.

5. Edmund L. Andrews, "U.S. Warns of Phone Industry Lag," *New York Times*, October 23, 1991.

6. Council of Economic Advisers, *Economic Report of the President* (Washington, D.C.: U.S. Government Printing Office, 1991 and 1992), p. 286 (1991) and p. 314 (1992).

7. Organization for Economic Cooperation and Development, *National Accounts, Detailed Tables, Volume II, 1977-1989* (Paris: OECD, 1991).

8. Council on Competitiveness, "Competitiveness Index 1991," (Washington, D.C.: Council on Competitiveness, 1991), p. 8.

9. Council on Competitiveness, *Gaining New Ground: Technology Priorities for America's Future* (Washington, D.C.: Council on Competitiveness, 1991), p. 1.

10. Andrew Pollack, "U.S. Chip Makers Stem the Tide in Trade Battles with Japanese," *New York Times*, April 9, 1992.

11. Council on Competitiveness, *Gaining New Ground*, pp. 7-9.

12. National Science Board, *Science and Engineering Indicators, 1991* (Washington, D.C.: U.S. Government Printing Office, 1991), p. 313.

13. Ibid., p. 342.

14. *Economic Report of the President,* 1992, p. 338.

15. U.S. Department of Labor, Bureau of Labor Statistics, unpublished data.

16. For 1982 and 1987 figures, see *Economic Report of the President,* 1992, p. 416, and for 1991 figure, U.S. Department of Commerce, Bureau of Economic Analysis.

17. *Economic Report of the President,* 1992, p. 385.

18. U.S. Congress, Congressional Budget Office, *The Economic and Budget Outlook: Fiscal Years 1993-1997* (Washington, D.C.: Congressional Budget Office, 1992), p. 65.

19. *Economic Report of the President,* 1992, p. 396.

20. U.S. Department of Commerce, Bureau of Economic Analysis, *Survey of Current Business,* various issues.

21. The figure for 1991 comes from *Economic Report of the President,* 1992, p. 385, and the 1992 projection comes from U.S. Congress, Congressional Budget Office, *An Analysis of the President's Budgetary Proposals for Fiscal Year 1993* (Washington, D.C.: Congressional Budget Office, 1992), p. 1.

22. Board of Governors of the Federal Reserve System, "Flow of Funds Accounts, Seasonally Adjusted Flows," Annual Revisions, January 31, 1992.

23. *Economic Report of the President,* 1992, p. 398.

24. Federal Reserve, "Flow of Funds Accounts."

25. Ibid.; *Economic Report of the President,* 1992, p. 326.

26. Federal Deposit Insurance Corporation.

27. Milt Freudenheim, "Health Costs Up 12.1% Last Year, a Study Says," *New York Times,* January 28, 1992.

28. Families USA Foundation study cited in Hilary Stout, "Average U.S. Family is Spending 11.7% of Income on Health Care, Study Finds," *Wall Street Journal,* December 11, 1991.

29. National Leadership Coalition for Health Care Reform, *Excellent Health Care for All Americans at a Reasonable Cost* (Washington, D.C.: National Leadership Coalition, 1991), p. 13.

30. Gene Steuerie, "Economic Perspectives," *Tax Notes,* March 9, 1992, p. 1287.

31. Walter B. Maher, statement of Chrysler Corporation before the

Senate Democratic Policy Committee on Health Care Reform, December 12, 1991.

32. A. Foster Higgins and Co., Inc., *Health Care Benefits Survey 1990* (Princeton: A. Foster Higgins and Co. Inc., 1990), as cited in National Governors' Association, *A Healthy America: The Challenge for the States* (Washington, D.C.: National Governors' Association, 1991), p. 11.

33. U.S. Bureau of the Census, Current Population Survey, cited in Robert Pear, "34.7 Million Lack Health Insurance; Studies Say Number is Highest Since '65," *New York Times*, December 19, 1991.

34. U.S. Congress, Congressional Budget Office, *Selected Options for Expanding Health Insurance Coverage* (Washington, D.C.: Congressional Budget Office, 1991), pp. 1, 7, and 9.

35. Clifford Krauss, "Under Political Steam, Health-Care Issue Gains Wider Support in Congress," *New York Times*, January 12, 1992.

36. U.S. Bureau of the Census, cited in Jason DeParle, "Number of People in Poverty Shows Sharp Rise in U.S.," *New York Times*, September 27, 1991.

37. U.S. Department of Commerce, Bureau of the Census.

38. Jason DeParle, "Fed by More Than Slump, Welfare Caseload Soars," *New York Times*, January 10, 1992.

39. U.S. Department of Agriculture, cited in "Record 25 Million People on Food Stamp Rolls," *New York Times*, March 29, 1992.

40. *Survey of Current Business*, various issues.

41. Ibid.

42. U.S. Department of Labor, Bureau of Labor Statistics, cited in Robert D. Hershey, Jr., "U.S. Unemployment Increases to 7.1%, Worst in 5 1/2 Years," *New York Times*, January 11, 1992.

43. Maggie Mahar, "Blue Collar, White Collar: Good Jobs Are Vanishing Throughout the Economy," *Barron's*, May 11, 1992.

44. U.S. Department of Labor, Bureau of Labor Statistics.

45. Don Terry, "Cuts in Public Jobs May Hurt Blacks Most," *New York Times*, December 10, 1991.

46. Joseph R. Meisenheimer II, Earl F. Miller, and Leo G. Rydzewski, "The Labor Market in 1991," *Monthly Labor Review* 115 (February 1992), p. 10.

47. *Economic Report of the President*, 1992, p. 330.

48. Ibid.

49. Lawrence Mishel and David Frankel, *The State of Working America, 1990-1991 Edition* (Armonk, N.Y.: Economic Policy Institute Series, M.E. Sharpe, Inc.), pp. 72-73.

50. Ibid., p. 53.

51. Sylvia Nasar, "Fed Gives New Evidence of 80's Gains by Richest," *New York Times*, April 21, 1992.

52. See George C. Lodge, *Perestroika for America: Restructuring Business-Government Relations for World Competitiveness* (Boston: Harvard Business School Press, 1990).

53. U.S. Department of Commerce, *Statistical Abstract 1991*, p. 751.

2. THE AMERICAN SYSTEM, 1945-90

1. Calculations based on Council of Economic Advisers, *Economic Report of the President* (Washington, D.C.: U.S. Government Printing Office, 1987 and 1991), p. 280 (1987) and pp. 289 and 379 (1991).

2. John Maynard Keynes, *General Theory of Employment, Interest, and Money* (New York: Harcourt Brace Jovanovich, 1964).

3. Statement of Senate Committee on Education and Labor, hearings on the National Labor Relations Board, cited in Thomas A. Kochan, Harry C. Katz, and Robert B. McKersie, *The Transformation of American Industrial Relations* (New York: Basic Books, 1986), p. 26.

4. The Cuomo Commission on Trade and Competitiveness, *The Cuomo Commission Report: A New American Formula for a Strong Economy* (New York: Simon and Schuster, 1988), pp. 99-102.

5. Beth Stevens, "Blurring the Boundaries: How the Federal Government Has Influenced Welfare Benefits in the Private Sector," in Margaret Weir, Ann Schola Orloff, and Theda Skocpol, eds., *The Politics of Social Policy* (Princeton: Princeton University Press, 1988), p. 134.

6. George F. Kennan, *Memoirs: 1925-1950* (Boston: Atlantic-Little Brown, 1967), cited in Robert Kuttner, *The End of Laissez-Faire: National Purpose and the Global Economy After the Cold War* (New York: Alfred A. Knopf, 1991), p. 47.

7. For a similar interpretation of the Bretton Woods system, see

Stephen A. Marglin and Juliet Schor, eds., *The Golden Age of Capitalism: Reinterpreting the Postwar Experience* (Oxford: Clarendon Press, 1990), p. 9.

8. Kuttner, *End of Laissez-Faire*, p. 42.

9. The material in this paragraph comes from Ira C. Magaziner and Robert B. Reich, *Minding America's Business* (New York: Harcourt Brace Jovanovich, 1982), pp. 265-66.

10. Nomura Research Institute, *NIR Review*, February 1991, cited in Office of Technology Assessment, *Competing Economies: America, Europe, and the Pacific Rim* (Washington, D.C.: U.S. Government Printing Office, 1991), p. 243.

11. Office of Technology Assessment, *Competing Economies*, p. 241.

12. Cited in Wassily Leontief, "Forget the Free Market," *New York Times*, March 7, 1992.

13. *The Cuomo Commission Report*, p. 36.

14. Magaziner and Reich, *Minding America's Business*, p. 266.

15. Nomura Research Institute, cited in Office of Technology Assessment, *Competing Economies*, p. 243.

16. *Economic Report of the President*, 1992, p. 341.

17. Paul Starr, *The Social Transformation of American Medicine* (New York: Basic Books, 1982), p. 333.

18. Michael Harrington, *The Other America: Poverty in the United States* (New York: Macmillan, 1962).

19. *Economic Report of the President*, 1992, p. 300.

20. Ibid, p. 366.

21. Marglin and Schor, *The Golden Age of Capitalism*, p. 18.

22. OECD, *Economic Outlook, Historical Statistics*, 1960-1989.

23. *The Cuomo Commission Report*, p. 36.

24. Michael Bruno and Jeffrey Sachs, *The Economics of Worldwide Stagflation* (Cambridge: Harvard University Press, 1985), pp. 176-77; Angus Maddison, *Phases of Capitalist Development* (New York: Oxford University Press, 1982), pp. 135-44.

25. Maddison, *Phases*, pp. 136 and 144-46.

26. *Economic Report of the President*, 1992, pp. 340 and 366.

27. Ibid., p. 340.

28. Paul Krugman, *The Age of Diminished Expectations: U.S. Economic Policy in the 1990s* (Cambridge: MIT Press, 1990), p. 12.

29. Maddison, *Phases*, p. 152.

30. William Lazonick, *Competitive Advantage on the Shop Floor* (Cambridge: Harvard University Press, 1990), p. 21.

31. Ibid., p. 282.

32. *The Cuomo Commission Report*, p. 41.

33. World Bank, cited in *The Cuomo Commission Report*, p. 44.

34. U.S. Congress, Congressional Budget Office, *The Economic and Budget Outlook: Fiscal Years 1993-1997* (Washington, D.C.: Congressional Budget Office, 1992), pp. 120-21. Inflation is measured with respect to prices in 1982.

35. Barry Bosworth and Gary Burtless, "Effects of Tax Reform on Labor Supply, Investment, and Saving" *Journal of Economic Perspectives* 1 (Winter 1992), pp. 4-5.

36. Cited in Benjamin Friedman, *Day of Reckoning: The Consequences of American Economic Policy* (New York: Random House, 1988), pp. 128-29.

37. *Economic Report of the President*, 1992, pp. 32 and 328.

3. INVESTMENT: THE FOUNDATION OF ECONOMIC STRENGTH

1. Lawrence M. Chimerine and Robert B. Cohen, *Investment: The Fast Track to a Strong Recovery* (Washington, D.C.: Economic Strategy Institute, 1991), p. 1.

2. Council on Competitiveness, "Competitiveness Index 1991," p. 8.

3. U.S. Congress, Congressional Budget Office, *How Federal Spending for Infrastructure and Other Public Investments Affects the Economy* (Washington, D.C.: Congressional Budget Office, 1991), p. 14.

4. Ibid.

5. Jeff Faux and Todd Schafer, "Increasing Public Investment: New Budget Priorities for Economic Growth in the Post-Cold War World," Economic Policy Institute, 1991, pp. 6-7.

6. Samuel K. Skinner, "Investing in U.S. Transportation Infrastructure: The Key to Economic Strength and Productivity," speech delivered before the Harris County Toll Road Authority, *Vital Speeches of the Day* 56 (September 15, 1990).

7. See David Alan Aschauer, *Public Investment and Private Sector Growth: The Economic Benefits of Reducing America's "Third Deficit"*

(Washington, D.C.: Economic Policy Institute, 1990), p. 20 and elsewhere; Alicia H. Munnell, "Why Has Productivity Growth Declined?" *New England Economic Review,* January/February, 1990.

8. Alan S. Blinder, *Growing Together: An Alternative Economic Strategy for the 1990s* (Knoxville, Tenn.: Whittle Direct Books, 1991), p. 72.

9. The Economic Policy Institute and Felix Rohatyn have made similar proposals.

10. Calculation based on Texas Transportation Institute, "Roadway Congestion in Major Urban Areas, 1982 to 1987," Research Report 1131-2, 1989, and on U.S. Department of Transportation, *The Status of the Nation's Highways and Bridges* (Washington, D.C.: U.S. Government Printing Office, 1989), both cited in Office of Technology Assessment, *Delivering the Goods* (Washington, D.C.: U.S. Government Printing Office, 1991), pp. 3-4 and 90; Aschauer, *Public Investment and Private Sector Growth,* p. 39.

11. Samuel K. Skinner, "Investing in U.S. Transportation Infrastructure."

12. U.S. Department of Transportation, "The 1991 Status of the Nation's Highways and Bridges," cited in Faux and Schafer, "Increasing Public Investment," p. 16.

13. U.S. Department of Transportation, Federal Aviation Administration, *Airport Capacity Enhancement Plan* (Washington, D.C.: DOT/FAA, 1988 and 1989), pp. 1-11(1988) and 1-10 (1989); U.S. Department of Transportation, Federal Aviation Administration, *FAA Aviation Forecasts, Fiscal Years 1990-2001* (Washington, D.C.: FAA-APO, 1990), pp. 5 and 7. These are cited in Office of Technology Assessment, *Delivering the Goods,* p. 121.

14. American Association of State Highway and Transportation Officials, *New Transportation Concepts for a New Century,* cited in Faux and Schafer, "Increasing Public Investment." These numbers are adjusted for inflation since 1989.

15. Daniel Patrick Moynihan, "How to Lose: The Story of Maglev," *Scientific American,* November 1989, p. 130.

16. Malcolm W. Browne, "New Funds Fuel Magnet Power for Trains," *New York Times,* March 3, 1992.

17. Karen Wright, "The Shape of Things to Go," *Scientific American,* May 1990, pp. 98 and 100.

18. Office of Technology Assessment, *Delivering the Goods,* pp. 138-39.

19. D. P. Sheer, *Assured Water for the Washington Metropolitan Area,*

Interstate Commission on the Potomac River Basin, 1983, as cited in Wade Miller Associates, Inc., *The Nation's Public Works: Report on Water Supply* (Washington, D.C.: National Council on Public Works, 1987), p. 48.

20. Office of Technology Assessment, *Delivering the Goods*, p. 139.

21. Apogee Research, *America's Environmental Infrastructure: A Water and Wastewater Investment Study* (Washington, D.C.: The Clean Water Council, 1990). Apogee's original estimates in 1988 dollars were adjusted for inflation between 1988 and 1992.

22. Robert B. Cohen and Kenneth Donow, *Telecommunications Policy, High Definition Television, and U.S. Competitiveness* (Washington, D.C.: Economic Policy Institute, 1989), p. 44.

23. Commerce Department, cited in Edmund L. Andrews, "U.S. Warns of Phone Industry Lag," *New York Times*, October 23, 1991.

24. Cohen and Donow, *Telecommunications Policy*, pp. 39-41.

25. R. Braumbaugh, A. Carron, and R. Litan, "Cleaning Up the Depository Institutions Mess," *Brookings Papers on Economic Activity* 1 (1989), pp. 241 and 251; Federal Deposit Insurance Corporation, *Annual Report 1989* (Washington, D.C.: FDIC, 1990), p. 101; Kenneth H. Bacon, "FDIC Seeks Rise in Premium for Insurance: Nation's Banks Would Pay an Average of 22% More to Cover Their Deposits," *Wall Street Journal*, May 13, 1992.

26. William Greider, *The Trouble with Money: A Prescription for America's Financial Fever* (Knoxville, Tenn.: Whittle Direct Books, 1989), p. 52; Stephen Rousseas, "Can the U.S. Financial System Survive the Revolution?" *Challenge*, March/April 1989, p. 41.

4. INDUSTRIAL PREEMINENCE

1. Joseph Raphael Blasi and Douglas Lynn Kruse, *The New Owners: The Mass Emergence of Employee Ownership in Public Companies and What it Means to American Business* (New York: Harper Business, 1991), p. 8.

2. "Can America Compete?" *The Economist*, January 18, 1992, pp. 66-68.

3. Council of Economic Advisers, *Economic Report of the President* (Washington, D.C.: U.S. Government Printing Office, 1992), p. 420.

4. U.S. Department of Labor, Bureau of Labor Statistics, "International Comparisons of Hourly Compensation Costs for Produc-

tion Workers in Manufacturing, 1975-90," November 1991, Report 817, pp. 6-7.

5. Ira C. Magaziner and Mark Patinkin, *The Silent War: Inside the Global Business Battles Shaping America's Future* (New York: Random House, 1989), p. 300.

6. Ibid., pp. ix-x.

7. Steven Greenhouse, "There's No Stopping Airbus Now," *New York Times,* June 23, 1991, business section.

8. Magaziner and Patinkin, *The Silent War,* p. x.

9. Jean-Claude Derian, *America's Struggle for Leadership in Technology* (Cambridge: MIT Press, 1990), pp. 64-65.

10. National Science Board, *Science and Engineering Indicators, 1991* (Washington, D.C.: U.S. Government Printing Office, 1991), pp. 313 and 318.

11. This discussion is based on Commission on the Skills of the American Workforce, *America's Choice: High Skills or Low Wages!* (Rochester, N.Y.: National Center on Education and the Economy, 1990), pp. 37-39.

12. Sally Klingel and Ann Martin, eds., *A Fighting Chance: New Strategies to Save Jobs and Reduce Costs* (Ithaca: Cornell University Press, 1988), pp. 13-32.

13. Commission on Skills, *America's Choice,* pp. 33-36.

14. Sidney P. Rubinstein, "Quality and Democracy in the Work Place," *Quality Progress* 21 (April 1988), pp. 25-28.

15. John Ryan, "Labor/Management Participation: The A. O. Smith Experience," *Quality Progress* 21 (April 1988), pp. 36-40.

16. Peter Lazes, Leslie Rumpeltes, Ann Hoffner, Larry Pace, and Anthony Costanza, "Xerox and the ACTWU: Using Labor-Management Teams to Remain Competitive," *National Productivity Review* 10 (Summer 1991), pp. 339-49 .

17. These are the three key factors identified by David I. Levine and Laura D'Andrea Tyson, "Participation, Productivity, and the Firm's Environment," in Alan Blinder, ed., *Paying for Productivity* (Washington, D.C.: The Brookings Institution, 1990), pp. 103-237.

18. The information about American *keiretsu* is drawn mostly from Kevin Kelly and Otis Port, "Learning from Japan," *Business Week,* January 27, 1990, pp. 52-60.

19. Peter DuBois and Richard Callicrate, "Growth of Employee Own-

ership Programs in the United States," Community Economic Stabilization Corporation (CESCO), February 1991.

20. David Osborne, *Economic Competitiveness: The States Take the Lead* (Washington, D.C.: Economic Policy Institute, 1987), p. 6.

21. Commission on Skills, *America's Choice*, p. 9.

22. Ibid., p. 62 and 64.

23. Magaziner and Patinkin, *The Silent War*, pp. 67-100.

24. Commission on Skills, *America's Choice*, p. 49.

25. Ibid., pp. 53-56.

26. Ira C. Magaziner and Robert B. Reich, *Minding America's Business* (New York: Harcourt Brace Jovanovich, 1982), pp. 344-45.

27. Magaziner and Patinkin, *The Silent War*, p. 9.

28. Michael T. Jacobs, *Short-Term America* (Boston: Harvard Business School Press, 1992), pp. 225-31.

29. Steve Lohr, "Recession Puts a Harsh Spotlight on Hefty Pay of Top Executives," *New York Times*, January 20, 1992.

30. Ibid.

31. William Taylor, "Can Big Owners Make a Big Difference?" *Harvard Business Review* 68 (September/October 1990), pp. 70-82.

32. Ibid.

33. Michael Dertouzos, Richard Lester, and Robert Solow, *Made in America: Regaining the Productive Edge* (Cambridge: Massachusetts Institute of Technology, 1989), p. 77.

34. Ibid., p. 69.

35. Clyde Prestowitz, "Let's Make a Real Deal with Japan," *Wall Street Journal*, January 2, 1992.

36. Dertouzos et al., *Made in America*, p. 40.

37. See Council on Competitiveness, *Gaining New Ground: Technology Priorities for America's Future* (Washington, D.C.: Council on Competitiveness, 1991).

38. Magaziner and Patinkin, *The Silent War*, pp. 380-94.

39. National Science Board, *Science and Engineering Indicators*, p. 308.

40. Philip Shapira, *Modernizing Manufacturing: New Policies to Build Industrial Extension Services* (Washington, D.C.: Economic Policy Institute, 1990), p. 20.

41. Ibid., p. 47.

42. U.S. Congress, Congressional Budget Office, *The Economic Effects of Reduced Defense Spending* (Washington, D.C.: Congressional Budget Office, 1992), pp. 23-25.

43. Jeff Faux and William Spriggs, *U.S. Jobs and the Mexico Trade Proposal* (Washington, D.C.: Economic Policy Institute, 1991).

44. Lawrence M. Chimerine and Robert B. Cohen, *Investment: The Fast Track to a Strong Recovery* (Washington, D.C.: Economic Strategy Institute, 1991), p. 13.

45. The information in this section is based on David Osborne, *Economic Competitiveness: The States Take the Lead* (Washington, D.C.: Economic Policy Institute, 1987).

5. ECONOMIC INCLUSION: THE CHALLENGE OF INNER-CITY POVERTY

1. William Julius Wilson, *The Truly Disadvantaged: The Inner City, the Underclass, and Public Policy* (Chicago: University of Chicago Press, 1987), p. 61.

2. Nicholas Lemann, "Balkanization by Caste and Class," interview with William Julius Wilson, *New Perspectives Quarterly* 8 (Summer 1991), p. 27.

3. Sheldon Danziger and Peter Gottschalk, "Earnings Inequality, the Spatial Concentration of Poverty, and the Underclass," *American Economic Review* 77 (May 1987), pp. 211-15. See also John Kasarda, "The Regional and Urban Distribution of People and Jobs in the U.S.," National Research Council, Committee on National Urban Policy, National Academy of Science, 1986. Cited in Wilson, *The Truly Disadvantaged*, pp. 41-42.

4. David T. Ellwood, "The Spatial Mismatch Hypothesis: Are There Teenage Jobs Missing in the Ghetto?" in Richard B. Freeman and Harry J. Holzer, eds., *The Black Youth Employment Crisis* (Chicago: University of Chicago Press, 1986), p. 11. Ellwood has documented the outmigration of low-skill jobs and the influx of high-skill ones in the Chicago labor market.

5. Wilson, *The Truly Disadvantaged*, pp. 49 and 60.

6. Lemann, "Balkanization by Caste and Class," p. 31. In this interview, Wilson refers to this group as the underclass.

7. Ken Auletta, *The Underclass* (New York: Random House, 1982), p. xiii.

8. J. S. Catterall, "On the Social Costs of Dropping Out," *High School Journal* 71 (1987), pp. 19-30; Center for Population Options, "Estimates of Public Costs for Teenage Childbearing." Both cited in Carnegie Council on Adolescent Development, *Turning Points: Preparing American Youth for the 21st Century* (New York: Carnegie Corporation of New York, 1989), p. 29.

9. "America's Wasted Blacks," *The Economist,* March 30, 1991, p. 17.

10. State of New York, *Executive Budget 1991-92*, pp. 267-68.

11. Catterall, "On the Social Costs of Dropping Out," pp. 19-30; Center for Population Options, "Estimates of Public Costs for Teenage Childbearing." Both cited in Carnegie Council on Adolescent Development, *Turning Points*, p. 29.

12. For a discussion of some of the indicators of competitiveness and an explanation of our competitive difficulties, see the Cuomo Commission on Trade and Competitiveness, *The Cuomo Commission Report* (New York: Simon and Schuster, 1988), p. 19. See also the Commission on the Skills of the American Workforce, *America's Choice: High Skills or Low Wages!* (Rochester, NY: National Center on Education and the Economy, 1990).

13. *The Cuomo Commission Report*, p. 123.

14. The Committee on Economic Development (CED), for example, has issued a series of reports on investing in disadvantaged children. See *Investing in Our Children: Business and the Public Schools* (New York: CED, 1985); *Children in Need: Investment Strategies for the Educationally Disadvantaged* (New York: CED, 1987); and *The Unfinished Agenda: A New Vision for Child Development and Education* (New York: CED, 1991). See also the Ford Foundation Project on Social Welfare and the American Future, *The Common Good: Social Welfare and the American Future* (New York: Ford Foundation, 1989); The William T. Grant Foundation, *The Forgotten Half: Pathways to Success for America's Youth and Young Families* (Washington, D.C.: The William T. Grant Commission on Work, Family and Citizenship, 1988); and State of New York, Task Force on Poverty and Welfare, *A New Social Contract: Rethinking the Nature and Purpose of Public Assistance*, December 1986. In many cases, these studies focus on future labor markets. Our view is that current inner-city conditions intensify today's competitiveness problems. Moreover, we feel that other task forces have not paid sufficient attention to the issue of the social development of children growing up in urban poverty.

15. "America's Wasted Blacks," *The Economist*, p. 12.

16. After dropping in the early 1980s, violent crime increased by 9 percent in the last half of the decade. See "What's Ahead," *U.S. News & World Report,* January 6, 1992, p. 39.

17. U.S. Department of Commerce, Bureau of the Census, *Statistical Abstract of the United States, 1991* (Washington, D.C.: Government Printing Office, 1991), p. 179.

18. National Commission on Children, *Beyond Rhetoric: A New American Agenda for Children and Families* (Washington, D.C.: National Commission on Children, 1991), pp. 119-20.

19. James P. Comer, "Educating Poor Minority Children," *Scientific American*, November 1988, p. 6.

20. See Lisbeth B. Schorr with Daniel Schorr, *Within Our Reach: Breaking the Cycle of Disadvantage* (New York: Doubleday, 1988), Chapter 2 and the studies cited therein.

21. See, for example, the above-mentioned reports of the Committee for Economic Development, and the Ford Foundation, *The Common Good.*

22. Comer, "Educating Poor Minority Children," *Scientific American*, p. 44.

23. Alan S. Blinder, *Growing Together: An Alternative Economic Strategy for the 1990s* (Knoxville, Tenn.: Whittle Direct Books, 1991), p. 39.

24. White House Task Force on Infant Mortality, *Infant Mortality in the United States*, draft, November 1989, p. 1.

25. See Schorr, *Within Our Reach*, p. 71.

26. Task Force on Infant Mortality, *Infant Mortality in the United States*, p. 44.

27. Institute of Medicine, Committee to Study the Prevention of Low Birthweight, Division of Health Promotion and Disease Prevention, *Preventing Low Birthweight* (Washington, D.C.: National Academy of Sciences, National Academy Press, 1985).

28. U.S. House of Representatives, Select Committee of Congress on Children, Youth, and Families, *Opportunities for Success: Cost-Effective Programs for Children, Update, 1990* (Washington, D.C.: U.S. Government Printing Office, 1990), p. 6.

29. Cited in Ian T. Hill and Trude Bennett, *Enhancing the Scope of Prenatal Services* (Washington, D.C.: National Governors' Association, 1990), p. 3.

30. Clifford Krauss, "Under Political Steam, Health-Care Issue Gains Wider Support in Congress," *New York Times*, January 12, 1992.

31. Select Committee on Children, Youth, and Families, *Opportunities for Success*, p. 7.

32. Ibid., p. 8. Another valuable but underfunded federal program is Chapter I. Chapter I picks up where Head Start leaves off, providing compensatory reading and mathematics assistance to disadvantaged children in grades K-6. But because of funding constraints, the program only reaches about half the eligible students.

33. J. Berrueta-Clement et al., *Changed Lives: The Effects of the Perry Preschool Programs on Youths Through Age 19* (Ypsilanti, Mich.: High/Scope Press, 1984), as cited in Schorr, *Within Our Reach*, p. 193.

34. Schorr, *Within Our Reach*, p. 195.

35. See R. Loeber and T. Dishion, "Early Predictors of Male Delinquency: A Review," *Psychological Bulletin* 1 (1983), pp. 68-99; L. N. Robins, "Sturdy Childhood Predictors of Adult Antisocial Behavior: Replications from Longitudinal Studies," *Psychological Medicine* 6 (1978), pp. 611-22; J. G. Bachman et al., *Adolescence to Adulthood: Change and Stability in the Lives of Young Men* (Ann Arbor: University of Michigan Institute for Social Research, 1978); D. S. Elliot et al., "An Integrated Theoretical Perspective on Delinquent Behavior," *Journal of Research in Crime and Delinquency* 1 (1979), pp. 3-27; J. G. Dryfoos, "Review of Interventions in the Field of Prevention of Adolescent Pregnancy," *Preliminary Report to the Rockefeller Foundation*, October 1983; A. L. Stroup and L. N. Robins, "Elementary School Predictors of High School Dropout Among Black Males," *Sociology of Education* 25 (Spring 1972), pp. 212-22; J. L. Kaplan and E. C. Luck, "The Dropout Phenomenon as a Social Problem," *Education Forum* 42 (1977), pp. 41-56; L. V. Klerman et al., "School Absence: Can it Be Used to Monitor Child Health?" in D. K. Walker and J. B. Richmond, eds., *Monitoring Child Health in the United States: Selected Issues and Policies* (Cambridge: Harvard University Press, 1984), pp. 143-52; and S. Phipps-Yonas, "Teenage Pregnancy and Motherhood: A Review of the Literature," *American Journal of Orthopsychiatry*, July 1980, pp. 403-31.

36. Schorr, *Within Our Reach*, p. 234.

37. Ibid., p. 231.

38. On reading tests, the average gain in Comer schools equaled that of the district as a whole at the second grade level. But at the fifth- and sixth-grade levels, the Comer schools had higher average scores. See Michel Marriott, "A New Road to Learning: Teaching the Whole Child," *New York Times*, June 13, 1990.

39. Schorr, *Within Our Reach*, pp. 240-45.

40. Carnegie Council on Adolescent Development, *Turning Points*, p. 41.

41. Ibid, p. 46.

42. U.S. Bureau of Labor Statistics, cited in Paul Duke, Jr., "Urban Teenagers, Who Often Live Isolated From the World of Work, Shun the Labor Market," *Wall Street Journal*, August 14, 1991.

43. Commission on the Skills of the American Workforce, *America's Choice*, pp. 2 and 48-49.

44. The MIT Commission on Industrial Productivity, "Education and Training in the United States: Developing the Human Resources We Need for Technological Advance and Competition," prepared by Richard Kazis for the Commission Working Group on Education and Training, *The Working Papers of the MIT Commission on Industrial Productivity*, Volume 2 (Cambridge: MIT Press, 1989), pp. 33-34.

45. The New York State Department of Economic Development administers programs to help minority enterprises develop "social capital." See Leon E. Wynter, "Workshops Are Helping Blacks Become Entrepreneurs," *Wall Street Journal*, December 19, 1990.

46. William T. Grant Foundation, *The Forgotten Half*, p. 25.

47. Commission on the Skills of the American Workforce, *America's Choice*, pp. 59-60.

48. For a discussion on how such a system might be implemented in the United States, see Robert I. Lerman and Hillard Pouncy, "Why America Should Develop a Youth Apprenticeship System," *Progressive Policy Institute Policy Report*, March 1990.

49. Rebecca M. Blank and Alan S. Blinder, "Macroeconomics, Income Distribution, and Poverty" in Sheldon H. Danziger and Daniel H. Weinberg, eds., *Fighting Poverty: What Works and What Doesn't* (Cambridge: Harvard University Press, 1986), p. 183.

50. For a discussion of the role of racism, see Wilson's *Truly Disadvantaged*. For other viewpoints, see Michael Reich, *Race and Inequality* (Princeton: Princeton University Press, 1984); Billy J.

Tidwell, *The Price: A Study of the Costs of Racism in America* (Washington, D.C.: National Urban League, 1990).

51. The estimates on the racial composition of the inner-city poor come from an unpublished paper by Ronald Mincey, "Underclass Variations by Race and Place: Have Large Cities Darkened Out the Picture of the Underclass?" (Washington, D.C.: The Urban Institute, February 1991).

52. Richard B. Freeman and Harry J. Holzer, "The Black Youth Employment Crisis: Summary of Findings," in *Black Youth Employment Crisis,* Freeman and Holzer, eds., p. 11. In this study of the labor markets in Chicago, Philadelphia, and Boston, Freeman and Holzer found that Boston, the city with both the highest quality of life and the tightest labor market, had a 10 percent higher employment rate among young black males than did either Philadelphia or Chicago.

53. See Sar A. Levitan and Frank Gallo, "Spending to Save: Expanding Employment Opportunities," Occasional Paper 1991-92, May 1991, Center for Social Policy Studies, George Washington University.

54. Henry Milner, *Sweden: Social Democracy in Practice* (New York: Oxford University Press, 1989), pp. 117-19.

55. Levitan and Gallo, "Spending to Save," p. 37.

6. RESTRUCTURING THE HEALTHCARE SYSTEM

1. Milt Freudenheim, "Health Costs Up 12.1% Last Year, a Study Says," *New York Times,* January 28, 1992.

2. National Leadership Coalition for Health Care Reform, *Excellent Health Care for All Americans at a Reasonable Cost* (Washington, D.C.: National Leadership Coalition, 1991), p. 13.

3. Organization for Economic Cooperation and Development, *OECD Health Data* (Paris: OECD, 1991); General Accounting Office, *Canadian Health Insurance: Lessons for the United States* (Washington, D.C.: General Accounting Office, 1991), pp. 16 and 35. See also General Accounting Office, *Health Care Spending Control: The Experience of France, Germany, and Japan* (Washington, D.C.: General Accounting Office, 1991), p. 16.

4. Walter B. Maher, statement of Chrysler Corporation before the Senate Democratic Policy Committee on Health Care Reform, December 12, 1991.

5. Families USA Foundation study cited in Hilary Stout, "Average U.S. Family is Spending 11.7% of Income on Health Care, Study Finds," *Wall Street Journal*, December 11, 1991.

6. Gene Steuerie, "Economic Perspectives," *Tax Notes*, March 9, 1992, p. 1287.

7. Congressional Budget Office, *Rising Health Care Costs: Causes, Implications, and Strategies* (Washington, D.C: Congressional Budget Office, April 1991), p. x.

8. A. Foster Higgins and Co., Inc., *Health Care Benefits Survey 1990* (Princeton: A. Foster Higgins and Co., Inc., 1990). Cited in National Governors' Association, *A Healthy America: The Challenge for States* (Washington, D.C.: National Governors' Association, 1991), p. 11.

9. Janice Castro, "Condition Critical," *Time*, November 25, 1991, p. 34.

10. Robert S. Miller, statement of Chrysler Corporation before the Senate Committee on Finance, February 25, 1991, p. 2; "Propping Up Detroit," *The Economist*, February 15, 1992, p. 75.

11. Castro, "Condition Critical," *Time*, pp. 36-38; Congressional Budget Office, *The Economic and Budget Outlook: Fiscal Years 1993-1997* (Washington, D.C.: Congressional Budget Office, 1992), p. 122.

12. Calculations by the National Association of State Budget Officers (Washington, D.C.: NASBO, 1992). Based on estimates developed by the Health Care Financing Administration and included in the president's 1993 budget. State expenditure base excludes local funds.

13. National Governors' Association, *A Healthy America*, p. 9.

14. Paul Starr, *The Social Transformation of American Medicine* (New York: Basic Books, 1982), pp. 198-234 and 290-378.

15. National Governors' Association, *A Healthy America*, p. 14.

16. Health Insurance Association of America, *Providing Employee Benefits: How Firms Differ* (Washington, D.C.: Health Insurance Association of America, 1990), p. 13. Cited in National Governors' Association, *A Healthy America*, p. 37.

17. Current Population Surveys, cited in Robert Pear, "34.7 Million Lack Health Insurance, Studies Say; Number is Highest Since '65," *New York Times*, December 19, 1991.

18. Congressional Budget Office, *Selected Options for Expanding Health Insurance Coverage* (Washington, D.C.: Congressional Budget Office, 1991), p. 9.

19. Clifford Krauss, "Under Political Steam, Health Care Issues Gain Wider Support in Congress," *New York Times*, January 12, 1992; Congressional Budget Office, *Selected Options*, p. 10.

20. Congressional Budget Office, *Rising Health Care Costs*, p. 20.

21. David A. Ridenour, "The Wrong Way to Health Care," *New York Times*, February 7, 1992.

22. National Leadership Coalition, *Excellent Health Care*, pp. 10-11; Pennsylvania Health Care Cost Containment Council, cited in Ron Winslow, "Data Spur Debate on Hospital Quality," *Wall Street Journal*, May 24, 1990.

23. Philip J. Hilts, "Bush Enters Malpractice Debate with Plan to Limit Court Awards," *New York Times*, May 13, 1991.

24. Congressional Budget Office, *Rising Health Care Costs*, p. xii.

25. See, for example, John C. Goodman, president, National Center for Policy Analysis, in "States Can Help," *Wall Street Journal*, December 17, 1991.

26. According to one estimate, the poorest 10 percent of households spend 19 percent of their income on healthcare while the wealthiest 10 percent spend only 8 percent. See Joel Cantor, "Expanding Health Care Coverage: Who Will Pay?" *Journal of Health, Politics, and Law* 15 (Winter 1990), pp. 755-78.

27. S. Wollhander and D. U. Himmelstein, "The Deteriorating Administrative Efficiency of the U.S. Health Care System," *The New England Journal of Medicine* 324, pp. 1253-58, cited in National Governors' Association, *A Healthy America*, p. 44 ; Congressional Budget Office, *Rising Health Care Costs*, pp. xiii-xiv.

28. Congressional Budget Office, *Rising Health Care Costs*, p. xii.

29. Our treatment of incremental and comprehensive reforms follows that of Robert Kerrey, "Why America Will Adopt Comprehensive Health Care Reform," *The American Prospect*, Summer 1991, p. 83.

30. Ian Hill and Janine Breyel, *Caring for Kids* (Washington, D.C.: National Governors' Association, 1991), cited in National Governors' Association, *A Healthy America*, p. 34.

31. General Accounting Office, *Canadian Health Insurance*, p. 5.

32. General Accounting Office, *Health Care Spending Control*, p. 5.

33. Congressional Budget Office, *Rising Health Care Costs*, p. 50.

34. U.S. Chamber of Commerce, cited in Kerrey, "Why America Will Adopt Comprehensive Health Care Reform," p. 88.

35. John Wennberg, "The Medical Care Outcome Problem: An Agenda for Action," policy paper, National Leadership Commission on Health Care, May 1987, cited in the Governor's Health Care Advisory Board, "Environmental Scan of Policy Trends and Strategic Issues," August 1991, p. 20.

36. General Accounting Office, *Canadian Health Insurance*, p. 7.

37. National Leadership Coalition, *Excellent Health Care*, pp. 25-26.

38. Ibid., pp. 30-31.

7. ECONOMIC IMPERATIVES AND A NEW
FOREIGN POLICY

1. Council of Economic Advisers, *Economic Report of the President* (Washington, D.C.: U.S. Government Printing Office, 1992), p. 421.

2. See Robert Kuttner, *The End of Laissez-Faire: National Purpose and the Global Economy After the Cold War* (New York: Knopf, 1991), pp. 8-10, 54-58, and elsewhere.

3. David Aaron and John Samples, "Proposal for an Economic Security Council," unpublished paper, November 1991.

4. See Jeffrey E. Garten, "Japan and Germany: American Concerns," *Foreign Affairs* 68 (Winter 1988/90), pp. 84-101, and Walter Russell Mead, "The United States and the World Economy," *World Policy Journal* 6 (Winter 1988-89), pp.1-45.

5. Cuomo Commission on Trade and Competitiveness, *The Cuomo Commission Report: A New American Formula for a Strong Economy* (New York: Simon and Schuster, 1988), p. 73.

6. Ibid.

7. Robert Z. Lawrence, "Efficient or Exclusionist? The Import Behavior of Japanese Corporate Groups," *Brookings Papers on Economic Activity* 2 (1991), pp. 311-30.

8. See Laura D'Andrea Tyson, *Who's Bashing Whom: Trade Conflict in High-Technology Industries* (Washington, D.C.: Institute for International Economy, forthcoming 1992).

9. See *The Cuomo Commission Report*, pp. 82-83.

10. Tyson, *Who's Bashing Whom*.

11. William W. Kaufman and John D. Steinbruner, *Decisions for De-*

fense: Prospects for a New Order (Washington, D.C.: The Brookings Institution, 1991), p. 54.

12. Ibid., pp. 54-55.

8. TOWARD A COMMUNITY OF THE AMERICAS

1. "Inter-American Relations: Neighbours," *The Economist*, May 23, 1992, pp. 26-27.

2. Inter-American Development Bank, *Economic and Social Progress in Latin America: 1991 Report* (Washington, D.C.: Johns Hopkins University Press, 1991), p. 9.

3. International Monetary Fund, *Direction of Trade Statistics*, March 1992.

4. Ibid. for export figures and U.S. Department of Commerce for GNP data.

5. Inter-American Development Bank, *Economic and Social Progress in Latin America: 1990 Report* (Washington, D.C.: Johns Hopkins University Press, 1990), p. 14.

6. Ibid., p. 311.

7. Inter-American Development Bank, *Economic and Social Progress in Latin America 1991*, pp. 276 and 314.

8. Economic Commission for Latin America and the Caribbean, *Economic Panorama of Latin America 1991* (Santiago: United Nations, 1992), p. 10.

9. Ibid.

10. Karin Lissakers, *Banks, Borrowers, and the Establishment: A Revisionist Account of the International Debt Crisis* (New York: Basic Books, 1991), p. 13.

11. Manuel Pastor, Jr., *Capital Flight and the Latin American Debt Crisis* (Washington, D.C.: Economic Policy Institute, 1989), pp. 1 and 8.

12. Inter-American Development Bank, *Economic and Social Progress in Latin America 1991*, p. 275.

13. Ibid., p. 273.

14. United Nations Development Programme, *Human Development Report 1991* (New York: Oxford University Press, 1991), pp. 140-41, 167, and 196.

15. Tim Golden, "Mexicans Head North Despite Rules on Jobs," *New*

York Times, December 13, 1991; David Johnston, "Border Crossings Near Old Record; U.S. to Crack Down," *New York Times*, February 9, 1992.

16. Matt Moffett, "Working Children: Underage Laborers Fill Mexican Factories, Stir U.S. Trade Debate," *Wall Street Journal*, April 8, 1991.

17. Material in this paragraph has been drawn from Lawyers Committee for Human Rights, *Human Rights and U.S. Foreign Policy: 1992 Report and Recommendations* (New York: Lawyers Committee for Human Rights, 1992).

18. Daniel Lazare, "The Drug War is Killing Us," *Village Voice*, January 23, 1990.

19. Robin Kirk, "Oh! What a Lovely Drug War in Peru," *The Nation*, September 30, 1991, p. 374.

20. Joseph B. Treaster, "Bush Sees Progress, but U.S. Report Sees Surge in Drug Production," *New York Times*, March 1, 1992.

21. Sonia Goldenberg, "War No More," *The Nation*, March 30, 1992, p. 401.

22. Human Rights Watch, *Human Rights in Mexico: A Policy of Impunity* (New York: Americas Watch, 1990); Human Rights Watch, *Unceasing Abuses: Human Rights in Mexico One Year After the Introduction of Reform* (New York: Americas Watch, 1991).

23. United Nations, *World Economic Survey 1991* (New York: United Nations Publications, 1991), pp. 162-64.

24. Salomon Brothers, "Private Capital Flows to Latin America: Volume Triples to $40 Billion in 1991," February 25, 1992.

25. Christopher Whalen, "Mexico's Government Creates Another Debt Crisis," *Wall Street Journal*, March 12, 1992.

26. For a Mexican viewpoint, see Roberto Salinas-Leon, "Don't Cry for Mexico's Current Account Deficit," *Wall Street Journal*, February 21, 1992.

27. Salomon Brothers, "Private Capital Flows to Latin America."

28. Ibid.

29. Arturo O'Connell, "The Argentine Economy: Short-and Medium-Term Prosperity," paper presented at the Project LINK System meeting, March 1992.

30. "Investment in Venezuela Sinks," *Wall Street Journal*, April 23, 1992.

31. "The Impatience in Venezuela," *The Economist*, February 8, 1992, p. 35.

32. Bruce Campell, *Canada Under Siege: Three Years into the Free Trade Era* (Ottawa: Centre for Policy Alternatives, 1992).

33. Bernard Wysocki, Jr., "Southern Exposure: Canada Suffers Exodus of Jobs, Investment and Shoppers to U.S.," *Wall Street Journal*, June 20, 1991.

34. See Jeff Faux and Richard Rothstein, "Fast Track-Fast Shuffle: The Economic Consequences of the Administration's Proposed Trade Agreement with Mexico," briefing paper, Economic Policy Institute, 1991, p. 6; Stephen Baker, David Woodruff, and Elizabeth Weiner, "Detroit South: Mexico's Auto Boom: Who Wins, Who Loses," *Business Week*, March 16, 1992, pp. 98-103.

35. See Walter Russell Mead, *The Low-Wage Challenge to Global Growth: The Labor Cost-Productivity Imbalance in Newly Industrialized Countries* (Washington, D.C.: Economic Policy Institute, 1990); Harley Shaiken, "The Universal Motors Assembly and Stamping Plant: Transferring High-Tech Production to Mexico," *The Columbia Journal of World Business* 26 (Summer 1991), pp. 125-37.

36. Jeff Faux and William Spriggs, *U.S. Jobs and the Mexico Trade Proposal* (Washington, D.C.: Economic Policy Institute, 1991).

37. Statement of Richard E. Feinberg before the Subcommittee on Western Hemisphere Affairs and the Subcommittee on International Economic Policy and Trade, Committee on Foreign Affairs, U.S. House of Representatives, Washington, D.C., at the hearing on the Enterprise for the Americas Initiative, February 27, 1991.

38. John T. Addison and W. Stanley Siebert, "The Social Charter of the European Community: Evolution and Controversies," *Industrial and Labor Relations Review* 44 (July 1991), pp. 597-99.

39. United Nations Development Programme, *Human Development Report 1991*, pp. 122, 128, and 174.

40. George E. Brown, Jr., J. William Goold, and John Cavanagh, "Making Trade Fair," *World Policy Journal* 9 (Spring 1992), p. 321.

41. See Seamus O'Cleireacain, "Labor Markets and the Social Dimension of 1992," September 1991 (revised version of paper presented at Seventh International Conference of Europeanists, Council for European Studies, Washington, D.C., March 1990), pp. 18-22; Addison and Siebert, "The Social Charter," pp. 608-14.

42. Addison and Siebert, "The Social Charter," pp. 598-600.

43. United Nations Development Programme, *Human Development Report 1991*, pp. 53-57.

44. Ibid., p. 54.

45. Statement of Jerome Levinson before the Subcommittee on International Development, Finance, Trade, and Monetary Policy of the Committee on Banking, Finance, and Urban Affairs, U.S. House of Representatives, June 12, 1991.

46. Cited in Economic Policy Council, *The International Labor Organization and the Global Economy: New Options for the United States in the 1990s* (New York: United Nations Association of the United States of America, 1991), especially pp. 68-72.

47. Ibid., especially pp. 36 and 47-48.

9. THE MACROECONOMICS OF
INVESTMENT-LED GROWTH

1. Congressional Budget Office, *Reducing the Deficit: Spending and Revenue Options* (Washington, D.C.: Congressional Budget Office, 1992), p. 5.

2. William W. Kaufmann and John D. Steinbruner, *Decisions for Defense: Prospects for a New Order* (Washington, D.C.: The Brookings Institution, 1991), pp. 2 and 7.

3. Congressional Budget Office, *The Economic and Budget Outlook: Fiscal Years 1993-1997* (Washington, D.C.: Congressional Budget Office, 1992), p. 11.

4. See Michael Bruno and Jeffrey Sachs, *The Economics of Worldwide Stagflation* (Cambridge: Harvard University Press, 1985), pp. 221-46.

5. Economic Policy Institute, "Press Advisory: Economists to Present Plan for Fixing the U.S. Economy," March 27, 1992.

6. David E. Rosenbaum, "States and Cities with Deficit Woes May Slow Rebound," *New York Times*, May 31, 1991.

7. Francis M. Bator and Robert Solow, "Two Ways to Wake Up the Economy," *New York Times*, December 4, 1991.

8. For a discussion of current plans for defense spending in 1997, see the Congressional Budget Office, *The Economic and Budget Outlook 1993-1997*, pp. 52-55.

9. The Internal Revenue Service, as cited in Michael Kinsley, "Accounts Receivable," *The New Republic,* June 8, 1992, p. 6.

10. General Accounting Office, *Canadian Health Insurance: Lessons for the United States* (Washington, D.C.: General Accounting Office, 1991), p. 7.

11. Congressional Budget Office, *The Economic and Budget Outlook*, p. 37.

12. Ibid., p. 38.

13. The growth effects were estimated with the Project LINK macroeconometric model of the global economy. One of the distinctive features of this model is that it incorporates the effects of public investment on growth.

10. CHOOSING OUR FUTURE

1. Bernard Shaw cited in Rudolph Flesch, ed., *The New Book of Unusual Quotations* (New York: Harper & Row, 1966), p. 43.

2. For a discussion of the one-sided approaches of the past, see E.J. Dionne, Jr., *Why Americans Hate Politics* (New York: Simon & Schuster, Inc., 1991).

ABOUT THE COMMISSION
AND ITS MEMBERS

THIS is the second major report on the nation's economic future published under the auspices of the Commission on Competitiveness established by Governor Mario M. Cuomo. The first report, *The Cuomo Commission Report: A New American Formula for a Strong Economy*, was released in 1988. That report analyzed America's difficulties in meeting economic competition from other nations and concluded that restoring our competitiveness was the key to America's future prosperity. It recommended that government play a positive role in restoring our ability to produce goods that would meet the test of international markets while enhancing our standard of living and quality of life. It emphasized that our economic policies should aim for high levels of sustainable economic growth, at home and globally. It called for far-reaching reforms in the private sector, a program it called A New American Formula, to restore our competitiveness. Lastly, the Commission's report predicted that if we did not become more competitive, we would decline as a nation.

The world has changed dramatically since the first report's publication. In the past four years the Cold War ended, the Soviet Union dissolved, the nations of Europe united into the single most prosperous region in the world, Japanese manufacturing and financial power continued to increase, and sweeping changes took place in the Third World, particularly in Latin America. At the same time, our nation's domestic problems worsened. The American economy sank into the longest recession of the postwar period. High unemployment, inadequate investment, and growing government deficits exacerbated the nation's social problems. Consequently, Governor Cuomo reconvened the Commission to take stock of the new global situation and our domestic problems, and to recommend policies that could take the nation in a new direction.

The Commission focused on the major issues where new policies were urgently needed: raising investment (both public and private), improving industrial competitiveness, reducing urban poverty, reforming our healthcare systems, developing a new international strategy to support domestic reform and protect economic security, and forging new relations with Latin America.

The Commission utilized a series of task forces to accomplish its work. Each task force included commissioners from a variety of backgrounds, as well as outside experts. Through meetings and correspondence during 1991 and 1992, the task forces formulated the practical policy recommendations that make up the body of this book.

Two of the task forces will also publish their work independently in the fall of 1992. The Task Force on Urban Poverty and Labor Markets will release *Ingredients for Success: A Strategy for Addressing the Crisis of the Inner City*. The Task Force on Latin America will issue *Toward a Community of the Americas*.

Biographies of the Commissioners

Lewis B. Kaden, chairman of the Commission, is a partner in the law firm of Davis Polk & Wardwell and served as chairman of the New York State Industrial Cooperation Council. Mr. Kaden is also an adjunct professor of law at Columbia Law School, chairman of the Twentieth Century Fund task force on financial markets and corporate governance, and a trustee of the Environmental Defense Fund, the Lawyers Committee for Human Rights, and Beth Israel Medical Center. Mr. Kaden served as counsel to the governor of New Jersey from 1974 through 1976 and was formerly a professor of law and director of the Columbia University Center for Law and Economic Studies.

Owen Bieber is president of the International Union, United Automobile, Aerospace, and Agricultural Implement Workers of America (UAW). Mr. Bieber, whose membership in the UAW began in 1948, is currently serving his third four-year term as president. He is also vice president and executive council member of the AFL-CIO, Chairperson of the AFL-CIO's Industrial Union Department's Committee on Reindustrialization, a member of the President's Advisory Committee for Trade Negotiations, and a board member of the National Association for the Advancement of Colored People (NAACP).

Donald P. Brennan is a member of the board of directors of Morgan Stanley & Co. and is the managing director of the firm's merchant bank. He currently serves on the boards of a number of industrial companies including Coltec Industries, Inc., and Fort Howard Corporation, and is chairman of the board of Waterford Wedgewood plc and Agricultural Minerals Corporation. Prior to joining Morgan Stanley in 1982, Mr. Brennan was vice chairman of the board of International Paper Company.

Edward J. Cleary is president of the New York State AFL-CIO. He began in 1949 as an apprentice in Local 3, International Brotherhood of Electrical Workers. He was elected president of that local in 1964. After having served for a number of years as secretary treasurer of the New York State Building Trades Council, he was elected New York State AFL-CIO president in 1984. Mr. Cleary serves as an executive board member of the New York City Central Labor Council, secretary of the Educational and Cultural Fund of the Electrical Industry, and director of the American Arbitration Association.

William C. Ferguson is chairman and chief executive officer of

NYNEX Corporation. Mr. Ferguson is a director and former chairman of the Business Council of New York State, Inc., and a member of the Conference Board. He serves on Governor Cuomo's Council on Fiscal and Economic Priorities, as well as the Governor's Business Advisory Board and the School/Business Alliance Task Force for New York State. Mr. Ferguson is on the boards of directors of NYNEX Corporation, CPC International and General Re Corporation.

Jeffrey E. Garten is a managing director of the Blackstone Group and the author of *A Cold Peace: America, Japan, Germany, and the Struggle for Supremacy*. Mr. Garten served as a managing director of Shearson Lehman Brothers where he directed their Japan office and oversaw the firm's investment banking business in Asia. During his banking career, he worked as an adviser to finance ministers and central bank governors in Peru, Costa Rica, and Panama. Mr. Garten also worked in the Nixon, Ford, and Carter administrations, holding senior staff positions on the White House Council on International Economic Policy, the White House Economic Policy Group, and the State Department policy planning staff. His articles have appeared in the *New York Times*, the *Wall Street Journal*, the *Los Angeles Times*, and *Foreign Affairs*.

Hernand V. Gonzalez, Jr., is national ethnic marketing manager for Pepsi-Cola Co. Previously Mr. Gonzalez has held various sales and marketing positions for the Pepsi-Cola Bottling Co. of New York. Prior to joining Pepsi-Cola, he worked for a number of economic development programs in New York. Mr. Gonzalez was also a member of the Hispanic Advisory Board during the Koch administration in New York City.

David D. Hale is senior vice president and chief economist for the Kemper Financial Companies. Mr. Hale is a member of the Financial Instrument Steering Committee of the Chicago Mercantile Exchange, the Security Exchange Committee's Task Force on Emerging Stock Markets, and a variety of government and private-sector economic policy research groups in Washington, Tokyo, and Bonn. He has written on a broad range of economic subjects for leading newspapers and magazines, and has frequently testified before congressional committees on domestic and international economic policy issues. Since 1990 he has been a consultant to the U.S. Department of Defense on how changes in the global economy are affecting U.S. security relationships.

Brad Johnson serves as Governor Cuomo's Washington counsel and director of the New York State Office for Federal Affairs in Washington, D.C. Mr. Johnson is also a member of the New York State Economic Affairs Cabinet and the Governor's World Trade Council, and he co-chairs the Governor's Task Force on Defense Spending and Economic Adjustment.

Eugene J. Keilin is senior partner of the investment banking firm Keilin and Bloom. Prior to founding Keilin and Bloom, Mr. Keilin was a general partner of Lazard Frères & Co. Mr. Keilin and his firm have provided financial advice to many of the largest trade unions in the United States and have been instrumental in many large employee ownership transactions. Mr. Keilin also has provided financial advice to the cities of Cleveland, Detroit, and New Orleans and to other city and state governments. He is a member of the board of directors (and chairman of the Finance Committee) of the Municipal Assistance Corporation for the City of New York and is a trustee of the Citizens Budget Commission.

Mitchell E. Kertzman is founder, chairman, and chief executive officer of Powersoft Corporation, a privately held company that develops and markets PowerBuilder, a graphic, client/server development environment, designed to build large-scale commercial and government applications. Mr. Kertzman served as 1990 chairman of the board of the American Electronics Association. He is a director of Intermetrics, Inc., the Massachusetts Computer Software Council, and the Massachusetts Taxpayers

Foundation. He is also a member of the Massachusetts High Technology Council and the Massachusetts Business Roundtable.

Lawrence R. Klein is the Benjamin Franklin Professor of Economics (emeritus) at the University of Pennsylvania and founded the Wharton Econometric Forecasting Associates. He is a principal investigator for Project LINK, an international research group for the statistical study of world trade and payments. He has served as president of the American Economic Association, the Eastern Economic Association, and the Econometric Society. In 1980 Professor Klein was awarded the Alfred Nobel Memorial Prize in economic science.

Perla Kuhn is senior partner of Kuhn and Muller, a law firm specializing in international trade and intellectual property law. Ms. Kuhn is a member of the North American Free Trade Association Committee of the American Exporters and Importers Association, the United States Trademark Association, and a director and vice president of the Argentine-American Chamber of Commerce in New York.

Karin Lissakers is director of Business and Banking Studies and adjunct professor of International Affairs at Columbia University's School of International and Public Affairs. Ms. Lissakers was deputy director of the policy planning staff of the U.S. Department of State for Economic Affairs; before that she was staff director of the Subcommittee on Foreign Economic Policy of the U.S. Senate Committee on Foreign Relations. Ms. Lissakers is chairperson of the New York Forum on International Business and a member of the Council on Foreign Relations. Her book *Banks, Borrowers, and the Establishment* was published in 1991.

Gerald W. McEntee is the international president of the American Federation of State, County, and Municipal Employees (AFSCME). Mr. McEntee is also a vice president of the AFL-CIO and a member of its executive council, and a co-founder and chairman of the board of the Washington-based Economic Policy Institute. He is a member of the National Commission on Children and is chairman of the AFL-CIO's Working Family Committee, vice president of Americans for Democratic Action, and a member of the boards of the American Arbitration Association and the Child Care Action Campaign.

Ira M. Millstein is a senior partner with Weil, Gotshal & Manges. He was formerly an adjunct professor at the New York University School of Law, Fellow of the Faculty of Government of the John F. Kennedy School of Government at Harvard University, and a Distinguished Faculty Fellow at the Yale School for Organization and Management. Mr. Millstein was chair of Governor Cuomo's Pension Investment Task Force, which published *Our Money's Worth*, and is now the chairman of the board of advisers at the Columbia University School of Law, Center for Law and Economic Studies. He is co-author of *The Limits of Corporate Power* and co-editor of *The Impact of the Modern Corporation*.

Ramon H. Orange is founder, president, and chairman of the board of Ebonex, Inc. Ebonex is a diversified contract manufacturing firm specializing in design, fabrication, assembly, and testing of metal fabricated assemblies, electromechanical assemblies, machined parts, and cable assemblies. Ebonex has been heavily involved in subway car refurbishment for New York City, New Jersey, Boston, Chicago, Washington, D.C., and, more recently, in the manufacture of automatic fare collection equipment for Washington, D.C. and New York City.

Addison Barry Rand is executive vice president of Xerox Corporation and was formerly president of the company's U.S. Marketing Group. Mr. Rand has held a variety of sales and marketing positions since joining Xerox in 1968. He is a director on the boards of Honeywell Inc., Abbott Laboratories, the College Recruitment Equity Fund, and the U.S. Chamber of Commerce.

Felix G. Rohatyn is a senior partner of the New York investment banking house, Lazard Frères & Co. He joined the firm in 1948 and became a partner in 1960. Mr. Rohatyn also serves as chairman of the Municipal Assistance Corporation for the City of New York. He is on the boards of directors of Pechiney S.A., Pfizer Inc., and Howmet Corporation. He was formerly a member of the Board of Governors of the New York Stock Exchange.

Robert E. Rubin is senior partner and co-chair at Goldman Sachs & Company. Mr. Rubin is on the board of directors of the New York Stock Exchange and the Harvard Management Co., Inc.; the board of trustees of the Carnegie Corporation of New York; and he serves on the Mayor's Council of Economic Advisers, the Governor's Council on Fiscal and Economic Priorities, and the Federal Reserve Bank of New York International Capital Markets Advisory Committee.

Stephen Schlesinger is director of international organizations for the New York State Department of Economic Development. He formerly served as special assistant to Governor Cuomo, advising him on international issues. He is the author of *The New Reformers* and co-author of *Bitter Fruit: The Untold Story of the American Coup in Guatemala*.

Jack Sheinkman is president of the Amalgamated Clothing and Textile Workers Union. He is also chairman of the board of the Amalgamated Bank, vice president of the AFL-CIO and its Industrial Union Department, vice president of the International Textile, Garment, and Leather Workers Federation, headquartered in Brussels, Belgium, and a member of the President's Committee for Trade Negotiations.

Lee Smith is executive director of the Commission and editor of its report. He also serves as the deputy commissioner for economic policy for the New York State Department of Economic Development and as director of Excelsior Capital Corporation, a not-for-profit corporation that develops economically targeted

investments for institutional investors. Previously he was ex-
ecutive director of the New York State Industrial Cooperation
Council and deputy commissioner and general counsel of the
New York State Department of Labor. He has been the editor of
a number of publications and reports, including: *Competitive
Plus, Our Money's Worth, The Cuomo Commission Report: A New
American Formula for a Strong Economy, A School is a Workplace,*
and *Getting a Piece of the Action.*

John J. Sweeney was elected to a fourth four-year term as president of the Service Employees International Union (SEIU) in
April 1992. He is also a vice president of the AFL-CIO and
chairman of its Health Care Committee. Mr. Sweeney was
appointed to the U.S. Department of Labor National Advisory
Commission on Work-Based Learning and is a member of the
National Leadership Coalition for Health Care Reform. He
recently served on the Advisory Council on Social Security and
has been a member of the board of trustees of Iona College. He
co-authored *Solutions for the New Work Force* and was awarded
the Alice Grant Labor Leader in Residence Chair by Cornell
University's School of Industrial and Labor Relations.

Vincent Tese is director of economic development for New York
State. He supervises the economic development activities of 22
state agencies, departments, authorities, and public benefit
corporations. Mr. Tese also holds the position of commissioner
of the State Department of Economic Development, chairman of
the State Job Development Authority, and chairman and chief
executive officer of the New York State Urban Development
Corporation. Previously he was state superintendent of banking. Prior to joining the Cuomo administration, Mr. Tese was a
general partner in the Sinclair Group Companies.

Laura D'Andrea Tyson is a professor of economics and business
administration and director of the Institute of International
Studies at the University of California, Berkeley. During the
1989-90 academic year, Ms. Tyson was the Henry Carroll Thomas

Participants: John Adams, executive director, Natu-
es Defense Council; Andrew Bartels, vice president,
he Chairman, American Express Company; David
rector, Mexico-U.S. Dialogos Program; Shafiqul Is-
fellow for international economics & finance, Council
Relations; Fred Jones, president, ABB Financial
nc.; Fred Krupp, executive director, Environmental
nd; Jerome Levinson, esq., Arnold & Porter; Thomas
y, assistant secretary for external affairs, The
n Institution; Abraham Lowenthal, founding pro-
ternational relations, School of International Rela-
versity of Southern California, executive director,
rican Dialogue; Jay Mazur, president, International
ment Workers Union; Doris Meissner, senior associ-
rnegie Endowment for International Peace; Michael
ecutive director, Lawyers Committee for Human
d John Sewell, president, Overseas Development

Ford Visiting Professor at the Harvard Business School. She is
on the advisory board of the Economic Strategy Institute, the
Conference Board Economics Colloquium, the Economic Policy
Institute Research Council, the Council on Foreign Relations,
and is a member of the *Los Angeles Times* board of economists.
Ms. Tyson is the author of numerous books and articles on the
economics of competitiveness. Her most recent book is *Who's
Bashing Whom: Trade Conflict in High Technology Industries*, which
will be published in 1992.

Lynn R. Williams is international president of the United Steelworkers of America, of which he has been a member since 1947.
He is also a vice president of the AFL-CIO's executive council
and vice president of the Industrial Union Department. Addi-
tionally, Mr. Williams serves as vice president of Americans for
Democratic Action, is a member of the steering committee of
the Council on Foreign Relations, and is on the board of directors of the American Open University.

Andrew J. Zambelli is secretary to the governor, serving as chief
of staff to Governor Mario M. Cuomo. Prior to joining the
Cuomo administration, Mr. Zambelli had a career in university
teaching and research. He is the author of a number of research
articles and paper presentations.

Members of the Investment Task Force

Commissioners: Felix Rohatyn, chair; Donald P. Brennan; William C. Ferguson; David D. Hale; Brad Johnson; Mitchell E. Kertzman; Lawrence R. Klein; Gerald W. McEntee; Ira Millstein; Jack Sheinkman; Vincent Tese; Laura D'Andrea Tyson; and Andrew J. Zambelli.

Additional participants: Patrick Bulgaro, director, N.Y.S. Division of the Budget and Jim Ruth, director of the Infrastructure Financing Project, Twentieth Century Fund.

Members of the Industrial Competitiveness Task Force

Commissioners: Mitchell E. Kertzman, chair; Owen Beiber; Donald P. Brennan; Edward J. Cleary; William C. Ferguson; Eugene J. Keilin; Ramon H. Orange; Addison Barry Rand; Jack Sheinkman; and Laura D'Andrea Tyson.

Additional Participant: George Lodge.

Members of the Poverty Task Force

Commissioners: Robert E. Rubin, chair; Hernand V. Gonzalez, Jr.; Eugene J. Keilin; Karin Lissakers; Ramon H. Orange; Lynn R. Williams; and Andrew J. Zambelli.

Additional Participants: Michael Dowling, director of Health, Education, and Human Services for the Governor, State of New York; David Hamburg, president, Carnegie Corporation of New York; Anthony Jackson, program officer, Carnegie Corporation of New York; Lewis Liman, associate, Cravath, Swaine, and Moore; Eric Ruttenberg, president, Tinicum, Incorporated; and Isabel V. Sawhill, senior fellow, The Urban Institute.

Members of the Healthcare Ta

Commissioners: John J. Sweeney, c Cleary; William C. Ferguson; He Johnson; Gerald W. McEntee; and

Additional participants: Dan E. B sioner, N.Y.S. Department of He director, N.Y.S. Assemblyman Ja Dowling, director of Health, Edu for the Governor, State of New Y director, Governor Cuomo's Health Maher, director, Office of Governr ration; Patricia M. Nazemetz, Corporation; Dr. Elena Nightingal dent, Carnegie Corporation; and Business Council of New York St

Members of the International S

Commissioners: Lewis B. Kaden Lawrence R. Klein; Karin Lissake Sheinkman; Vincent Tese; and La

Additional Participants: David Aar Company, Inc.; Robert Kuttner, c *pect;* Sherle R. Schwenninger, seni tute; Richard Bartel, Executive Edi Inc. and editor, *Challenge, The Ma*

Members of the Latin America

Commissioners: Karin Lissakers, ch Stephen Schlesinger; and Jack She

Additional ral Resour Office of Brooks, d lam, senio on Foreig Services, Defense F E. Lovejc Smithson fessor of i tions, Un Inter-Ame Ladies Ga ate, the C Posner, e Rights; ai Council.

STATEMENTS BY THE
COMMISSION MEMBERS

STATEMENT BY OWEN BIEBER

This Commission has made a valuable contribution to the debate over the direction of U.S. economic policy. It has identified the key problems confronting our nation: declining earnings, rising unemployment, and the proliferation of poverty-level jobs are all evidence that the economy is failing America's working people.

To halt the erosion in living standards, we must meet the challenge of a global economy. That will require change. We must alter government's and employers' attitudes about the role of unions. For more than a decade, starting with President Reagan's firing of striking air traffic controllers in 1981, much of corporate America has taken the offensive against the labor movement. Before 1981 the permanent replacement of striking workers was unthinkable. Since then it has become an increasingly common employer tactic. The National Labor Relations Board, stacked with antilabor appointees, has failed to stop corporations from violating the labor law, thereby tacitly encouraging an increasing proportion of employers to refuse outright to bargain with unions. This assault on unions and collective bargaining has certainly contributed to the decline in workers' living standards.

The Commission's strategy for economic renewal calls for improving the nation's ability to produce, which in turn re-

quires more employee participation and management cooperation, as well as recognition of the rights of unions to protect
workers' interests. As things now stand, we at the United
Automobile Workers are not optimistic about the number of
employers that will pursue meaningful, ongoing cooperation
with their workers. Nor are we confident about the attitude of
government toward unions. A strong labor movement can help
put our economy back on the "high road" by helping to forge
new workplace bargains that can support employee participation. This is why fundamental labor law reforms must be part
of any realistic strategy for economic renewal. Indeed, without
such reforms, the enduring labor-management-government cooperation needed to make the Commission's recommendations
a reality will remain elusive.

STATEMENT BY WILLIAM C. FERGUSON

It has been a privilege to participate in the work of Governor
Cuomo's Commission on Competitiveness. I applaud the
Commission's success in bringing together the diverse views of
members in a powerful, coherent, and practicable report.

I heartily endorse the report's overall prescriptions for
using the talents and resources of all Americans to promote
sustainable economic growth and development within a framework of individual and collective opportunity and responsibility. In particular, I support the Commission's emphasis on
infrastructure development as a means to employ American
workers in building a superior platform for our nation's long-
term economic growth, its ability to create jobs, and its competitiveness.

The one section of the Commission's report on which I
would like to offer a specific observation is that concerning
corporate governance (see pp. 109-113). It is important not to
lose sight of the fact that publicly owned corporations are
representative democracies, similar to America's local, state,
and federal governments. In corporations, share owners elect
representatives (directors) to oversee their interests. And, one

might note, the turnout for the annual elections of directors is much higher than in politics: usually over 80 percent of all eligible voters participate in corporate elections, whereas fewer than 50 percent normally vote in governmental elections.

Can corporate democracy be improved—and should it be? Absolutely. The Securities and Exchange Commission has recently proposed rules to standardize and clarify disclosure of executive compensation and to enhance communication among share owners. These are worthy objectives, and the Securities and Exchange Commission's process is appropriate to determine the specific means to achieve those aims. The report's recommendation that government get involved in training people to be directors and encourage large institutional investors to exert more influence on boards of directors is philosophically in conflict with traditional notions of representative democracy. We would all agree that individuals should be encouraged to run for public office and that all voters should be more active in the political process. But we would all, I hope, be outraged if someone proposed that a government agency start training people to be congressional candidates or that the government pass laws and regulations to give certain powerful special interests (institutional investors) advantages over individual voters in their ability to influence the political process. (The fact is that institutional investors, *under existing laws*, are increasingly exerting their influence over corporations.)

Also at odds with traditional notions of representative democracy (one share/one vote) is the concept that large institutional investors (such as pension fund trustees) should have a greater voice in the governance of the corporation than other share owners. Directors are elected to represent *all* share owners of the corporation, not particular groups of share owners whose interests may conflict with those of the corporation and its other share owners.

In particular, the suggestion that these large institutional share owners should have a greater role in the development of corporate strategy—the traditional responsibility of management—could have a detrimental effect on the accountability of management to its share owners. Should management be held accountable for a failed corporate strategy that was urged upon it by these large institutional investors? Or should these influential investors be held accountable by the less influential share owners? And what impact would greater participation in the corporate governance process have on the fiduciary responsibility of pension fund trustees to fund beneficiaries?

In short, we are on the right track in espousing the principle that corporate governance is and should be a representative democratic process. In recommending that corporate representative democracy be enhanced, however, we should not propose specific "solutions" that, in fact, would be antidemocratic.

STATEMENT BY JEFFREY E. GARTEN

It is not necessary to agree with every point of the Commission's report to grasp and support its basic conclusion: America has enormous potential, but the nation is on the wrong course, not marginally but fundamentally. Measured by what we once were as a nation, and by the trajectories of our most important competitors, we are fast losing ground economically and socially. Only the equivalent of a revolution in thought and action will suffice to change our direction. In my view this report should be the starting point for reassessing the kind of future we want and how we get there.

STATEMENT BY MITCHELL E. KERTZMAN

It was both stimulating and educational to sit on this Commission, and I am proud of our report. I do want to comment on several subjects about which I feel quite strongly.

The recommendations of the Commission, if implemented, would radically improve the country. I am, however, pessimistic about the future. What stands in the way is a political system that is almost completely dysfunctional. Before any of our recommendations stand a chance of being evaluated and, I hope, implemented, Americans must change that system.

Today one and only one thing concerns representatives in Washington: reelection. From the day a congressperson, senator, or first-term president wins election, he or she begins the next campaign. All too much time is spent raising money, usually from special interests. I know that the expression "special interests" brings to mind fat-cat lobbyists representing big business, but there are other special interests, such as the elderly, that also wield tremendous power in Washington. The obvious problem is the buying or renting of political influence. Proof of this is the unprincipled support by lobbying groups of incumbents, regardless of the politics of the candidates. The not-so-obvious problem is the amazing amount of time fundraising takes away from legislating. The public must remove money from American electoral politics.

Money, though, is not the only problem. The biggest enemy, to paraphrase Pogo, is us. Citizens send a clear message to their elected officials with their votes. The message sent so far is that voters do not hold them accountable for solving the big problems facing the country, such as those discussed in this report. Instead, they are held accountable for wish lists. For my industry, electronics, the wish list might include the R&D tax credit or federal funding for critical technologies. For the elderly, it probably centers on social security. Whatever the wish list encompasses, it costs the federal government money, either through direct spending or through tax credits. We must start holding individual representatives, senators, and the president personally accountable for solving the biggest problems facing the nation, like the deficit. This will only work if we *all* put our wish lists on the table at the same time and let the collective judgment of our elected officials set priorities. If we do not like what they do, we can throw them out, but let us start sending them the right message.

Finally I believe that the Commission has made a laudable but insufficient commitment to the reduction and elimination of the federal budget deficit. I believe that it would be possible to balance the budget over the years projected by the report.

This must be done if only to prove that we, as a nation, are capable of making hard choices for the greater good. We deny our generational responsibility if we do not lift this burden from the shoulders of our children and grandchildren. I know from my service on the Commission that time was precious and resources scarce, but I would feel remiss if I did not personally stand up for elimination of the deficit. From my Latin studies I remember the story of the Roman senator Cato the Elder, who would end any speech, no matter what the subject, with the same warning: "Carthage must be destroyed." I feel like a modern-day Cato the Elder, because I end this and every statement of public policy the same way. The deficit must be eliminated.

STATEMENT BY LAWRENCE R. KLEIN

The nation needs measures to address both the immediate problem of generating a strong recovery and the longer-term problems of restoring growth while simultaneously reducing the deficit. This report provides a much needed package of practical recommendations to meet these goals. The increase in public infrastructure investment is, I believe, crucial for both a strong recovery and for improving the nation's long-term prospects.

There are two topics, however, that could have received more attention. First, as a consequence of world political developments and especially the end of the Cold War, we will certainly see significant reductions in annual defense expenditures, leading eventually to smaller military establishments, with reduced personnel, facilities, and equipment. Some of the reductions are already taking place. One important question is what will be done with this "peace dividend." If the dividend were used solely to reduce the federal budget deficit, long-term interest rates would decline by about 1 percentage point, and this would stimulate enough investment to add $50 billion (1992 prices) to GNP by the year 2000. If the Federal Reserve accommodated this fiscal change by loosening the money supply, the increase in GNP could be realized much sooner.

All the savings from the defense budget will probably not be devoted to deficit reduction. If up to one-half of the defense reduction goes into needed infrastructure investment, then there will be added gains on the supply side. While defense spending on durable facilities or equipment does not produce an output of useful goods that go into the makeup of the national product, comparable spending on civilian fixed capital does indeed contribute to the production of such an output stream. Directing defense money into public infrastructure can produce a multiplier effect that is about one to one and one-half times as large as the multiplier of ordinary government expenditure; therefore the real contribution will be even larger than that suggested by conventional multiplier analysis.

The immediate effects of reducing military spending are almost certain to contain some economic disappointments for many people. Even the smooth and quick transition from war to peace in the reconversion after World War II was not free of income and production losses. A year or two passed before peacetime civilian activities were able to get the country on a sustained growth path. Scenarios for arms reduction by the Congressional Budget Office and others all show initial economic setbacks; short-run maladjustments and economic losses should be expected.

Direct investment of a good part of the peace dividend, as this report proposes, into public infrastructure, instead of letting it all go to deficit reduction, would bring even greater enhancement to economic growth of the United States—and much sooner.

In addition to some early perverse national effects of the defense cutbacks, there will also be some severe localized adjustment problems. When a defense plant or a military base closes down, it is virtually impossible to avoid a rise in unemployment and a loss of family income at the site. Nevertheless, analyses of base closings by the Pentagon show that in three to five years, civilian conversion can generate increased employment and in some cases take even less time. Thoughtful entrepreneurs have been able to anticipate the redirection of national security priorities and have shifted their own facilities appropriately to earn profits by producing civilian rather than military goods. Speeding up the adjustment process will require federal leadership and resources—resources that Washington has thus far been unwilling to provide.

The second area that could have received more attention is monetary policy and its connection with fiscal policy. Any program to restart growth risks generating fears of inflation, leading to higher interest rates. Because the federal debt is so large, higher interest rates will trigger increased federal spending for debt service, thus worsening the deficit. Therefore, to sustain a recovery and keep the deficit under control, Washington needs to have a mixture of fiscal and monetary policies that will keep interest rates low. To my mind, the best way for this to happen is for the executive branch to reach an understanding with the Federal Reserve. The Federal Reserve would agree to an accommodating monetary policy, provided that the executive branch implemented measures to raise net revenues and reduce the deficit once the recovery gathers steam. Without such a quid pro quo, I believe that today's low interest rates will not last.

Finally, revenue-raising measures need to restore progressiveness to the tax code. The progressive income tax provided one of the key automatic stabilizers of the postwar macroeconomy, reducing deficits when incomes began to grow rapidly and increasing them during a recession. Unless the nation acts now to restore progressiveness, we will make it difficult, if not impossible, to achieve significant deficit reduction as the economy begins to grow again.

STATEMENT BY GERALD W. McENTEE

It is my hope that many of this excellent report's recommendations become federal policy after the November elections.

This is a report that contains probably the best and most comprehensive analysis of the economic problems besetting our country. Governor Cuomo deserves the gratitude and respect of all of us in business and labor for demonstrating that a consensus is possible on America's economic future.

Declining investment in our people and our physical infrastructure, after nearly 50 years of the Cold War, makes it imperative that we reorder our priorities. Our states and cities are in chronic budget crisis, and despite sacrifices from taxpayers and public employees, the crisis will only deepen unless the nation secures a new federal partnership and funding.

I must dissent, however, from the call for more tax breaks for business, unspecified cuts in entitlement programs, and the reluctance to endorse a single-payer system for financing healthcare. And while I support the recommendation on employee participation in workplace decision making as far as it goes, I believe that a greater role for unions and individual employees in a workplace that "drives out fear," as called for by Dr. W. Edwards Deming, is essential to America's economic success in the 1990s.

This is hardly the time for new tax breaks for business. As the report so clearly demonstrates, the federal deficit is a growing threat to America's economic security. Certainly new investment is needed, both public and private. But the record of tax breaks for business and the wealthy over the past 12 years shows that tax incentives are little more than an added gift from government for actions that would be taken anyway. According to the work of Jane Gravelle of the Congressional Research Service and Robert McIntyre of Citizens for Tax Justice, this is particularly true of the net investment tax credit. The credits would be largest during strong growth periods when the economy and business investment are expanding, but they would contract when the economy also contracts. The net investment tax credit would be too big and too costly when it is not needed and too small when it might provide some stimulus to the economy.

It has been increasingly popular to call for entitlement cuts, on the theory that Americans must curb consumption; besides, the rich people who receive entitlements do not need them anyway. The point is not that entitlements are too generous, but that taxes are too low on wealthy corporations and individuals. Obviously more revenue is needed to reduce the deficit and increase investment. But with record-setting low taxes on the wealthy, the answer is to use the tax system for what it was designed to do and not to undermine support for a successful social insurance system. (I applaud the Commission's call for a 38 percent tax rate on incomes above $200,000, but the rate could be set at 40 percent, and by eliminating the investment tax credit, there would be more than enough revenue.)

Finally the Commission correctly calls for national health insurance. It recognizes the significant savings described by the General Accounting Office if America were to enact a system modeled on the single-payer approach used in Canada. Yet the Commission declines to endorse this model. While the next president and Congress may decide that the single-payer system is not politically feasible because of our entrenched private health insurance industry, it represents the best public policy by all accounts.

STATEMENT BY ROBERT E. RUBIN

I agree with most of the Commission's description of the United States' current economic situation and, more importantly, with its concern about the long-run economic outlook. I also believe the recommendations offer much that is useful and thought-provoking, although I have a few reservations. I feel that the process was refreshingly and remarkably free of political influence and ideological bias the process was open, collegial, and intellectually honest.

The report correctly argues that unless a number of long-term economic and social problems are addressed effectively, the United States is likely to experience unsatisfactory growth and standards of living and erosion of its world position. I agree with the report's focus on rebuilding the economic base, with emphasis on education, infrastructure, reclamation of the inner city, and reduction of the budget deficit. I would add increasing the savings rate, where the United States' compares very poorly to most developed nations.

Fundamental to dealing with many of the issues discussed in this report is creating public willingness to reject parochial interests and to sacrifice in the present in order to allocate resources to longer-term, problem-solving programs that will restore our economic vigor. This in turn can only be accomplished through strong political leadership. We must also recognize that most economic and social decisions are trade-offs and involve negative as well as positive impacts (though obviously policy decisions can be made to deal with negative impacts, as in worker adjustment assistance where jobs are lost because of free trade). In other words, we have to put aside our political predilection to seek painless solutions to difficult problems, because there are none.

My disagreements and reservations with regard to the report are small relative to its totality, and I have no views on certain matters which are technical and outside my experience (i.e., high-speed rail).

Domestic Issues

Incentives for moving business focus from short term to longer term seem desirable. At the same time, government planning is not an economically effective substitute for business decisions made in response to market forces, except with regard to areas where private market forces by their nature will not function effectively (e.g., environmental protection or certain kinds of research, where there are important public benefits that market forces will not reflect and so need to be promoted by public policy). In addition, there are areas where public policy could reduce or eliminate impediments to market forces. Also, though opportunities may exist for improving the system of corporate governance through adjustments, the current balance between shareholder direction and management flexibility does not seem greatly out of line.

On a more micro level, I strongly disagree with the federal government injection of equity capital into banks, and with encouraging banks to establish shareholdings so as to play a management role in other industries.

Finally, I chaired the Commission's task force on poverty, and I strongly agree with its conclusions: a) urban poverty affects all our lives enormously, as people who have been left out of society are lost as productive participants in the economy, require costly welfare programs, and contribute to crime and drug problems; b) there are programs that work, and this problem can be solved over time; and c) the approach should rely not on income transfers but rather the development of constructive behavioral norms and useful skills.

This is not a problem for the urban poor alone; our economy and our country will not work for any of us unless this crisis is solved.

International Relations

Free trade is crucial to world prosperity, to which our own well being is inextricably and irreversibly linked. While some countries may have formal and informal impediments to free trade, our major problems are domestic, as discussed in this report, and must be faced and overcome rather than using real or imagined trade barriers as a scapegoat. Of course, where significant trade impediments do exist, we should vigorously seek to have them reduced, and access to our markets can be a powerful tool. Policy should also recognize the job-creating and technology transfer benefits of foreign investment.

Finally, I think Mexico has made important political, social, and economic strides over the last several years. We should continue to pursue a free trade agreement with Mexico, subject to reasonable conditions and appropriate accompanying legislation to deal with workers and companies that are adversely affected.

Conclusion

I believe that the enormous change occurring in the international marketplace creates both significant opportunity and risk for the United States. The new world environment will be beneficial to us if our own economic and social systems are in order. Absent this, there is a significant chance that the United States' world standing will decline and its living standards will not meet reasonable expectations. My limited reservations notwithstanding, I think this report provides highly useful and persuasive guidance toward sensible policy, with greater specificity and substance than is usual in reports of this kind. Thus it should play a meaningful role in the policy dialogue in the complicated years ahead.

STATEMENT BY LAURA D'ANDREA TYSON

As this report indicates, the American economy faces both short-run and long-run problems. The two are quite different, but the policies proposed by the Commission are an effective antidote to both of them. In the short run, the problem is one of inadequate demand. We are growing at only half the speed typical of the first year of recovery from a long recession. In the long run, the problem is one of anemic productivity growth and therefore slow growth of incomes. Since 1973 American productivity has grown a third as fast as it did between 1948 and 1973. If we had maintained the level of productivity growth over the last two decades that we enjoyed during the previous two-and-a-half decades, today's median family income would be $47,000 rather than $35,000. As long as our productivity growth continues to lag behind that of our trading partners, we will be unable to pay ourselves higher real wages and remain competitive. Without higher productivity growth, nearly one-fifth of fully employed Americans will continue to earn family incomes that fall below the poverty line.

The obvious prescription for both the long-run wasting disease and the short-run recessionary headache from which the economy suffers is increased public and private investment in machinery, technology, infrastructure, and people. This prescription is at the heart of the recommendations made in this report. The Commission believes that investment should take precedence over both tax cuts and aggressive reductions in the federal budget deficit.

Tax cuts are proposed by many conservative thinkers on the grounds that America's economic ills are the result of too much government. But this diagnosis does not stand up to the facts. Taxes and government spending command smaller shares of national output in the United States than they do in almost all of the other advanced industrial societies. And most of these societies are doing better than the United States in ways that count. They have higher savings and investment rates, and their real wages have been growing faster for more than a decade.

Tax cuts are proposed by many Democrats as a way to cure the recession and deliver middle-income tax relief at the same time. But this logic is flawed. Income tax cuts will stimulate consumption, not investment, and will further denude the government of revenues to invest in the physical, human, and scientific capital on which future economic competitiveness depends. Tax cuts for the middle class are desirable as part of an overall tax package that increases tax rates on upper income groups and restores greater equity in the tax burden. But they are not justifiable as a means to stimulate the long-run growth of the economy.

No more justifiable is the balanced budget amendment or any other radical proposal for eliminating the federal budget deficit by draconian means. Slashing government spending or increasing taxes will only slow the economic recovery, exacerbating our short-run problem. And deficit reduction plans that further cut public investment will deprive us of the human and physical infrastructure required for a competitive economy in the 21st century. The share of the nation's economy invested by the federal government in education and training, children's programs, infrastructure, and civilian research and development plummeted 40 percent during the 1980s. We must reverse these trends, even as we find ways to reduce the overall deficit as the economy recovers.

This report provides recommendations to meet these challenges. Perhaps the most important of these recommendations is the establishment of an independent, bipartisan National Budget Commission to develop guidelines for gradual deficit reduction between now and 1997. In my opinion these guidelines will have to include two essential components: tax increases and a national healthcare plan that stops the ravaging of the nation's finances by a system that is out of control. Since our long-run economic problem is underinvestment, additional revenues should be raised by taxes on consumption. A gasoline tax and a national sales or value-added tax should be considered. Both kinds of taxes have been used effectively by the other advanced industrial societies. A gasoline tax has the extra advantage of promoting energy conservation in the United States, which remains the most profligate user of the world's energy resources.

Investment is one pillar of this report's recommendations. Teamwork is the other. Unlike many other reports on competitiveness, this one emphasizes cooperation as well as individual initiative. Government must cooperate with business, labor must cooperate with management, and the United States must cooperate with its trading partners. The restoration of American competitiveness must not come at the expense of the disadvantaged either at home or abroad. Indeed this report argues that competitiveness should not be viewed as a goal in itself, but as a means to building a just, caring society and a stable, prosperous world economy.

INDEX

343